OUST
—— THE ——
DICTATOR

OUST
THE
DICTATOR

USHER IN PEACE

MEHR A. KALAMI

OUST THE DICTATOR
USHER IN PEACE

iUniverse books may be ordered through booksellers or by contacting:

iUniverse
1663 Liberty Drive
Bloomington, IN 47403
www.iuniverse.com
844-349-9409

Because of the dynamic nature of the Internet, any web addresses or links contained in this book may have changed since publication and may no longer be valid. The views expressed in this work are solely those of the author and do not necessarily reflect the views of the publisher, and the publisher hereby disclaims any responsibility for them.

Any people depicted in stock imagery provided by Getty Images are models, and such images are being used for illustrative purposes only. Certain stock imagery © Getty Images.

ISBN: 978-1-6632-2343-2 (sc)
ISBN: 978-1-6632-2342-5 (e)

Library of Congress Control Number: 2021910220

Print information available on the last page.

iUniverse rev. date: 07/20/2021

"Stone walls do not a prison make,

Nor iron bars a cage:

Minds innocent and quiet take

That for an hermitage.

If I have freedom in my love,

And in my soul am free,

Angels alone, that soar above,

Enjoy such liberty."

Excerpts from "To Althea from Prison."
Richard Lovelace (December 9, 1617 - 1657)

CONTENTS

INTRODUCTION

I have penned this work with the cardinal aim to draw attention of nations of the world that untold calamities could befall mankind should the nations under tyrannical despots, puppet dictators, and totalitarian forms of regimes continue to hold unlimited sway on the nation and the country they misrule at the behest of the unscrupulous Political Mafia that propelled them to power.

I have examined the "Political Mafia", defined their deeds and crimes, reminded the reader of the terrible number of human loss in WWII and the dictators responsible for it. I have detailed the wanton murder of Jews and others during the years 1933 – 1945, named those who deny the Holocaust and at the same time named the "Righteous among Nations", people with compassion and altruism. I have focused on Donald J. Trump as the main subject of this work, while also calling out dictators in the past and present – and their inhuman deeds.

Mehr A. Kalami, Geneva, Switzerland

UPDATED DEVELOPMENTS

Lest it be late, let it be known that Trump, the individual who occupied the Oval Office, and who had a myriad of plenipotentiary and executive powers placed at his disposal has officially lost the presidential elections to Joseph Robinette Biden, a former Vice President under President Barack Obama, by a vast margin of votes, awarding Biden 302 Electoral College votes against Trump's 232 votes. President-elect Biden secured a total of 81,283,495 popularity votes as against Trump's 74,223,753. It dramatically ended Trump's vain attempt to overturn the closely monitored results. The November 3, 2020 presidential elections ousted this menace.

Republican politicians grudgingly accepted their defeat and Mitch McConnel the Senate majority leader accepted the validity of the election and Biden as the new President of the United States of America on December 15, 2020. Biden officially took the oath of Office at noon time on Wednesday, February 20, 2021.

Donald Trump was on the threshold of being created into a dictator, a tyrant, and a despot by those who believed in his false promises prior to the first election in 2016 when the Electoral College declared him the winner. In the four tumultuous years he was in Office, he had become synonymous with compulsive lying, falsity, thievery, crime, chaos, and corruption. In short, his unpopularity both in the country and throughout the global community hiked him further as the most desperate and disgraced individual to ever walk into the Oval Office.

The vainglorious Trump presided over an administration which appeared to be a bizarre form of "Ineptocracy" in addition to "Kleptocracy."

Fearing imminent defeat, his enablers had suggested him to invoke the "Insurrection Act" of 1807 on Monday June 1, 2020. This is an Act authorizing the employment of land and naval forces of the United States in case of insurrections within the territorial boundaries of the United States of America. There was not a single instance of such a development in any part of the country. It was a ploy and an excuse to delay either the presidential elections of 2020 or to reinstate Trump (the definite loser in the elections) to the Oval Office.

The last act of this doleful, fraudulent, tax-evading, draft-dodging, juvenile name-calling, and foul-mouthed individual was to grant pardons…pardons to convicted individuals, terrorists accused and sentenced to prison for murdering innocent and unarmed men, women, and children in Iraq, to black mailers, thieves, traitors, and scoundrels like himself. Trump the arch-charlatan and coward did it to the astonishment and chagrin of the global community. The educated people in the United States of America appeared dazed, enraged, and shocked. A criminal pardoning murderers and criminals. That is the true color of Trump.

A prominent federal judge in Iowa who warned against political corruption ridiculed Trump's pardons, including those issued to convicted Republican campaign operatives and former members of Congress. "It is not surprising that a criminal like Trump pardons other criminals", senior U.S. District Judge Robert Pratt of the Southern district of Iowa told the Associated Press in a brief phone interview on Monday, December 28, 2020. The judge said: "But apparently to get a pardon, one has to be either a Republican, a convicted child murderer or a turkey."

Trump is out and the only major blow to him, apart from losing the elections in a fair manner, is his debts that will deprive him of every cent he and his children have by way of his fraudulence.

All said, the deranged aspiring dictator in the last weeks of his stay in the White House decided to augment his infamy and ego even after Biden defeated him by more than seven million popular votes.

On the 6th of January 2021, when the presidential certification was held as a formal recognition of Joe Biden as the new President, pre-arranged violence by nearly fifty thousand armed terrorists with flags bearing the name of Trump, blessed and encouraged by Trump himself, his eldest son, and a few Republican Senators, were unleashed on the Capitol Building. The fifty thousand assembled terrorists in a small area presents an agonizing fact and summative assessment as to how many millions of terrorists in the country may be masquerading as normal citizens. That day will forever live in infamy, a bleak day, and a permanent stain on American History.

The unruly mob entered the Capitol Building overwhelming a handful of security officials who withstood a physical attack while waiting for assistance from other law enforcement personnel. The mob, brandishing weapons, ransacked and vandalized the building, broke windows, stole official letters and items on desks as souvenirs. An unarmed woman rioter lost her life in addition to three others who were on a rampage. A law enforcement officer lost his life, and 140 other officers were injured, some permanently disfigured. Trump, his eldest son Donald Trump Jr., Jared Kushner (Trump's son-in-law), Ivanka Trump, Rudi Giuliani (Trump's personal Attorney), Josh Hawley (Senator from Arkansas), and Rafael "Ted" Cruz (Senator from Texas) were grossly guilty and responsible for planning, blessing, guiding, and goading this criminal and blood-shedding insurrection and horror.

Trump did not condemn their terrorism and hooliganism in the faintest vein, but instead spoke of them in an endeared manner. Thus overnight, Trump's regime turned the United States of America into a third world nation, even condemned by desperate and notorious regimes. This shocked the global community and several leaders of the world denounced Trump.

BEFORE ANYTHING ELSE

Before anything else, allow me to address the honored readers thus:

I have researched this work from the foundation of my personal knowledge and experience as to what corrupt politics enacted by corrupt politicians could do to create havoc and turmoil in this world. I have degrees in both Political Science and Economics and have worked in this field for many years. Most of the sources of information for this book are academic and self-evident. I have not sought the assistance of any person in thinking what to write and no individual has influenced me on this subject. I have not ever asked for the approval from any individual on the subject matter of this book, nor have I solicited guidance regarding how to begin, continue and end this literary work.

In all truth, condemning humankind's evil against mankind does not merely constitute an opinion, but a school of thought that combines eschatology with cosmology and spiritual approach to life that could be considered as "logos logic" seeking prosperity, peace, and bliss for mankind by challenging the evils of created despotism and tyranny.

Under no circumstance, have I ever thought of preparing this work anticipating laurels, reward of any kind, or praise from any source or individual. I have not played and will never play into the desires of any individual, party, society, or group. I write independently. I am independent of any society or organization and party.

This work relates to the urgency in "Ousting the Dictator", whoever, whenever and wherever he or she is.

My simple thoughts would be to reflect the quotes of Iran's famed astronomer, scientist mathematician, philosopher and poet, Hakim Omar Khayyam (May 18, 1048 – December 4, 1131):

"The Moving Finger writes, and having writ,
Moves on: nor all your piety nor Wit
Shall lure it back to cancel half a line,
Nor all your tears wash out a Word of it."

(Hakim Omar Khayyam Neyshaburi. From the original in Persian, translated into English by Edward Fitzgerald in 1859)

At times I am agnostic, but most of the times I am a believer in the Omnipresent, the Omnipotent and the Omniscient One; as in monotheistic religions; Zoroastrianism, Judaism, Jainism, Buddhism, Christianity, Islam, Sikhism, Baha'ism and hold in esteem words of wisdom from sages and "masters". Finally, I prefer to be an Omnist.

I have maintained a distance from those using organized religion and belief as a "crutch" and means to rain hardships and torments on fellow human beings practicing a faith or belief other than theirs.

I have always paid special attention to reasonable sermons from religious guides, including among others, spiritual leaders (Unity Church), Muslim clergymen preaching equality, compassion and understanding (from a pulpit of a Mosque belonging to any School of Islamic Thought), Christian preachers (Catholic and others) delivering the message of peace and help, Jewish Rabbis whether Neturei Karta or of other denominations spreading the sermon of understanding and solace among humankind, or scholars, guides and teachers following the Baha'i Faith, inviting the world towards unity and oneness in all aspects of life.

In all truth this work must be considered as *"Researched, Compiled and Written"*, by me.

Any income from this writing which will constitute my share will be unfailingly handed to Saint Jude Children's Research Hospital.

Mehr A. Kalami

CHAPTER ONE

DICTATORS AND ENABLERS

The Tyrant, Despot, Dictator, and His Enablers, Their Theatrics, and a Simple Reminder to Them

The dictator, or most plainly speaking, the cruelty embedded in a human being is in reality unambiguous. This evil is both inborne within a person, but mostly abetted and created by unscrupulous Internationals.

Over the millennia, hundreds, perhaps thousands of definitions have been created for a dictator. There is no accurate definition. There is no perfect or complete designation and description accorded to the individual who orders mass scale murders, initiates wars, destroys lives, and slaughters people practicing a certain religion or creed. Usually, an obscure individual makes his presence felt, through the aegis of his enablers, who are either from within the country, regional, or from a distant land, who claims to be the "redeemer of the unjustly treated population" and once in the seat of power unleashes murder, mayhem, and bloodshed throughout the country where he is, pleading that he is just creating law and order.

Before going further, one must consider the role of "Stochastic Terrorism" that has played a significant role in creating dictators and despots on earth. Before the era of electronics and advanced mass communications, rumors and hearsay played a pivotal role in creating a dictator, but as advancements were made, radio and television including the internet played a salient role in creating a murderous regime to satisfy the needs of "The Internationals".

"Stochastic Terrorism" is the use of mass communications to incite random lone wolves to carry out unpredictable violent acts. The Stochastic terrorist is certain that his inflammatory rhetoric will stir up violence – he just does not know exactly what will happen, or who will participate, or where or when. Stochastic Terrorists in the USA include conservative radio and television talk-show hosts. *Russet Research Institute.*

To sum up, the characteristics of a dictator and a despot can be defined as having the properties of cruelty, evil, cold-bloodedness, and ruthlessness all merged into one. There is no such definition as an "enlightened dictator", or a "merciful dictator." All dictators are a curse to mankind, whether military, theocratic or so-called democratic.

Who and what type of an individual is a tyrant and a dictator and what are his shenanigans, his ploys, and his various methods of deceits, obfuscations, and bamboozlements? Albeit the fact of being aware of being a puppet and a front man for the Internationals, he continues to act as a self-made strongman. He is in short, the evil coward, actor and showman struggling to appease his masters while tormenting the citizens of the country he professes to safeguard and protect and to meet their needs through false promises.

These marionettes are trained to chant the "mantra" of needing progress, law and order and prosperity for the masses at regular intervals to large crowds assembled and paid for the occasion. The dictator is ushered on a stage while the thousands assembled go into a frenzy of cheering and praising the lackey at a signal by the "sloganeer", usually the floor director(s) stationed at strategic locations within the crowd who in turn willfully reacts to the taglines. The crowd is well trained in coordinating with the speaker of the occasion. The minions in all their speeches have a partially uniform script laid out for them which they confidently tell the paid crowd; "It is me and me alone who can bring you bliss, prosperity, glory and richness in life. Nobody can do such things better that me.

Nobody has ever done it better than me. I am the best you can ever get in the history of this country."

The sane crowd outside the paid assembled agitators often ask themselves as to what this "self-glorifying" individual has ever done or is in the process of doing that they consider worthwhile.

In Theocracies, several more statements are usually added by the dictator who speaks as though it is a "joint dictatorship" by the clergy; "We will guide you toward perfection. We will shed away your ugly and ungodly past. We will cleanse your mind and existence of all the sins you have committed in the past. We will create a new form of existence for you in this world and prepare you for the "day of Judgement". With us you need not worry about anything!" If in an Islamic form of Theocracy, the clergyman-dictator will attribute everything to "Allah" and if Christian fanatics administer it; they thank Jesus (considered as God) for whatever is happening, while in a Hindu operated Theocracy, dozens of gods and goddesses are invoked for thanks.

After being well seated in power, the theocratic regime's tyrant will commence with threats and terrible consequences for those disobeying his orders and laws. Usually in an Islamic Theocracy, death is the only prescription for disobeying the orders of the clergy or for planning a revolt. Special courts, set up throughout the country for the unlucky persons considered as defaulters, hastily arrive at a standard verdict. The sentence is death, which is carried out immediately. The victim has no right to defend himself or herself. The court decided the verdict before any trial begins. "Allah has willed that you be executed" are the final words of the Islamic judge who till a few years earlier was either a cobbler, an aggressive beggar in the streets, or even an ex-convict sentenced for robbery or burglary or for an assortment of crimes. He is the appointed judge!

The dictator is merciless, unemotional, and impersonal. He cares the least for the welfare and well-being of the nation. He only thinks of his rewards from his masters.

In the twenty first century, in several countries, such persons are not too difficult to find. Petty and major tyrants, despots, dictators, and aspiring dictators exist. Even "joint-dictatorships" could be traced in certain countries where the enablers of the puppet dictator have a share in the loot and destruction of the nation and its wealth.

In the United States of America, the public easily recognized Trump as the most dangerous, evil, and cruel person to be stationed in the White House. He had, in the fourth week of August 2020, reflected his desire to be in the White House till the year 2034! He had been in the White House since January 2017.

As stated, Trump was trounced in the November 3, 2020 elections. Joe Biden won by over seven million popular votes and received an appreciable margin of 306 to 232 of the total 538 available electoral votes. Presidential election laws require a total of 270 electoral votes to pronounce the winner of the presidential elections.

Since then, Trump did whatever he could to stunt the States from certifying the winner (Joseph Robinette Biden) and to have a smooth transition of power as the American Constitution requires. Through attorneys he challenged the results of several states which pronounced Biden as the winner. In the days following his defeat, Trump also claimed that he would run for Office on November 5, 2024.

In many cases, especially in the USA, either an archaic Society or even duplicitous "donors" who have made billions of dollars in questionable businesses, particularly construction activities, gambling casinos, prostitution, pornographic industry and even drugs, propel the ruling head of a country into Office.

That "leader in Office" is no more than a "political prostitute" ever subservient to his master or masters who have placed him in Office through a supposed election. He is in private the servitor of those persons who have provided him the seat of power and will do as they order him, depending on the "whims and fancies" of the masters behind the curtain. He is that "dictator" in the making! He is just an "embellished lackey," puppet, tool, and a pawn. He or she will do at the bidding of those "behind-the-curtain" forces who are the real masters. In simple terms, most of the United States of America's presidents are just "front-men" to distract the general population and the world in general from the people who really run the country according to their personal agendas.

At the present there are a dozen or more dictators in office throughout the world…in various countries of the world. Some satisfy the end result of their unlimited powers to subjugate the local population of the country, whom they pretend to serve, while enriching themselves and their cronies, while others not only torment and murder the nation but also create havoc and tumult in countries, far from their own borders.

Conspicuous cases of dangers threatening world peace are the globally outlawed Theocratic Republic in Tehran, the much-feared Kim "dynasty" in Pyongyang, and the administration in Moscow. The past unpopular administration of a mentally disturbed individual in Washington D.C. was potentially another factor haunting global tranquility. As such, these petty dictators in Tehran and Pyongyang are incapable of creating a global genocide but may indirectly be the cause of it; a cause that creates excuses for dangerous super-powers to have the reasons to intervene while taking the unbridled advantage to destroy that country under the garb of playing the modern day "Robin Hood!"

It would be logically befitting to term the regime in Tehran and Pyongyang as dystopian while the past administration in Washington sought to slowly creep towards the same rule as in Tehran, Moscow, and Pyongyang.

All said, one can rightfully conclude that these forms of rule where dystopia prevails, the administrators wage a ceaseless war against the population they outwardly profess to serve. Upon the slightest move against his despotic rule, the dictator declares an unending war against the very same nation he pretends to bring prosperity, thus drowning the larger percentage of the population in misery, bondage, poverty, death, and destruction.

MEHR A. KALAMI

Definition of Terms

Comeuppance

"A deserved rebuke or chastisement." *Webster's New International Dictionary*

It may be argued that the term "comeuppance" may be applied to those nations who have knowingly and wittingly, either through a lack of thought and immorality, brought upon themselves an undemocratic administration headed by a tyrant of their own choosing. They may later claim their ignorance and regret at being misled through propaganda and deceit. They may even deny knowing the dictator whom they may claim has been thrust into their lives. They may even end up by condemning him or her but never addressing themselves as the chief culprit who took to the streets hailing and praising the aspiring dictator.

Socialism

"any of various economic and political theories advocating collective or governmental ownership and administration of the means of production and distribution of goods." *Merriam Webster Dictionary*

> "Socialism' is a scare word they have hurled at every advance people have made in the last twenty years.
> Socialism is what they called public power.
> Socialism is what they called Social Security.
> Socialism is what they called farm price support.
> Socialism is what they called bank deposit insurance.
> Socialism is what they called the growth of free and independent labor organizations.
> Socialism is their name for almost anything that helps all the people."

Harry S. Truman. Speech, October 10, 1952

"Socialism" means that society pools its resources to provide things for everyone, In the United States of Americas today, that includes:

Fire Departments, Police, Ambulances, Public Schools, Public Hospitals, Student Loans, Veterans' Benefits, National Weather Service, Road and Bridge Construction, Unemployment Insurance, Bank Deposit Insurance, Medicare, Social Security, FEMA, GI Bill, National Parks, Food and Drug Safety, NASA, Hazardous waste Disposal and Clean-up, Sewers, Military, and many other services to the needy nation.

Capitalism

"an economic and political system in which a country's trade and industry are controlled by private owners for profit, rather than by the state."
Definitions from Oxford Languages

Capitalism and financial considerations, if unchecked form the negative pillars of such governments, especially in the United States of America who claim democracy shields capitalism and the individual capitalist acts strictly in accordance with democratic laws. The term "Democracy" lacks any form of a perfect definition or any operational standard! The capitalist henceforth claims freedom to exploit and financially subjugate the working class according to his designs. He is unopposed in any court of laws. This is his form of democracy.

Through capitalism, many political objectives could be realized. This is what happened and is happening in the United States of America. More than two billion dollars are spent each presidential election year to choose, rather than elect a president. Those few controlling the finances buy the media to promote their candidate of choice. The public has no choice. Then for the next four years that selected president who is usually fraudulently placed into power is subjected to a barrage of accusations and "mal-behavior" till he is either boycotted or condemned as a villain by the masses, including those who voted for him. Most are unaware that "voting and votes" have the least political implications and effects as the whole drama is nothing but a big sham thrown upon the US citizens and forced to believe that voting the US president is indeed a factuality and something that could be credited as the real democratic approach to democracy in the land of the free and the brave, that is the United States of America! In truth, it is neither the land of the free nor the brave, where millions of Native Americans and Negro Slaves have been massacred!

Dictatorship

"a form of government in which absolute power is concentrated in a dictator or a small clique." *Merriam Webster Dictionary*

Words to All the Dictators, Tyrants and Aspiring Dictators

Know well,

Comprehend in depth the ever-burgeoning wrath of the masses and the vengeance of the souls whose lives you ended in the name of power, authority, and state ideology.

Know well,

The haunts of celestial reprisals lurking near your stately seat of power that will befall you, your enablers, your henchmen, and your entire family irrespective of their age and whether they are innocent or not.

Know well,

That the blood you spilled under the guise of safeguarding your philosophies, will eventually serve to eradicate that philosophy; especially the religious beliefs and restrictions you have imposed on the general population, albeit the benign roots and nature of that religion. That religion and its tenets will gradually ablate.

Know well,

Tyrants and dictators can never be redeemed. They are created out of violence and bloodshed and end violently. An attritional revolt by the masses scaling the dictator's sanctuary to mercilessly deal with the despot and his enablers. The citizens will continue by hunting down the individual mafia bosses to mete out the same justice that was subjected to the innocent people whose country they overtook with deceit. There is no escape.

And finally, a personal message to the cruel dictator and tyrant:

You the tyrant, you the dictator, and you the aspiring dictator shall be done and dealt unto as you have done to others. Your evil motto of "spread falsity, fear, backwardness and superstitious beliefs, keep them sick, impoverished, hopeless, and hunger stricken, while encouraging the misled masses to continue clinging to religion as a means of salvation and bliss in life – after - death" will not work indefinitely. Your practices and motto will undoubtedly end immediately after your life is ended. And the entire scenario will not end peacefully, more blood will be spilled due to you the dictator. You must also consider the terrible revenge exacted on your entire family members, every single one of them, whether an infant, adult or aged.

Those Who Hold the World Hostage and Control All Developments, from Politics to Terrorism

In all sincerity, one may defy the term of "Ousting the Dictator" as a futile attempt of whipping a dead horse! Many argue that what the "bosses" of the "political mafia" created; the tormented masses cannot undo. Only the bosses can undo what they created. The "Political Mafia" has existed and exists in most major countries of the world and mainly operate in countries with geo-political importance and untold mineral wealth. It is this institution behind the curtain that holds sway over the entire world! They, in unison agree to appoint selected dictators and through them, create wars and skirmishes causing the death of millions; pitting soldiers against so-called enemy soldiers who never knew each other, nor are they aware of the reasons Leaders sent them to kill and be killed!

While the dictator is secretly counseled by a chosen *consigliere*, he outwardly behaves and acts as if he is the "master of the realm" he surveys. He only serves the interest of his masters with potential powers to manipulate the situation through him, the puppet dictator of their choice. The question of majority votes is meaningless. And to add, it is always the minority that misrules the majority!

Washington, Pyongyang, and Tehran are some of the main places where the power brokers select the dictators and place them in power, just to destroy those countries and to create havoc and mayhem within their nation.

Most individual dictators, who were once unknown, some born out of wedlock, and some began in abject poverty with little or no education, fringe rabble-rousers or at most, professional agitators, and peripatetic provocateurs, understand they are merely a tool, pawn, and a "yes-man" to the bosses and enablers behind the curtain; a detested leech to the nation where they are appointed, their lifeline solely depending on faithfully serving their master's interests. In his mind the dictator believes he is the seat of power, while in truth, and within him, he is also very aware that he is merely the "political servitor" of his masters behind the curtain, who are often located far away from the country where their chosen dictator acts at their behest!

Consequently, the dictator exploits the forgotten poor to pay the rich, while the poor continue to suffer throughout their life. In recent years such a situation in particular relates to Trump, the once boisterous and "problem child," later a glorified realtor, a controversial and even disliked television reality showman, an alleged rapist and child molester, master of skullduggery, charlatan, mentally unstable, corrupt, revengeful, and a foul mouthed individual, parachuted into the White House by those individuals identified as "holding the world" as hostage; those who control armament and other crucial industries, finance, politics and terrorism through their minions and selected hands!

In the United States of America, the "Political Mafia" appointed Trump whom they were assured of his fickle nature, poor judgmental skills, murky and shady past, volatile temper, financial setbacks, matrimonial problems, suffering from various medical issues, foremost of them all being (allegedly) frontotemporal dementia and a host of drawbacks, more conspicuously related to social life, money, and finance. He was finally chosen among dozens of "candidates" to be their docile lackey that they earlier earmarked to benefit their enterprises. After having vested in him a halo of superhuman glory through the mass media, they would have him do their bidding through "advisors," so-called savants and "experts" carefully chosen to orchestrate a parallel administration while presenting him as the only and most capable person to bring prosperity to the United States of America. The "front-man" candidate was "whelped" through nearly a billion dollars generously supplied as "donation" to his election campaign. While the former reality tv star, professional liar, and proven fraudster seriously believed in his popularity before the general elections, it was in truth, the ubiquitous Russian mafia orchestrating the US presidential elections in 2016!

In the article, *Donald Trump, 'The Perfect Target': Russia Cultivated Trump as Asset for 40 Years – Ex-KGB Spy*, (The Guardian dated Friday, January 29, 2021) David Smith sheds further light on the role of the "Political Mafia" in the creation of a servitor and a puppet. Excerpts from the article are self-explanatory.

> "Donald Trump was cultivated as a Russian asset over 40 years and proved so willing to parrot anti-western propaganda that there were celebrations in Moscow, a former KGB spy has told the Guardian."

> "Yuri Shvets, posted to Washington by the Soviet Union in the 1980s, compares the former US president to 'the Cambridge five,'

the British spy ring that passed secrets to Moscow during the second world war and early cold war."

"In 1987, Trump and Ivana visited Moscow and St Petersburg for the first time. Shvets said he was fed KGB talking points and flattered by KGB operatives who floated the idea that he should go into politics."

An unbiased reading of the entire article throws light as to how and why subjects favorable to the selectors are chosen. Donald Trump was one such person who had wittingly and willingly embraced the very concept of a puppet for business and money.

As recently as the third week of August 2020, papers and documents from the Federal Bureau of Investigation (FBI) proved the Russian meddling of the 2016 Presidential elections, favoring Donald J. Trump.

One may clearly understand the mental prowess of Trump by listening and reading his statements, most of which could be dismissed as self-embellishment, meaningless, unrelated, insulting, opprobrious, misleading, accusatory, incomplete, utter falsehood, lies and pure rubbish!

For centuries, the Mafia Bosses' struthious philosophy of never being discovered and pointed to as the source of being a scourge on mankind through their ill-conceived wealth, has ablated. The world is gradually identifying this global menace created and operated by global Imperialism, Communism and Colonialism, simply through the unlimited wealth at their disposal. They create unpopular and even murderous administrations whichever and wherever it serves their interests. Theocracy, Communism, Fascism, Kleptocracy, Frenetic Democracy, Oligarchy, and a host of other types of governments regularly discovered and chosen for the unlucky nations of whose benign and popular administrations they decide to replace. (They chiefly bankroll sacerdotal revolutions and uprisings as was the case in Iran when they toppled the modernizing, prosperous and farsighted reign of the Pahlavi Monarchy to replace it with Ruhollah Mousavi-Mostafavi, an obscure clergyman.)

Such are the cruel, vile, vicious, and murderous schemes of the Political Mafia comprised of billionaires and the ultra-rich. Their secret homework, apart from their never-ending greed, is to create chaos, commotion, crime, and corruption wherever they decide; they acquire it through bankrolling their contacts in those targeted countries who are omnipresent and ever prepared for such an event.

From the point of inductive or deductive logic, experience has proved that assassinations, bloodshed, wars, "false flags," revolutions, destruction and continued tensions throughout the globe undoubtedly feed the insatiable greed of those ruling the world and holding the world hostage.

Judging from the past one hundred years of US political developments, President Franklin Delano Roosevelt (January 30, 1883 – April 12, 1945) could be judged as a conspicuous example of one whose election campaign was untarnished and whose term in office unblemished and acclaimed as the most beneficial to the American nation. By the same token, it must be stated that most of the US presidents are actors, jesters and puppets chosen to distract the public from the realities facing the country while diligently and unfailingly serving their mafia bosses, some who are in the country and some abroad!

History mentions dozens of individuals unscrupulously manipulating and ruling the world at any age or time within the last one hundred years. They are grossly guilty of manipulating geo-politics to suit their demands, "appointing" their men in various countries, turning them into dictators; seated comfortably in power just to perform at their bidding. The end of these dictators is self-evident; escape and live in hiding, be murdered, imprisoned, or beaten to death by an angry mob at any appropriate time and place!

Nathan Mayer Rothschild (September 16, 1777 – July 28, 1836), a prominent banker, businessman and financier, the wealthiest person of the Rothschild family, once said; "I care not what puppet is placed on the throne of England to rule the Empire. The man who controls Britain's money supply controls the British Empire and I control the British money supply."

The Rockefellers, the Astors, the Duponts, Sheldon Adelson, Haim Saban, Bill Gates, Jeff Bezos, Larry Ellison, Michael Bloomberg, Warren Buffet, Carl Icahn, Rupert Murdoch, Mark Zuckerberg, Carlos Slim, Donald Bren, Sergey Brin, Larry Page and Bernard Arnault, are, but a few names of the billionaires involved in having a hand in elections of the heads of State, whether directly or indirectly, in most of the countries in the world. Billionaires in the United States of America exceed six hundred and seventy individuals as of early 2020. They regularly "contribute" to their willing tools seated in power, just to safeguard their personal interests which translates into a steady stream of wealth into their already swollen coffers. So long as their appointed puppets hold together the reins of power on their behalf and money flows in, the puppet dictator exists. Even at the cost of human lives and sanctity! Some of these individuals ae deceased, but their heirs continue to follow their principles.

A Prominent Former Governor of the State of Minnesota Briefly Presents his Views on the American Presidency

James George Janos (aka Jesse Ventura), a former Governor of the State of Minnesota, and prior to that a "professional wrestler," an investigative journalist, and a former Navy Seal, addressed the upper one percent, who, through their financial backing, appoint Presidents; thereby ruling the United States of America:

> "You control our world. You have poisoned the air we breathe, contaminated the water we drink, and copy-righted the food we eat. We fight in your wars, die for your causes, and sacrifice our freedoms to protect you. You have liquidated our savings, destroyed our middle class, and used our tax dollars to bailout your unending greed. We are slaves to your corporations, zombies to your airwaves, servants to your decadence. You have stolen our elections, assassinated our leaders, and abolished our basic rights as human beings. You own our property, shipped away our

jobs, and shredded our unions. You have profited off of disaster, destabilized our currencies, and raised our cost of living. You have monopolized our freedom, stripped away our education, and have almost extinguished our flames. We are hit…we are bleeding…but we have no time to bleed. We will bring the giants to their knees and you will witness our revolution!"

The "Political Mafia" is strong and existing! Ousting the dictators throughout the world is a challenge to humanity ever since civilization commenced thousands of years ago. The cardinal aim of this writing is to call on the nation of those countries that are being destroyed through tyrannical and murderous regimes, whether dominated by the evils of theocracy, military, or billionaire charlatans seated in power, to defiantly yet courageously stand up and be counted.

The cruelty and misdeeds of global Imperialism, Communism and Colonialism must end. Short of violence or any bloodshed, the public needs to utilize every step available to oust the evils of tyranny and dictatorship and to halt the murderous invasion of any country by internal invaders and hirelings acting on the orders of their foreign based Mafia Bosses.

Ending the murderous yoke of dictatorships, especially despotism under Theocracy will be difficult to achieve without bloodshed. The chief reason is the vast number of brainwashed fanatics acting under the orders of their leader whom they have been made to believe is either supernatural, an anointment and appointment of God, the exalted one, the "all knowing, all wise" and many other attributions appeasing him, albeit the leader is a former obscure, semi-literate and an ignorant individual, a scoundrel, a charlatan and perhaps a roadside beggar. This relates to Iran, a country virtually destroyed by the evils of Islamic Theocracy through the clergymen created by Imperialism and Colonialism. Overthrowing the Kim dynasty in North Korea would be facing the same obstacles and challenges as that of the clergy dominated dictatorship in Iran.

A ray of hope to end dictatorship in the United States of America is however through the "ballot box."

I have taken the opportunity and the privilege to present my thoughts and feelings. Through my writings, I have a hope that Freedom of Expression can finally evince the nature of dictatorial laws and administration wherever Imperialism, Fascism, Colonialism and Communism have planted their puppets. Peace on Earth and goodwill towards mankind!

There is a need to remind that the needy and impoverished, the old and feeble, and the voiceless are the continuous targets of cruelty and misery throughout the world. From the poor and homeless person in the streets, uncertain if a morsel of bread would arrive for the day and without a fixed place to rest at night, to those living in utter poverty and hunger in hovels, all are among the exploited of the earth. There is no "rich country" and "poor country." Experts measure richness in terms of the scant minority of a nation in any country who are well off financially, not exceeding two percent of the entire population, while reflecting misleading and falsified figures as official government statistics of that country. Prosperity, wealth, and riches in true essence belong to those one or two percent who have successfully enslaved the public to serve them and to add to their already wealthy status.

As is well known, and to repeat, there are no set of rules and regulations binding and governing the laws of democracy. The Political Mafia "selects" most of the governments and administrations in countries either with geo-political importance or with mineral wealth. They control powerful countries that could subjugate and invade certain strategic countries under one pretext or the other and later install a puppet administration, who will diligently work for their interests. The degree of terror and misery spread by governments upon its own citizens for whom they are elected to serve requires an encyclopedia.

Author, political activist, human rights and environmental causes advocate, Suzanna Arundhati Roy renders her words of wisdom thus:

> "As the disparity between the rich and the poor grows, the fight to corner resources is intensifying. To push through their 'sweetheart deals,' to corporatize the crops we grow, the water we drink, the

air we breathe, and the dreams we dream, corporate globalization needs an international confederation of loyal, corrupt, authoritarian governments in poorer countries to push through unpopular reforms and quell the mutinies. Corporate Globalization - shall we call it by its name? Imperialism-needs a press that pretends to be free, it needs courts that pretend to dispense justice."

Roy disputes U.S. claims of being a peaceful and freedom-loving nation, listing China and nineteen Third World "countries that America has been at war with – and bombed – since World War II," as well as previous US support for the Taliban movement and the Northern Alliance (whose track record is not vastly different from the Taliban's).

In her final analysis, Roy sees American-style capitalism as the culprit:

"In America, the arms industry, the oil industry, the major media networks, and the U.S. foreign policy, are all controlled by the same business combines."

On her views on Narendra Modi, the Prime Minister of India, Roy in 2013, called Narendra Modi's nomination as prime minister a "tragedy." She said that business houses were supporting his candidacy because he was the "most militaristic and aggressive" candidate. She has argued that Modi has control over India to a degree unrecognized by most people in the western world; "He is the system. He has the backing of the media. He has the backing of the army, the courts, a majoritarian popular vote. Every institution has fallen in line."

Roy has on numerous occasions expressed deep despair for the future, calling Modi's long-term plans for a highly centralized Hindu State "suicidal" for the multicultural subcontinent."

Recently, Roy has opined on the rampant spread of the Coronavirus Virus.

"What is this thing that has happened to us? It is a virus, yes. In and of itself it holds no moral belief. But it is definitely more than a virus...It has made the mighty kneel and brought the world to a halt like nothing else could. Our minds ae still racing back and forth, longing for a return to 'normality,' trying to stitch our future to our past and refusing to acknowledge the rupture. But the rupture exists."

And amid this terrible despair, she said that this challenge offers us a chance to rethink the doomsday machine we have built for ourselves. "Nothing could be worse than a return to normality. Historically, pandemics have forced humans to break with the past and imagine their world anew."

In keeping up with the harmony of the subject matter of this literary work, "Ousting the Dictator," I find it most appropriate to reflect my dedication to human beings who lost their most precious gifts; their lives, while confronting the evils of subjugation in all forms, whether slavery, imprisonment and even execution for even intimidating the dictator, or fighting injustice and human exploitation.

No person deserves the initial esteems more than a once enslaved Ghanaian woman named Breffu and Christian, her companion, who in early November 1733 on the Danish Island of Jan, in the West Indies heroically stood up against their Danish enslavers and tormenters, the Kroyer family, originally from Denmark. Breffu and her companions entered the opulent home of the Kroyers and slaughtered this family who had most cruelly treated dozens of slaves earlier, either for disobedience or petty errors.

Preferring death rather than be captured and tortured to death, Breffu chose suicide in May 1734.

Breffu's heroism is a remembrance to mankind to stand up and be counted, to stand up and combat injustice and any dictatorial law.

Injustice and wanton murder of African Americans was and is an ugly face of reality throughout the country of the United States of America, beginning when the country was a part of the British Empire and continuing even after the country formed an independent country. Even today, people of African origin are brutalized and killed without any justified reason, right in the streets. In courts, harsh punishments are rendered to them for petty crimes.

Even after the American wars for independence, United States statesmen, politicians, and thinkers never accepted African Americans as equals for bizarre and unacceptable reasons. In all simple truth anti African sentiments in the United States of America is not recent. It dates back to more than two centuries ago and includes those who are considered as outstanding American politicians.

The enslaved Africans gladly embraced Christianity, their masters' religion, naively thinking that since they were Christian converts, life would be ameliorated for them by the slave masters. They were absolutely wrong. The owners did not care, they still treated the slaves as lesser humans.

Examining some of the statements by so-called stalwarts of American politics one feels shocked at their thoughts.

Benjamin Franklin (January 17, 1706 – April 17, 1790). Scientist, author, inventor, politician, and political philosopher.

> "Why increase the sons of Africa, by planting them in America where we have so fair an opportunity, by excluding all blacks and tawnies, or excluding the lovely black and red."

Thomas Jefferson (April 13, 1743 – July 4, 1826), President of the United States of America.

> "I advanced it, therefore, as a suspicion only that the blacks whether originally a distinct race or made distinct by time or circumstance, are inferior to the whites in the endowments of both body and mind."

Abraham Lincoln, (February 12, 1809 – April 15, 1865) President of the United States of America.

> "There is a physical difference between the white and the black races which I believe will forever forbid the two races living together while they do remain together...there must be a position of superior and inferior, and I as much as any man am in favor of having the superior position assigned to the white race."

Henry Rose Berry (1797 – December 15, 1867). Member of the Virginia House of Representative. He owned four slaves. Barry made the below mentioned statements after the bloodiest slave insurrection in American history. Nat Turner (October 2, 1800 - November 11, 1831) a slave and self-proclaimed prophet, initially met with six other slaves and later with more in the third week of August 1831 where they planned the mass murder. That night they rampaged through the streets of Jerusalem, Virginia, where they axed, shot, and bludgeoned fifty-five whites, mostly women and children. They also massacred ten black slaves. The rebellion was promptly suppressed on the morning of August 23, 1831. In retaliation, militias and mobs from the area murdered nearly 120 slaves and free blacks. Nat Turner was captured after six weeks in hiding. He was tried on November 5, 1831 for "conspiring to rebel and making insurrection;" he was convicted and sentenced to death. He was hanged on November 11, 1831 in Jerusalem, Virginia and his corpse was drawn and quartered. Historians claim that he was beheaded as an example to frighten other would-be rebels and his headless remains buried in an unmarked grave.

In the aftermath of the grisly murders by African slaves, Henry Rose Berry in his speech dated early January 1832 to members of the Virginia State Legislature said:

> "We have as far as possible, closed every avenue by which the light may enter the slave's mind. If we could extinguish the capacity to see the light, our work would be complete. They would be then on the level of beast of the fields, and we should then be safe."

In 1919, several decades after the evils of slavery was banned in 1865, two hundred and thirty-seven mass lynching of Black farmers and sharecroppers in the State of Arkansas were carried out by white vigilantism. The Black people were murdered because they wanted a fair compensation for the crops they produced and harvested. The perpetual shame of mankind's cowardice in murdering the African American farmers will always be reprehensible. It will always be a blot on American history. Authorities have never ascertained who provoked and ordered this wanton murder. The government officials did not care to investigate the murderers. They were not interested.

Around that same time was the "Tulsa Race Massacre" (May 31 - June 1, 1921), when thugs and hooligans murdered many United States citizens of African origin and burned their homes to the ground. More than seven hundred people were admitted to hospitals and nearly six thousand black residents of the city interned at large facilities for several days. A 2001 state commission examination of the event was able to confirm thirty-six dead, twenty-six black and ten white. Those who chronicled the events claim that more than a hundred died of their gunshot wounds, although this has not been substantiated. Nevertheless, dozens lost their precious lives.

While remembering Breffu's heroic stand against despotism, let us also remind ourselves of courageous and heroic Jewish women in the 1930's and 40's, who most bravely and fiercely (rather than beg and plead with murderous Nazi elements) walked towards their imminent death and into the gas chambers with an infant in arm and a child in their hand. Stands by such glorious Jewish mothers must and should stand as an outstanding paragon of courage; to face injustice with a fighting spirit. Their daring stand destroyed the spirit of the joint dictators of the evil Nazi dictatorship who claimed supremacy over the weak, the meek and the defenseless. Millions, more than six million innocent Jewish lives were deliberately destroyed by the evilest regime in the twentieth century.

This modest work is also dedicated to:

- The more than ten to twelve million lives of the Nation of Congo destroyed by the mentally disturbed and cruel Leopold II of Belgium (April 9, 1835 – December 17, 1909). Leopold II openly encouraged looting of the mineral and natural resources of the Congo, while systematically murdering and maiming the population.

- The hundreds of millions of human lives that have been sacrificed at the altar of crime, chaos, war mongering, territorial aggrandizement, evil mindedness with cruelty and corruption since the early 1900's. This relates to dictators replaced by other dictators who committed and continue to commit murder, including the most atrocious and vile acts against millions of people. Such were and are individuals in any given country who were jubilantly welcomed as heroes and liberators by those very same people who initially empowered and glorified him or her, and who later labelled themselves as victims of those same individuals they wittingly and even knowingly hailed as their leader. The "chosen" leader and savior later turned into a murderer and a merciless dictator with plenipotentiary powers, amenable only to himself and it is those original supporters who now beg that same dictator to just let them live! Just to be alive! Just to exist!

- The millions of soldiers who fought under the banner of the individual dictator to "defend" their homeland against imagined enemies, far, far away from the territorial boundaries of their own country!

- The millions of those defenseless human beings, men, women, and children, mostly those who followed the Jewish faith, who were murdered in cold blood for simply following a religion other than those practiced by much of the population in any given country, simply because the dictator had willed it so. Lest it be late, Adolf Schickelgruber Hiedler-Hitler, the tyrannical dictator's deeds ultimately ended with the death of nearly forty-five million human beings in World War Two, and it also served to end his own cruelty filled life!

An unbiased research states that the figure of "six million Jews murdered" is in reality nearly seven million Jewish men, women, and children. Those murdered in small towns and villages in the then occupied Soviet Union by the Nazis were counted as Soviet citizens rather than Jews. Those shot and gassed in extermination and concentration camps are only considered.

- The thousands of writers, authors, poets, sportsmen, journalists, and columnists who have been attacked, thrown into prisons, or executed through a summary trial in any form of dictatorship, be it military, theocratic, or even an outwardly form of democracy as being practiced in the United States of America.

Conspicuous among the dozens of murders of journalists throughout the countries of the world is that of Saudi Arabian journalist and writer Jamal Khashoggi who was murdered in the Saudi Arabian consulate in Istanbul, Turkey in October 2018.

In one of the eighteen interviews Trump had with Bob Woodward, prominent writer, Trump had wittingly boasted that he had saved the (explicit) of Saudi Arabia's Crown Prince, Mohamed bin Salman. Bin Salman has been identified as the person who had directed the murder of journalist Khashoggi through his operatives at the Saudi Arabian Consulate in Istanbul, Turkey. The Central Intelligence Agency (CIA) had concluded that Khashoggi, a frequent critic of the Saudi royal family, was murdered in the Saudi Arabian consulate in Istanbul, Turkey, in October 2018 on the direct orders of bin Salman.

Mass media reports that Trump knew very well, the criminal deed of Prince bin Salman and chose to hide it through reasons known to himself, but mainly said to relate among others, with Salman's father, King Abdulaziz, bestowing the top civilian honor gold medal on Trump on May 20, 2017 among several costly gifts. The Saudi King is noted for his ruthless behavior. This gift was among eighty-three items Trump received from the Saudi Ruler, including tiger fur-lined robes, several swords and daggers, gold embroidered dresses and an expensive artwork.

Of importance is the fact that US federal law bans government employees from accepting any gift from a foreign government valued at more than three hundred ninety dollars. Trump and several members of his entourage may have also received gifts, but existing laws prohibit them from keeping the gifts. The topic of Saudis lavishly gifting Trump paved the possibility of his offspring to have some form of business venture in Saudi Arabia which may have been a strong factor and motive in Trump protecting Prince bin Salman's crime. Nevertheless, Trump participated, even if indirectly, in bin Salman's crime by protecting him.

Trump has knowingly participated in hiding the identity of the person who ordered the gruesome murder of a journalist. The much-loathed Crown Prince is the de facto ruler of Saudi Arabia, albeit his senile father is the official king of the country. Turkish authorities never found Khashoggi's body. He was dismembered at the orders of bin Salman according to Turkish investigation reports. Donald J. Trump most shockingly sided with a murderer and a petty tyrant and the son of a ruling tyrant. This is the Wahabi School of Islam which teaches and permits the rulers of Saudi Arabia to murder any imagined enemy or any individual they dislike through any means possible including hired thugs. Often, they cling to invented Islamic canonical laws to justify their crimes.

The Saudi crown prince is often compared to the indecent, cruel, extravagant, and boisterous sons of Saddam Hussein Tikriti, the executed tyrant of Iraq. Saddam's sons died through violence as they had lived.

While recognizing those who suffered at the hands of barbaric people; the past and present dictators, it is also encouraging to know those who believe in true altruistic values benefitting humanity.

Among the hundreds, or the thousands, one such person is Ashton Kutcher (prominent American actor) whose non-profit organization "Thorn;" Digital Defenders of Children, of which his ex-wife Demi Moore is a co-founder, has taken a huge leap in helping victims of human trafficking. The organization's efforts have been so effective that with their help, law enforcement has been able to identify 5,894 child sex trafficking victims. They also rescued another 103 children from grievous situations of sexual abuse in 2017.

In February 2017, Kutcher gave a fifteen-minute speech on modern-day slavery to the Senate Foreign Relations Committee in the hope of compelling Congress to take concrete steps towards ending the horrors faced by women and children around the world. In his speech, Kutcher not only spoke about the rights of these women and children that have constantly been violated but also touched upon how he has been trolled and criticized for the stand that he has taken. He has often been told to "stick to his day job" (he is known as an actor), by these critics but he says what he does now and what his organization stands for is his day job. He also recounted horrific incidents of young children under the age of ten being raped and content being shared on the dark internet. The Department of Homeland Security had also enlisted the help of his organization in trying to track down the perpetrator of a seven-year-old victim who they had been trying to nab for the past three years. (Source: Notes from "48 Hours" television program). While Ashton Kutcher will also be eternally remembered in the annals of written history as a name worthy of respect, it would only be befitting to compare his noble deeds to those who were and are always considered the "Righteous Among the Nations."

If the moral and spiritual duties of those honored as "Righteous Among the Nations" were mainly considered to save precious lives of Jews, Gypsies, Slavs and others in mortal danger during the Second World War under the sadistic dictator, then in the present days of uncertainty and immorality, Ashton Kutcher's organization (to include the equal contributions of his former wife, Demi Moore) should and must be hailed as a landmark in fighting the evils of child abduction, forced slavery, human trafficking and other ills plaguing humanity. This nefarious crime is virtually rampant throughout the world, even in the so-called modern and industrialized countries who continuously claim to be the bulwark against such odious deeds.

The untiring and courageous Anuradha Koirala of Nepal, who follows the spiritual teachings of Mother (Saint) Theresa, single-handedly rescued abused and abandoned women and children throughout Nepal from a life of misery and torment. She, together with her volunteers, rescued eighteen thousand girls from sex trafficking. Most of these girls were destined to be smuggled to the rich Arab Sheikhs in Saudi Arabia, Dubai, Abu Dhabi,

Riyadh, and Bahrein's royal family members scattered throughout the tiny Island of Bahrein. The governments of Qatar, Oman and specifically His Majesty King Abdullah II of Jordan have outlawed, eschewed, and unequivocally condemned such a barbaric act. Many in the Muslim world consider His Majesty King Abdulla II as the leader of the Muslim World.

It is also undeniable that there are millions of others in this world, although less conspicuous than Ashton Kutcher, who with their limited funds and possibilities continue to endlessly contribute their modest share in ameliorating the lives and living standards of humanity in distress throughout the world. Thousands, even millions throughout the world have taken the cue from Ashton Kutcher in saving lives and returning dignity to those who have lost their faith in fellow humankind.

Let all awakened consciences join in respecting Sir Nicholas George Winton, British humanitarian (May 19, 1909 - July 1, 2019) and a very courageous person who dared imminent dangers to rescue children from certain death. Winton most daringly saved the lives of 650 Jewish children from occupied Prague, then the capital of Czechoslovakia, by transporting them to England by train and ferry during the Holocaust.

And yet another hero to remember was French Resistance hero Georges Loinger. (August 29, 1910 – December 28, 2018). Loinger in a courageous move rescued some 350 Jewish children and helped them escape into neutral Switzerland. Special esteems to the courageous nation of Switzerland who helped save innocent lives.

Let us also remember the "Children of Tehran!" More than a thousand Jewish children, some of them just ten or less who were safely brought to Iran at the wishes of the late Shah of Iran during the war years and holocaust in Nazi occupied Europe. Also, included in the group were a few hundred aged men and women. His Majesty Mohammad Reza Pahlavi, Light of the Aryans, welcomed the large group and instructed all comfort be placed at their disposal.

Historian, writer, chronicler of historical events in Iran and academic, Dr. Shojaeddin Shafa (December 4, 1918 – April 17, 2010) quoted the

Shah who with his entourage welcomed the Jews who were assisted to escape Nazi occupation forces through arrangements earlier made with the Iranian Diplomatic Corps throughout occupied Europe where Jewish lives were endangered. Dr. Shafa in early 1976 at a gathering in Tehran University recalled that in mid-1942; "In the lawns of the Marble Palace in downtown Tehran, His Majesty walked towards some of the aged and some who were in wheelchairs and welcomed them, some in English and mostly in French, promising them all protection while assuring of their safety. In a short speech he addressed them:

> "Greetings to you my honored Jewish friends, brothers and sisters. You are today in the same land where Cyrus our Great King welcomed you nearly two and half thousand years earlier. You chose to come to this country having faith in our words, promising to protect you. We shall keep up to your expectations at all costs. If Cyrus the Great (601 BC. – December 4, 530 BC. Founder of the Achaemenid Empire, invaded Babylonia in 538 BC, and freed the Jews from captivity) liberated the honorable Jews from captivity and helped rebuild their temples and even invited them into Iran (then a vast empire) then why should we not respect Cyrus the Great and his noble deeds, our own conscience and human instincts and the ancient Zoroastrian teachings of 'Good Words, Good Thoughts and Good Deeds,' but aspire to do even more with whatever possibilities we have. As the true descendants of this great King who was the first to recognize, declare and proclaim human rights as inseparable from humankind, it is our moral and spiritual duty to offer our services and help. We must do it! We will do it with a greater zeal! Such a proclamation by the great King undoubtedly forms the most outstanding pillars and part of human history. Posterity and history will judge us if we do not hasten to take the required steps to ameliorate their situation which is endangered. It is no secret that our Jewish brothers and sisters have been subjected to the most horrifying brutality. Welcome you all to the land where the remains of Cyrus, Darius, Xerxes, Cambyses, Daniel, Esther, and Mordechai are laid to rest. Feel at home."

At the end of the war and the declaration of the State of Israel, many were flown to Tel Aviv, but many preferred to live in Iran and join the Jewish community there.

In modern times, special honor and gratitude goes to such respected heads of state; President of the French Republic, His Excellency Emmanuel Jean-Michael Frederic Macron, a philosopher, a visionary and a far-sighted politician, staunch supporter of Human Rights seeking to ameliorate living conditions of humankind, in the true tradition of the French nation. His Majesty King Felipe VI of Spain, who like his father, His Majesty King Juan Carlos I, has always attached special importance to human lives and their well-being. His Majesty King Felipe VI is considered one of the strongest supporters of Human Rights throughout the world. Ere it be forgotten, the popular succeeding governments of Switzerland in the past centuries, who have always and unfailingly come to the succor of mankind in need and aid, deserves a special tribute.

Last, but not the least, a word of gratitude to the dozens of the heroic Israeli doctors and nurses who have continued and continue to treat the sick and terminally ill Palestinians in need of special medical attention.

Quotes and Poems

It would only be too befitting for the reader of this Chapter to judge for themselves as to what degree these quotes and poems relate to the dictators, despots and tyrants or the aspiring dictators in the twenty first century, who imitate the cruel and war-mongering dictators of the past. I feel sure that mankind has yet to take a cue from the words of sagacity and admonishments from these thinkers, philosophers, and men of letters to create a world devoid of the miseries plaguing humankind for thousands of years, where the maligned, mentally ill tyrants, despots and dictators have indulged in cruelties, mass murders, territorial aggrandizements, enslavement, imprisonment, and limitations of every kind.

Reinforcing the truth that dictators, tyrants, and evil beings are not born, they are created! Since such individuals rise and grab power through deceit, falsity, violence, crime, and chaos, they will eventually be rid by the very nation they have harmed and destroyed, in the same manner.

I have reflected only a portion of the quotes and statements. Nevertheless, most were spoken in extempore, but suggest the reader to research the entire statements of these persons.

Admonishments to the Public

Epitaph on a Tyrant
Perfection, of a kind, was what he was after,
And the poetry he invented was easy to understand;
He knew human folly like the back of his hand,
And was greatly interested in armies and fleets;
When he laughed, respectable senators burst with laughter,
And when he cried the little children died in the streets.

W.H. Auden (1907 – 1973)

"A tyrant must put on the appearance of uncommon devotion to religion. Subjects are less apprehensive of illegal treatment from a ruler whom they consider god-fearing and pious. On the other hand, they do less easily move against him, believing that he has the gods on his side."

Aristotle

"Wherever they burn books, in the end will also burn human beings."

Christian Johann Heinrich Heine, Essayist, journalist, and poet. (December 13, 1797 – February 17, 1856)

"The secret of Freedom lies in educating people, whereas the secret of tyranny is in keeping them ignorant."

Maximilien Robespierre, French Lawyer (May 6, 1758 – July 28,1794)

"In order to rally people,
Governments need enemies.
They want us to be afraid, to hate, so we will rally behind them.
And if they do not have a real enemy, they will
invent one in order to mobilize us."

Thich Nhat Hanh/Nguyen Xuan Bao, Vietnamese monk, (1926-)

"Choose your leaders with wisdom and forethought.
To be led by a coward is to be controlled by all that the coward fears.
To be led by a fool is to be led by the opportunists who control the fool.
To be led by a thief is to offer up your most
precious treasures to be stolen.
To be led by a liar is to ask to be told lies.
To be led by a tyrant is to sell yourself and those you love into slavery."

Octavia E. Butler, (June 22, 1947- February
24, 2006). *Parable of the talents.*

"You only have power over people as long as you don't take everything away from them. But when you've robbed a man of everything, he's no longer in your power – he's free again."

Alexander Solzhenitsyn. (December 11, 1918 – August 3, 2008)

"As a nation, we began by declaring that 'all men are created equal, except negroes.' When the Know-Nothings get control, it will read 'all men are created equal, except negroes, and foreigners, and Catholics.' When it comes to this I should prefer to emigrating to some county where they make no pretense of loving liberty - to Russia, for instance, where despotism can be taken pure, and without the base alloy of hypocrisy."

Lincoln Letters. Abraham Lincoln, 16th US President. (February 12, 1809 – April 15, 1865)

"Those who are capable of tyranny are capable of perjury to sustain it."

Lysander Spooner. American abolitionist, entrepreneur, essayist, legal theorist, political philosopher, Unitarian, and writer. (January 19, 1808 - May 14, 1887)

"The president is a nationalist, which is not all the same thing as a patriot. A nationalist encourages us to be at our worst, and then tells us that we are the best. A nationalist, 'although endlessly brooding on power, victory, defeat, revenge,' wrote Orwell, tends to be 'uninterested in what happens in the real world.' Nationalism is relativist, since the only truth is the resentment we feel when we contemplate others."

Timothy Snyder (August 18, 1969) *On Tyranny: Twenty lessons from the Twentieth Century.*

Danilo Kis, the Serbian writer speaking on nationalism said, "Nationalism has no universal values, aesthetic or ethical. A patriot, by contrast, wants the nation to live by its ideals, which means asking us to be our best selves. A patriot must be concerned with the real world, which is the only place his county where his country can be loved and sustained. A patriot has universal values, standards by which he judges his nation, always wishing it well – and wishing that it would do better."

Danilo Kis (February 22, 1935 – October 15, 1989)

"The wisest thing in the world is to cry out before you are hurt. It is no good to cry out after you are hurt; especially after you are mortally hurt. People talk about the impatience of the populace; but sound historians know that most tyrannies have been possible because men moved too late. It is often essential to resist a tyranny before it exists."

G.K Chesterton (May 29, 1874 – June 14, 1936).

"A democracy which makes or even effectively prepares for modern, scientific war must necessarily cease to be democratic. No country can be really well prepared for modern war unless it is governed by a tyrant, at the head of a highly trained and perfectly obedient bureaucracy."

Aldous Huxley (July 26, 1894 – November 22, 1963) From his writings; *"Ends and Means."*

"When you make men slaves, you deprive them of half of their virtue, you set them in your own conduct an example of fraud, rapine and cruelty, and compel them to live with you in a state of war; and yet you complain that they are not honest or faithful."

Olaudah Equiano (1745 – March 31, 1797)

"In every age it has been the tyrant, the oppressor and the exploiter who has wrapped himself in the cloak of patriotism, or religion, or both to deceive and overawe the People."

Eugene Victor Debs. (November 5, 1855 – October 20, 1926)

"During the next hundred years, the question for those who love liberty is whether we can survive the most insidious and duplicitous attacks from within, from those who undermine the virtues of our people, doing in advance the work of the Father of Lies."

On several occasions, Michael Novak told his audience that there is no such thing as truth, they teach even the little ones." Novak compared truth as a bondage. Believe what seems right to you. There are as many truths as there are individuals. "Follow your feelings. Do as you please. Get in touch with yourself. Do what feels comfortable." He repeatedly cautioned those who speak in this way prepare the jails of the twenty-first century saying that they do the work of the tyrants.

Michael Novak (September 9, 1933 – February 17, 2017)

"There will be in the next generation or so, a pharmacological method of making people love the servitude, and producing dictatorships without tears, so to speak, producing a kind of painless concentration camp for entire societies, so that people will in fact have the liberties taken away from them, but will rather enjoy it, because they will be distracted from any desire to rebel by propaganda or brainwashing, or brainwashing enhanced by pharmacological methods. And this seems to be the final revolution."

Aldous Huxley (July 26, 1894 – November 22, 1963)

"Break your silence and the tyrants will wet themselves." and,
"I am what stands between humanity and the crisis – I am what stands between humanity and discrimination and disparities - I am what stands between humanity and dictators."

Abhijit Naskar, (October 9, 1991) One of the world's celebrated Neuroscientists, and an untiring advocate of global harmony.

"There are two ways to be fooled. One is to believe what isn't true. The other is to refuse to accept what is true."

Søren Aabye Kierkegaard, Danish philosopher, theologian, poet, and social critic. (May 5, 1813 – November 11, 1855)

"Tyrannies are perpetuated by diffident men who do not possess the courage to act out their beliefs."

Stanley Milgram (August 15, 1933 – December 20, 1984) *Obedience to Authority.*

MEHR A. KALAMI

"You want a picture of the future? Imagine a boot trampling a human face. The moral to be drawn from this nightmarish situation is simple. Don't let it happen. It depends on you."

George Orwell (June 25, 1903 – January 21, 1950)

"Of all the tyrannies that affect mankind, tyranny in religion is the worst, every other species of tyranny is limited to the world we live in; but this attempts to stride beyond the grave and seeks to pursue us into eternity."

Thomas Paine (January 29, 1737 – June 8,1809)

"Pity the nation whose people are sheep,
And whose shepherds mislead them.
Pity the nation whose leaders are liars, whose sages are silenced,
And whose bigots haunt the airwaves.
Pity the nation that raises not its voice,
Except to praise conquerors and acclaim the bully as hero
And aims to rule the world with force and by torture.
Pity the nation that knows no other language but its own
And no other culture but its own.

Pity the nation whose breath is money
And sleeps the sleep of the too well fed.
Pity the nation – oh, pity the people who allow their rights to erode
and their freedoms to be washed away.
My country, tears of thee, sweet land of liberty."

Lawrence Ferlinghetti (born March 24, 1919 – February
22, 2021) Poet, Painter, Socialist Activist.

"When you tear out a man's tongue, you are not proving him a liar, you are only telling the world that you fear what he might say."

George Raymond Richard Martin (September 20, 1948)

"Throughout history, it has been the inaction of those who could have acted, the indifference of those who should have known better, the silence of the voice of justice when it mattered most, that has made it possible for evil to triumph."

Emperor Haile Selassie I (Ge ez, born Lij Tafari Makonnen, July 23, 1892 – August 27, 1975, son of Makonnen Wolde-Mikael Guddisa and Princess Yeshimebet Ali Abba Jifar, daughter of the renowned Oromo ruler of Wollo, Ali Abba Jifar.)

"That until the philosophy which holds one race superior and another inferior is finally and permanently discredited and abandoned; That until there are no longer first-class and second-class citizens of any nation; that until the color of a man's skin is of no more significance than the color of his eyes; That until that day, the dream of lasting peace and world citizenship and the rule of International morality will remain but a fleeting illusion, to be pursued but never attained."

Emperor Haile Selassie I

"We must stop confusing religion, and spirituality. Religion is a set of rules, regulations, and rituals created by humans which were supposed to help people spiritually. Due to human imperfection religion has become corrupt, political, divisive, and a tool for power struggle. Spirituality is not theology or ideology. It is simply a way of life, pure and original as given by the Most High. Spirituality is a network linking us to the Most High, the universe, and each other."

Emperor Haile Selassie I

"We know they are lying,
They know they are lying,
They know we know they are lying,
We know they know we know they are lying,
But they are still lying."

Aleksandr Isayevich Solzhenitsyn (December 11, 1918 – August 3, 2008) Russian novelist, philosopher, poet, historian.

"When ignorant folks want to advertise their ignorance, you don't have to do anything, you just let them talk."

Barack Obama (August 4, 1961) 44th President of the United States of America.

"We should soundly reject language coming out of the mouths of any of our leaders that feeds a climate of fear and hatred or normalizes racist sentiments; leaders who demonize those who don't look like us or suggest that other people, including immigrants, threaten our way of life or refer to other people as sub-human. Or imply that America belongs to just one certain type of people."

Barack Obama, August 5, 2019.

"We must especially beware of that small group of selfish men who would clip the wings of the American Eagle in order to feather their own nests."

Franklin D. Roosevelt. (January 30, 1882 – April 12, 1945) 32nd President of the United States of America between March 4, 1933 and April 12, 1945.

"We are a nation of many nationalities many races, many religions-bound together by a single unity of freedom and equality. Whoever seeks to set one nationality against another, seeks to degrade all nationalities."

Franklin D. Roosevelt.

"The liberty of a democracy is not safe if the people tolerated the growth of private power to a point where it becomes stronger than the democratic state itself. That in its essence is fascism: ownership of government by an individual, by a group, or any controlling power."

Franklin D. Roosevelt.

"Tyrants are always fond of bad men, because they love to be flattered, but no man who has the spirit of a freeman in him will lower himself by flattery, good men love others, or at any rate do not flatter them. Moreover, the bad are useful for bad purposes; 'nail knocks out nail,' as the proverb says."

"It is characteristics of a tyrant to dislike everyone who has dignity or independence, he wants to be alone in his glory, but anyone who claims or likes dignity or asserts his independence encroaches upon his prerogative and is hated by him as an enemy to his power. Another mark of a tyrant is that he likes foreigners better than citizens and lives with them and invites them to his table; for the one are enemies, but the others enter into no rivalry with him."

Aristotle, "Politics." C. 350 BCE

"America today feels like 1929 or 1930 Berlin. Things that couldn't be said five years ago in public are now normal discourse. Trump is an enabler. He's a sick, very disturbed individual. Appeasement of Fascism is what led to everything."

Stephen B. Jacobs, Buchenwald Concentration Camp survivor.

"Dictators ride to and fro on tigers from which they dare not dismount. And the tigers are getting hungry."

Winston Churchill (November 30, 1874 – January 24, 1965) *While England Slept*, 1938

"Trump is incompetent, dishonest and profoundly indecent. His staggering incapacity for moral leadership in this unprecedent moment is hard to overstate. His empty boasting, dishonesty, blame gaming, lack of empathy and fragile ego are a deadly combination of traits right now."

Stephen Edward Schmidt (September 28, 1970) American communications and public affairs strategist who has worked for Republican political campaigns.

"I'll bet no future President will ever hang Trump's portrait in the White House. It will be impossible to shower even false praise on the most vile of men. His Presidency will be like Chernobyl. Something to be sealed off. A poison to be contained."

Stephen Edward Schmidt.

Note: In the second week of May 2020, Trump had refused to unveil the portrait of former President Obama, as is customary of the person seated in the White House.

"Either the United States will destroy ignorance. Or ignorance will destroy the United States."

William Edward Burghardt Du Bois (February 23, 1868 – August 27, 1963) American sociologist, socialist, historian, civil rights activist, Pan-Africanist, author, writer, and editor. First African American to earn a doctorate. Du Bois was also one of the founders of the National Association for the Advancement of Colored People. (NAACP) in 1909.

"I found much that was alarming about being a citizen during the tenures of Richard Nixon and George W. Bush. But whatever I may have seen as their limitations of character or intellect, neither was anything like as humanly impoverished as Trump: ignorant of government, of history, of science, of philosophy, of art, incapable of expressing or recognizing subtlety or nuance destitute of all decency and wielding a vocabulary of seventy-seven words that is better called Jerkish than English."

Philip Roth (March 19, 1933 – May 22, 2018) Author.

"One of the saddest lessons of history is this: If we've been bamboozled long enough, we tend to reject any evidence of the bamboozle. We're no longer interested in finding out the truth. The bamboozle has captured us. It's simply too painful to acknowledge, even to ourselves that we've been taken. Once you give a charlatan power over you, you almost never get it back."

Carl Edward Sagan (November 9, 1934 – December 20, 1996) Astronomer, planetary scientist, cosmologist, astrophysicist, astrobiologist, author, poet, and science communicator.

"A fascist is one whose lust for money or power is combined with such an intensity of intolerance towards those of other races, parties, classes, religions, cultures, regions or nations as to make him ruthless in his use of decent or violence to attain his ends."

Henry Agard Wallace (October 7, 1888 – November 18, 1965) 33rd Vice President of the United States of America, 1941 – 1945.

"An evil enemy, will burn his own nation to the ground…to rule over the ashes."

Sun Tzu (544 – 496 BC) Chinese general, military strategist, philosopher.

Words of Wisdom

"The root of joy is gratefulness. It is not joy that makes us grateful; it is gratitude that makes us joyful."

Brother David Steindl-Rast, born Franz Kuno Steindl-Rast (July 12, 1926), Catholic Benedictine Monk, author, and lecturer.

"We can reject everything else: religion, ideology, all received wisdom. But we cannot escape the necessity of love and compassion. This, then is my true religion, my simple faith. In this sense, there is no need for temple or church, for mosque or synagogue, no need for complicated philosophy, doctrine, or dogma. Our own heart, our own mind, is the temple. The doctrine is compassion. Love for others and respect for their rights and dignity, no matter who or what they are: ultimately these are all we need."

Dalai Lama

"You exist in time, but you belong to eternity-You are a penetration of eternity into the world of time-You are deathless, living in the body that is born and dies-Your consciousness knows no death, no birth-It is only your body that is born and dies-But you are not aware of your consciousness-You are not conscious of your consciousness-And that is the whole art of meditation; Becoming Conscious is Consciousness itself."

Words of wisdom from Osho (December 11,1931 – January 19, 1990)

History and War

History bears witness that since the birth of the United States of America as an independent country on July 2, 1776, with the declaration of independence, the country has been at war for ninety three percent of the time of its existence. (On July 4, the Continental Congress formally adopted the Declaration of Independence, which had been written largely by Thomas Jefferson. Though the vote for actual independence took place on July 2, 1776, from then on, the 4th became the day that was celebrated as the birth of American Independence). There was calm and peace throughout the country between 1796-1797 and again between 1807-1809 and yet another period of calm between 1828 to 1830. Some historians opposed to war and destruction ask whether the United States of America is a truculent bully.

A state of comparison exists between United Kingdom and the United States of America. During its tenure as the so-called policeman of the world between 1815, after the Napoleonic Wars, to 1914, the outbreak of the First World War, the country was at war for all but fifteen years. That means eighty five percent of the time, but if one takes the timeframe of all American history from 1776 till today (late 2020) then the United Kingdom was at war for all but twenty-three years, amounting to ninety percent of the time, almost the same as the United States of America.

On October 10, 2019, Newsweek reported that the USA has spent six trillion dollars on wars that killed half a million people since the 9/11 tragedy where three thousand lives perished, perpetrated by terrorists, fifteen of the nineteen of them who were Saudi Arabian citizens who adhered to the school of "Wahabism" considered an offshoot of mainstream Islam.

The world-wide terrorist group who committed this gruesome crime are in fact being led by a "joint command" of terrorists. They have a leader; whose real identity is unknown. He is their form of a dictator. He is replaced as soon as he is either killed or dies! Such a blood-shedding phenomenon is only achieved by a dictator, or a puppet dictator or an aspiring dictator!

Since the dawn of mankind's presence on Planet Earth, humanity has always been in one way or the other desirous of hierarchy, leading to some form of dominance…dominance to sway power and to control and in most of the cases to just rule, whether the immediate family, group, society or even a nation. The exact timing of the commencement of such a behavior is unknown and cumbersome a task to assess. It is since time immemorial; human behavior, instincts and feelings have not changed!

In modern times, humanity had and still has that potential and propensity on a larger scale to enact and create situations, much more dangerous, hundreds, if not, thousands of times more dreadful than even eight decades ago. With the invention of mass-scale destructive weaponry, death, destruction, and bloodshed on an unbelievably colossal scale will be the results should countries with such weapon systems decide to wage war. Usually, it is time and often, that a country with weapons of mass destruction wages war with a country far weaker and even poverty stricken that reason, logic and syllogism defy!

Imagine the unthinkable; the breakage of a war between two neighboring nuclear armed mortal enemies; Pakistan with a population exceeding two hundred million and India with a population of one billion and four hundred million! The human casualty would cause the death of at least two hundred million on both sides, if not much more! These two countries have been at war with each other on at least four occasions.

We could name hundreds of wars, battles, skirmishes, and conflicts. Such horrifying developments yet conspicuous in the annals of written history are many, just too many to list. They number in the thousands. Some, many of them can never be skipped. They caused blood to flow and lives lost, cities razed, and societies slaughtered. They tell us the carnage these human errors have caused in their statistics. Some of the several hundred are the battles of Thermopylae (6000 casualty 480 BC), Kadesh (Unknown casualty 1274 BC), Marathon (8000 casualty 490 BC).

Documents including historical facts speak of the gradual increase of human losses in wars, as the years went by, due to improvements in weaponry. Other battles that created untold human losses are Cannae, Pharsalus, Carrhae, Alesia, Bosworth, Hastings, Trebia, Issus, Gaixia, Adrianpole, Cunaxa, Corinth, Teutoburg Forest, Platea, Hydaspes, Zama, Salamis, Wars of the Carnatic, Napoleonic, Boer, and hundreds more. None of the soldiers in the opposing armies knew each other!

The Persian-Roman Wars is certainly a blot on humankind since this was the longest War history has ever recorded. The Wars were fought in various regions of the Persian and Roman Empire. More than two million dead. 62 BC – 628 AD. The Wars continued for 694 years! Again, none of the soldiers in the opposing armies knew each other!

The "Hundred Years War" was a series of conflicts waged from 1337 to 1453 by the House of Plantagenet, rulers of the Kingdom of England, against the French House of Valois, over the right to rule the Kingdom of France. Most notable war during the Middle Ages, where five generations of kings from two rival dynasties fought for the throne of the largest kingdom in Western Europe. Historians have suggested that more than a million soldiers and half that number in civilian casualties. Once again, none of the soldiers in the opposing armies knew each other!

Between the years May 22, 1455 - June 16, 1487 (32 years, 3 weeks, and 4 days) on English soil was fought "Wars of the Roses" or initially called "The Cousins' War" between two rulers; the House of Lancaster and the House of York. In one major Battle of Towton where over 50,000 soldiers fought, more than 25,000 lost their lives. The exact number of casualties of the bloodiest battle on English soil could not be ascertained, nevertheless, it has been suggested by various historian to number in the hundreds of thousands. As usual in all wars and conflicts, none of the soldiers in the opposing armies knew each other!

More and more Wars, whose dimensions and magnitudes were immense, where mankind were manipulated by their leaders to kill, kill, and kill and be finally killed. For whom and for what? For the leader now turned dictator or for whom? Some of these human created disasters whose ability to destroy and kill increased in "geometrical proportion' compared to the wars, of the past were: The Two World Wars, Korea, Vietnam, Iran – Iraq, Gulf Wars, India - Pakistan and hundreds more in the African Continent where real records of human carnage can never be tracked.

To better comprehend the depth of misery and bloodshed, wars, battles, and conflicts caused then and now with more advanced weaponry packing massive destructive power, the subsequent lines will give a more precise idea of the extent mankind's folly has sunk.

World War I

Mankind's folly fell to abyssal depths when either due to territorial and economic conflicts or simply due to sheer stupidity, World War I commenced in the Balkans in late July 1914 and ended in November 1918, leaving 17 million dead and 20 million wounded. None of the soldiers in the opposing armies knew each other!

Historians reasoned if the terrible conflict could have been averted or if the situation was out of control, when a few generals and politicians decided that war was the answer! Strangely enough, with the absence of reason and basic logic, this terrible crisis was triggered by the assassination of Archduke Franz Ferdinand by a Bosnian-Serb nationalist Gavrilo Princip who had been supported by a nationalist organization in Serbia.

The German historian Michael Freund described Franz Ferdinand as "a man of uninspired energy, dark in appearance and emotion, who radiated an aura of strangeness and cast a shadow of violence and recklessness ... a true personality amidst the amiable insanity that characterized Austrian society at this time."

Franz Ferdinand's sometime admirer Karl Kraus put it, "he was not one who would greet you...he felt no compulsion to reach out for the unexplored region which the Viennese call their heart." His personal relations with Emperor Franz Joseph were tense; the emperor's personal servant recalled in his memoirs that "thunder and lightning always raged when they had their discussions."

To repeat, the terrible "Great War" that took 17 million lives and wounded 20 million all began at the death of a mentally unstable and an inept individual! None of the soldiers in the opposing armies ever knew each other!

World War II

This terrible event in written history commenced on September 30, 1938 with the invasion and occupation of the Czech part of Czechoslovakia. One major excuse was the German Fuehrer's claim to the Sudetenland where large numbers of German speaking people lived. Germany invaded Poland on September 1, 1939 – October 6, 1939. This time Danzig (Gdansk) the port city in Poland was the target, where also many German speaking population lived. The Germans accused the Poles and the Czechoslovakians of grossly mistreating the German population.

The participants were Adolf Hitler, Benito Mussolini, and the Japanese ruling hierarchy. Generalissimo Francisco Franco Bahamonde, the dictator in Spain chose to be neutral.

It is a known fact that this war was fought on land, sea and air in Europe, Asia, Africa, and South America. World War II was the deadliest military conflict in history. An estimated total of 70 – 85 million people perished, or about 3% of the 1940 world population which was estimated to have been 2.3 billion.

Some conspicuous reasons both in the very distant past and, especially now, is chiefly to usurp territories, pillage and loot the natural, and mineral resources of the country being attacked or invaded. Although in many cases territorial aggrandizement may not be the main cause, the true intentions are masked under various guises. Under various pretexts, false flags, unfounded claims and reasons, war is initially commenced through political activities, leading to threats, then border conflicts and finally full-scale war where the unsuspecting youth of the countries involved are sent to their certain deaths while serving the designs of armament manufacturers in bankrupting the financial coffers of the countries involved in the wars. All done by the so-called heads of state, while they take their orders by their "handlers" who helped elect them to the seat of power!

Direction of the World vs US

While the sane and cultured world has many enlightened leaders and could be rightfully termed as leaders of the Free World in their own rights; Emmanuel Macron, Justin Trudeau, Angela Merkel, Felipe VI, The Collective Democracy in Switzerland and many other major figures, the other side of the political spectrum in majority of the countries of the world presents a very doleful picture that virtually eclipses the numbers of benign and progressive leaders! The USA is most unfortunately regressing into a lawless State where unruly thugs freely attack the ordinary public that they believe do not conform with their standards of thoughts.

I will concentrate on the subject as to how a progressive society like the USA, once referred to as a bastion of humanity and Leader of the Free World has abysmally sunk into a war-mongering nation under the "management" of a poorly tutored bully who successfully dodged his compulsory Military Service under various excuses of poor health and who was placed into the Oval Office through the incorrect method of Presidential Elections. How an individual and his appointed thugs threatened war and destruction on other countries for refusing to be subservient to him and his appointees. They belittled and insulted other nations of the world for their religious beliefs and faiths; these threats and insults were also used against the US Nation in general!

Former president Jimmy Carter in a lecture directed to Trump on April 13, 2019 said: "We have wasted, I think, three trillion dollars on military spending. China has not wasted a single penny on war and that's why they're ahead of us. In almost every way." (In relation to Trump increasing hundreds of billions of dollars on the military budget.)

"This president's cruelty is matched by the cowardice of his enablers, who inflict just as much damage on the nation and its ideals. Men and women in elected office shouldn't get a presumption of normalcy. They must answer for their silence in the face of bigotry and misogyny." Dan Rather, writer, popular journalist.

"Scientists and inventors of the USA (especially in the so-called 'Blue-State that voted overwhelmingly against the present individual in the Oval Office) have to think long and hard whether they want to continue research that will help their government remain the world's superpower. All the scientists who worked for Germany in the 1930s lived to regret that they directly helped a sociopath like Hitler murder millions of people. Let us not repeat the same mistakes over and over again." Piero Scaruffi

"Nobody has ever recommended a dictatorship aiming at ends other than those he himself approved. He who advocates dictatorship always advocates the unrestricted rule of his own will." Ludwig Von Mises...Omnipotent Government

"It was one of the greatest errors in evaluating dictatorship to say that the dictator forces himself on society against its own will. In reality, every dictator in history was nothing but the accentuation of already existing state ideas which he had only to exaggerate in order to gain power." Wilhelm Reich, The Mass Psychology of Fascism

"Ignorance is an evil weed, which dictators may cultivate among their dupes, but which no democracy can afford among its citizens." William Beveridge

CHAPTER TWO

DICTATORS

He, the dictator wields all powers, with the so-called elected officials being nothing less than a group of thugs, acting at the behest of the dictator.

Thus, a dictator is created but not born. It could be asked as to how a dictator, essentially one single person, a single human being in all frailty, is able to dictate, order and even define the lives and livings of millions of people whom he controls and is not in the least amenable to his acts and deeds! He just sends them to die through wars and border conflicts, just to appease his masters who helped "whelp" him into power!

The power of "suggestion" coupled with false promises, lies and deceit plays a salient role in embellishing the future dictator in the minds and eyes of the public. Although lacking any academic credentials or even simple general knowledge, the supposedly elected and popular ruler, through widespread terror, has reserved for himself the role of the "ultimate decider" concerning every affair of the country, from lifestyle of the entire nation, their religious practices, and views; including strict limitations as to what they should eat, drink, wear, and speak. Such is the case rampant in the Theocracy in Tehran, considered to be the most anti-human regime in the country's history, perhaps in modern history throughout the world.

Research has proved the existence of similarities between the cruel regimes of Kim Jong-un in Pyongyang, the Theocratic clergy republic in Tehran, and the former Trump administration in Washington. They are and were all engaged in a war of "attrition" against the very same nations they were supposed to care and protect. In most simple terms, they have all unilaterally declared war against the very same nation they swore to defend and respect. The worst offender cannot be singled out. Any individual, group or party who opposes the dictatorial administration are considered as traitors and could expect the worst form of punishment.

The freedom of a nation reeling under the tormenting yoke of theocracy is not limited to what they should not do but only what they can do and should do! Political Thinkers identify such forms of government as maniacal, evil, and murderous sacerdotal theocracies. It appears a challenge to find a microcosm of benign aspect within their rule. This includes all religiously inclined regimes, whether Buddhist, Christian, Islamic or Hindu.

Dictators are created by human beings themselves and not through some ethereal or extra-terrestrial forces. Foreign powers with arcane agendas have played a pivotal role in overthrowing stable and modernizing Monarchies and other forms of Governments for their own benefit. Destabilizing and then toppling them is usually a US tactic! They create a "savior" in an unknown person for the nation whose government they desire to overthrow for their own interests!

In cases of modern day "classical dictators," there existed and exist Adolf Schickelgruber-Hiedler-Hitler (Adolf Hitler), Benito Mussolini, Pol Pot, Heng Samrin, Isaias Afewerki, Mao Zedong, Stalin, Omar al-Bashir (ousted and disgraced), Saddam Hussein Tikriti, Meles Zanawi Asres (former Prime Minister of Ethiopia succeeded Mengitsu Haile Mariam, a tyrant), Teodor Obiang Nguema Mbasago (President of Equatorial Guinea, who openly practices cannibalism), Paul Kagame, Robert Mugabe, succeeded by Emmerson Dambudzo Mnangagwa, Yoweri Museveni (President of Uganda), Clergyman Khamenei who has replaced clergyman Khomeini, an advocate to further uphold the values of his brand of Islam, Kim-il-sung, Kim Jong-il, Kim Jong-un, and dozens and dozens of such individuals.

Again, some deceased, some ousted and some still clinging to the gall of power!

Time and again, history has proved that it is the vociferous paid agitators who hail the future dictators with a paean of praise as saviors and invest in them a halo of superhuman glory even though few in that particular country have any knowledge about that "replacement."

Of interest is that not one of these so-called leaders had any academic credentials worthy to mention! Once seated firmly in power, the deceitful "leader" commences his dictatorial deeds of cruelty. The very same people who had earlier chanted poems of glorification and paens of praise to him now beg for their lives. The puppet head of state will now follow the orders of those who swept him to power.

Peaceful co-existence is out of the picture since creation of puppet regimes' main aim is to create "business" and further the goals of Imperialism. The only method is to keep up the tempo of tension, to create war...a war between their newly created "client state" through their puppet and any neighboring country that the puppet regime is at loggerheads. This will eventually enrich the armament industry of those power wielders in various forms; often selling their obsolete weapon systems to both warring parties while simultaneously emptying the treasury of the puppet regime. Under this strategy both parties of the war undergo death and destruction.

Lying, obfuscation and deceit through mass media has become the "tools of the trade" in both the past as in modern times. It has been successfully used in Germany, Italy, Iran, Greece, Cambodia, Afghanistan, Ethiopia and elsewhere to overthrow Monarchy or any other form of legitimate and popular government that has advocated peace and prosperity.

In most cases, the USA is grossly guilty of toppling any legitimate government, especially in Iran (through the aegis of the Carter Administration), where Monarchy, prevailed for more than two and half millennia. Undeniably true that International Imperialism promoted and authored a takeover of the country by ethnic minorities, claiming descent from the Prophet of Islam!

This is what International Imperialism wants and this is what Global Colonialism plans all the way. Communism, Marxism, Maoism and Trotskyism went to their graves as was expected. But Imperialism and Colonialism are most unfortunately there to stay!

In the USA too, such tactics, chiefly obfuscating the general population with false promises have been widely used before and during elections, whether Presidential or others! Only during the 2016 Presidential elections, it has been noted that the major candidates of the Republican Party have openly called for fraudulent tactics, "gerrymandering," (for local State and countrywide elections) violence, intimidation and even the use of force to win. Vote rigging, and other tricks are usually applied to assure a certain candidate wins, regardless of his questionable past and present.

Listed are the dictators, some alive, some dead and many of them executed and some leading a life of misery in exile. A list of present-day dictators, their deeds, and lifestyles reflect the horrors the world is imminently facing: wars, death, bloodshed, and destruction.

I have reflected these names together with the number of human beings they either killed through personal orders or were directly and indirectly responsible for these deaths. Researched figures reflect the degree of cruelty, evil and destruction inherent within mankind. I have left the reader with the liberty of either condemning or condoning any of these individuals. Their nefarious, odious, and notorious lifestyles and philosophies are self-explanatory. Lives of a few despots, including their deeds against humankind are presented. The numbers next to their names are in millions of human lives they destroyed to maintain their position.

Pol Pot - 2.4, Kim Il sung - 1.6, Saddam Hussein - 2, Slobodan Milosevic, Karadzic and Mladic exceeding 1 million, Heng Samrin - 1, Enver Pasha - 2.5, Ho Chi Minh - 1.7, Yahya Khan 2 - 12, Vladimir Lenin - 4, Napoleon - 3, Emperor Leopold 10 to 12 million, Julius Jacob von Haynau (?), Chiang Kai-shek – 10, Adolf Hitler - 17-20, Stalin - 40-62, Mao Ze Dong - 45-75, Ruhollah Khomeini - 1.5-2, Ali Khamenei – 125,000, Paul Kagame - 500,000-1,000000, Ronald Reagan and George HW Bush

(?)...Bill Clinton (?)...., George Walker Bush - 1, Robert Mugabe (?), Mobutu Sese Seko (unknown thousands), Omar al Bashir (Handed over to the International Criminal Tribunal), Mengutsu Haile Mariam - 1, Teodoro Obiang Nguema - Tens of thousands, King Mswati III (unknown thousands), Isaias Afewerki (?), Aleksandr Lukashenko (Unknown number), Islam Karimov (unknown thousands), King Abdulla, Saudi Arabia (unknown thousands), Hideki Tojo - 4, Emperor Hirohito - 6, Chiang Kai-Shek - 10.

The Dictators Who Were

In this Chapter, several cruel individuals who seized power and proclaimed themselves either as "paramount leader" or dictator, who knowingly and willfully oversaw the deaths, murders, and destruction of hundreds of thousands and even millions of their own compatriots are reflected.

Whether they have presided over the death of a few of their own compatriots or even more, and as said, hundreds of thousands, or in millions, written history has already referred to them as blood-thirsty murderers and tyrants, unworthy as being categorized as normal human beings in any sense.

Detailed are these dictators to remind mankind for posterity that what commences from an individual prattling revenge, animosity and hatred laced with false promises of ameliorating the nation's ills and shortcomings by pointing to a certain group or groups either practicing religious beliefs or a faith which is in the minority compared to those practiced by the majority of the nation can magnify into untold miseries for the nation.

The dictator's inebriated posture filled with toxic references to the minorities who had no role in the least for any imagined ills and shortcomings of the nation is accepted as a postulated fact without the least care to investigate the undeniable truth.

To refrain from either categorizing them either as a "lesser or worst dictator," they are not placed in a particular order. A dictator is a dictator irrespective of the number of human lives he has taken.

Mao-Zedong *Chairman Mao* (December 26, 1893 – September 9, 1976) He was a Chinese communist revolutionary who has been termed as the founding father of the People's Republic of China which he ruled with an iron hand from its establishment in 1949 until his death in 1976.

While Mao has been presented as a controversial figure, he is regarded as one of the most important and influential individuals in modern world history. He is also regarded as a political intellect, theorist, military strategist, poet, and visionary.

Mao is undoubtedly the worst dictator history has ever chronicled. He simply ordered his army of supporters to massacre any form of opposition either to him as a person or his plans.

During the late phase of the Chinese Civil War, between 1947-1951, there were mass killings of landlords as part of the program called "Land Reform," to redistribute land and properties to the peasant class and landless workers. This resulted in the death of millions of people. The actual number of people killed in the land reform campaign is believed to be lower than Ren Bishi's (April 30, 1904 – October 27, 1950) estimate of thirty million. Bishi was the Secretary General of the Politburo of the Communist Party of China.

During the economic and social campaign dubbed as the "Great Leap Forward" by the Communist Party of China under the leadership of Mao between the years 1958 to 1962 aimed to rapidly transform the country from an agrarian economy into a socialist society through rapid industrialization and collectivization, China experienced the greatest famine in its history. This deed under Mao is said to have caused the starvation and death of twenty to forty-three million people. Historians have made the case that the great leap forward was a genocidal campaign along class lines.

Another genocide perpetrated by the Communist Party under Mao was the notorious "Cultural Revolution," that took place in China between 1966 and 1976 which was a sociopolitical movement set into motion by Mao personally. The stated aim was to preserve true Communist ideology throughout the country by purging remnants of capitalist and traditional elements from Chinese society, and to re-establish Maoist thought as the dominant ideology within the Party. Writers and historians have documented the death of nearly ten million people during this catastrophic "Cultural Revolution!"

Harry Wu, famed Chinese-American human rights activist (February 8, 1937 – April 26, 2016) in one of his speeches stated: "those killed were targeted on the basis of class rather than ethnicity, therefore terming the campaign 'genocide' is incorrect and the neologism 'classicide' is more accurate. Throughout the next thirty years of social and economic transformation in Maoist China, class-motivated mass killings continued resulting in the deaths of nearly ten million members of the landlord class."

Harry Wu in his memoirs wrote:

> "My youth was one of peace and pleasure. Then in 1949 came the communist revolution, led by Mao. My life changed dramatically. During my teen-age years, my father lost all his properties. We had money problems. The government took over all the property in the country."

In early October 2009, Wu met the Dalai Lama in Washington. After that meeting, Wu spoke about the mass murder of Tibetans who had challenged the Chinese Army when they overran Tibet.

By all estimates, Mao Zedong could be rightfully called the most cruel and evil dictator who ever lived and directly participated in the deaths of nearly seventy-five million human beings! In the annals of written history there was never such an individual under whose cruel rule such an unimaginable number of human beings perished.

Immediately after his death, Mao's fame ablated into infamy. Hundreds of millions of Chinese who had lost their family members gradually began to loathe and even hate him and his ideologies.

Joseph Vissarionovich Stalin (born Ioseb Besarionis dze Jughashvili, December 18, 1878 – March 5, 1953) Stalin, a Georgian revolutionary and Soviet politician who led the Soviet Union after the death of Lenin in 1924 until his own death in 1953, was considered a cold-blooded murderer. He succeeded Lenin as the General Secretary of the Communist Party of the Soviet Union.

Under Stalin, "Socialism in One Country" (A theory put forth by Stalin and Nikolai Bukharin, the Bolshevik revolutionary who was later executed at the orders of Stalin for conspiring to overthrow the Soviet State in 1938) became a central tenet of the party's dogma. The theory held that given the defeat of all the communist revolutions in Europe in 1917-1923 except Russia, the Soviet Union should begin to strengthen itself internally.

Through the Five-Year Plans, the country underwent agricultural collectivization creating a centralized command economy and rapid industrialization. This led to significant disruptions in food productions that contributed to the famine of 1932-33. Between five and seven million people perished due to starvation. Historians have debated if the government had intended the famine and subsequent deaths to occur. To eradicate accused "enemies of the working class," Stalin instituted the "Great Purge" in which over a million were imprisoned and at least seven hundred thousand executed between 1934 and 1939.

At the onset and during the Second World War, Stalin had issued orders to execute dozens of senior military officers including thousands of military personnel who had refused orders to murder civilians in occupied territories. Several dozens of mass killings took place within the territorial boundaries of the Soviet Union as well as in countries the Soviets had occupied during World War II. The numbers have been described to be in the millions. No statistics have been provided.

However official records reveal 799,455 documented executions in the Soviet Union between 1921 and 1953; 681,692 of these were carried out between 1937 and 1938, the years of the Great Purge. But according to Michael Ellman (Economist), the best modern estimate for the number of repression deaths during the Great Purge is 950,000-1.2 million, which includes executions, deaths in detention, or soon after their release. In addition, while archival data shows that 1,053,829 perished in the Gulag from 1934 to 1953, the current historical consensus is that of the 18 million people who passed through the Gulag system from 1930 to 1953, between 1.5 and 1.7 million died as a result of their incarceration.

Historian and archival researcher Stephen G. Wheatcroft and Michael Ellman attribute roughly 3 million deaths to the Stalinist regime, including executions and deaths from criminal negligence. Wheatcroft and historian Robert Davies estimate famine deaths at 5.5 to 6.5 million while scholar Steven R. Rosefielde gives a number of 8.7 million.

The American historian Timothy D. Snyder in 2011 summarized modern data, made after the opening of the Soviet archives in the 1990's and concludes that Stalin's regime was responsible for 9 million deaths, with six million of these being deliberate killings. He notes that the estimate is far lower than the estimates of 20 million or above which were made before access to the archives.

On February 4, 1989, a Soviet weekly newspaper published the most detailed accounting of Stalin's victims yet presented to a mass audience, indicating that about 20 million died in labor camps, forced collectivization, famine, and executions.

The estimates, by the historian Roy Medvedev, were printed in the weekly tabloid "Argumenti i Fakti," which has a circulation of more than 20 million. In all, Mr. Medvedev calculated about 40 million victims of Stalin's repressions, including those arrested, driven from their land or blacklisted. Although the accounts and statistics of Stalin's terror is inexact and contentious science, Mr. Medvedev's estimates are in line with Western calculations that have long been disparaged by more official Soviet historians.

In a 2016 Kiev International Institute of Sociology poll, 38% of respondents had a negative attitude of Stalin, 26% a neutral one and 17% a positive. 19% refused to answer.

All said, Stalin is accused of ordering the deaths of between forty-two to sixty million people!

Pol Pot (born Saloth Sar May 19, 1925 - April 15, 1998) A Cambodian and a Marxist-Leninist, educated in elite schools and moved to France in the 1940's where he joined the French Communist Party. On his return to Cambodia in 1954, he joined the Marxist-Leninist Khmer Viet Minh organization in its guerilla war against King Norodom Sihanouk. Following the retreat of the Khmer Viet Minh's retreat in 1954, he fled to North Vietnam but later returned to Cambodia to regroup his forces. In 1968 he re-launched the war against the Cambodian government. Aided by the North Vietnamese military, his forces advanced and controlled all of Cambodia by 1975, when he achieved the title Secretary General of the Khmer Rouge (followers of the Communist Party of Kampuchea). He consistently received Chinese support as a bulwark against Soviet influence in the region.

Once in total control of the country, Pol Pot began his reign of terror, exacting a terrible bloodbath against the population who had not earlier supported his cause of Marxism -Leninism, as presented in the writings of Mao Zedong and Joseph Stalin. He has been internationally denounced for his role in the Cambodian genocide, regarded as a dictator guilty of crimes against humanity.

He first renamed the country as the Democratic Kampuchea and sought to create an agrarian socialist society. He ordered to forcibly relocate the urban population to the countryside to work on collective farms. Those who refused were summarily shot. Pol Pot's philosophy of eliminating the slightest discontent among the public earned him the title of the murderer-in-chief of Phnom Penh. Entire families were slaughtered under his orders, even if one had opposed him. Mass killings were a widespread practice by his forces under his direct orders. Malnutrition, strenuous working conditions, and the absence of proper medical services caused the laborers to die in the rice paddies due to exhaustion. Bodies of young children, as young as nine, the old and the feeble were discovered dead in the paddy fields throughout the country.

Although lacking proper statistics as to the number of deaths, scholars believe the number to exceed 3 million.

The Marxist-Leninists unhappy with Pol Pot's method of governing the country directly asked for Vietnamese intervention after Pol Pot's troops attacked several Vietnamese villages where there was a heavy civilian casualty. They installed a rival Marxist-Leninist faction opposed to Pol Pot and renamed the country the People's Republic of Kampuchea.

Pol Pot and his Khmer Rouge escaped to the Thai border, sometime in early 1993. Another faction opposed to him and led by Ta Mok, also a mass murderer, ordered Pol Pot be put under house arrest where he apparently committed suicide in 1998.

His last years were spent in total obscurity in a shanty dwelling where he was provided with the most meagre means of living. Ta Mok's personnel taunted and treated him with disdain. Years later, news surfaced that he was physically assaulted and regularly slapped by guards while under detention.

During his last days, he was suffering from various incurable ailments and was visibly frail. He walked with his hands folded, with an aura of absolute innocence, not mentioning or regretting even once the millions he ordered to be killed.

Saddam Hussein Tikriti, (April 28, 1937 – December 30, 2006) Saddam Hussein could be well considered as being the most bloodthirsty of any Arab ruler in the annals of Arab history in the past century. He seized power by deposing his ailing elder cousin Ahmed Hassan al Bakr on July 16, 1979 and overnight proclaimed himself as the sole administrator of Iraq. Prior to this date, he was the real power behind the al Bakr regime.

He created a security apparatus as cruel as himself. Many fellow Arab rulers and governments throughout the Arab world condemned the brutality of his dictatorship. Most conservative figures place the figure of those killed during interrogations at nearly two thousand and those executed by his security apparatus to exceed three hundred thousand.

Saddam Hussein's invasion of Iran resulted in the death of at least 800,000 Iranian military personnel in addition to more than two hundred thousand civilians and the destruction of at least twelve townships and three major cities. This also included over three hundred villages and border settlements on the Iraqi side of the border. Similarly Iraqi losses were reported to be more than half a million dead in addition to tens of thousands of civilian casualties. Saddam Hussein also attacked Iraqi Kurds with chemical weapons which killed at least four thousand. Saddam did not hesitate to use chemical weapons against the military personnel and civilian population in Iran. Both parties to this long war proclaimed victory.

It must be also said that in one of the longest modern-day wars (Iran–Iraq War, September 22, 1980 – August 20, 1988), all Arab countries, except for Syria and Algeria, extended their unequivocal support to their Arab brother Saddam Hussein Tikriti and his regime with men, money, and materials. On the contrary, at the outset of the Iraqi regime's invasion of Kuwait, every Arab country condemned Saddam.

His invasion of Kuwait resulted in the death of at least ten thousand Kuwaitis and the liberation of Kuwait by the US Armed forces resulted in the death of at least forty thousand Iraqi troops. The second attack on Iraq under George Walker Bush resulted in the estimated death of another two hundred fifty thousand Iraqi soldiers and civilians. The exact figures are still clouded in controversies.

Under no circumstances Saddam Hussein could ever be praised as a benign individual. He was as cruel as any dictator whether in the past or the present. His invasion of Kuwait and pillaging the wealth of that country hastened his downfall with both Arab countries and the United States of America taking steps to halt his further ambitions. Interventions by the Arab countries and the USA cost the Iraqi Army and the civilians of Iraq a heavy toll in men and materials. However, it must be mentioned that neither the United States of America nor governments of major countries strongly condemn the Iraqi dictator when he used chemical weapons on military as well as civilian populations in Iran, including Kurdish populations in his own country. Condemnations came however late, but only after a massive human toll.

Saddam Hussein, trembling and shaking and muttering unclear words was led to the gallows on December 30, 2006. This is how the life of this dictator ended!

Kim Il-Sung (April 15, 1912 – July 8, 1994) Often referred to as the Kim Dynasty in North Korea. The Korean Communist leader with his special brand of Communism is responsible for the deaths of at least 1.6 million North Koreans who were opposed to his ideologies and his strict rule.

An extremely uncompromising and a cruel individual, Kim Il-Sung, meted out harsh retributions against his enemies, sometimes wiping out entire families, even if one person in that family opposed him. The exact number of human tolls during his tenure in office, including the Korean War reached more than two million!

His son and successor Kim Jog-il was as ruthless as his father and his son and successor Kim Jong-un is as murderous as his father and grandfather.

On August 29, 2019, the Supreme People's Assembly of the Democratic People's Republic of Korea, changed their Constitution to solidify Kim Jong-un's rule. Earlier in July 2019, in a new Constitution he was named head of State and commander-in-chief of the military.

Kim is now the Head of State with plenipotentiary powers to do and act as he pleases! Historians agree that Kim, the third-generation hereditary leader, rules North Korea with an iron fist and the title change will mean little to the way he wields power.

"Dear Respected Leader," or "The Marshal" as Kim Jong-un is addressed, has claimed to have a nuclear button at his "disposal."

In Far East Asia, Kim Jong-un does not warn his opponents in advance. He sends his hired hordes to simply massacre and deal violently against those conspiring against him and his dictatorial regime. Kim is often shown on screen surrounded by professionally hired young girls and ladies weeping and hysterical at his presence, just infatuated at his glory and looks. In simple truth the "beloved leader and marshal" is profoundly despised by the vast majority, even those accompanying him in his tours of the country and industrial and military installations who hold a small notebook scribbling the "on-the-spur instructions and words of wisdom" of the dictator.

Ho Chi Minh (May 19, 1890 – September 2, 1969) Born Nguyen Sinh Cung, this North Vietnamese dictator was another self-styled hero fighting Imperialism. Some 1.7 million human lives were lost under the regime headed by Ho Chi Minh.

Clergyman Seyed Ruhollah Mousavi Mostafavi (Ruhollah Khomeini aka Grand Ayatollah, Imam, September 24, 1902 – June 3, 1989)

Little is known about the parental and maternal origins of Ruhollah Khomeini. He has never spoken about them. What has been researched is that his ancestors migrated towards the end of the eighteenth century from their residence in Nishapur/Neishabur, Khorasan Province, western Iran, to The Kingdom of Awadh – a region in the modern state of Uttar Pradesh, India. For history's sake, it must be mentioned that as a "Seyed," his entire forefathers migrated to Iran from one or the other Arab country. Ruhollah Khomeini's ancestors upon leaving Iran, settled in Kintoor, near Lucknow, the capital of Awadh.

Khomeini's paternal grandfather, Seyed Ahmad Mousavi Hindi (the Indian), was born in Kintoor. He left Lucknow (India) in 1830 and migrated to Iraq, where he wrote in his memoirs that Iraq was his ancestral land, as he was a Seyed. In 1834 he visited Iran (then referred to as Persia) and settled in Khomein, a city south west of Tehran in Markazi Province. He continued to be called "Hindi" (the Indian). There are also claims that Seyed Ahmad Mousavi departed from parts unknown in Kashmir, rather than Lucknow.

Khomeini's Assault on Modern Iran

"Khomeini's assault on modern Iran through agitation and obfuscation commenced somewhere in early 1963." Dr. Shojaeddin Shafa.

> "Before that he studied under the guardianship of Ayatollah Abdul Karim Haeri Yazdi (1859 – January 30, 1937). Clergyman Haeri Yazdi studied in various seminaries in Iraq. Iranian Historians claim the British monitored his movements in Iraq and found him a pleasant and a willing servitor to the British Crown. Upon his return to England from India, Lord Curzon (January 11, 1859 – March 20, 1925), Viceroy and Governor-General of India, was informed of this clergyman who would be an asset in creating a wedge between the then Imperial Government and the common population, thus weakening the central government and preparing grounds needed to colonize Iran under the British rule, finally linking British dominions from south west Asia to Central Asia. Iranian Historians also claim that upon the proposals of Lord Curzon to the British Crown, a sum of one hundred thousand Pounds Sterling (equals to more than 1.2 million US dollars in 2020) was handed over to Clergyman Haeri Yazdi in Qom, by a member of the British Consulate in Tehran. The money was discreetly paid in 1920 to expand the then Feyziyeh Seminary in Qom to churn out more and more clergymen who would agitate against the Central Government, weaken it and either turn the country into a chaotic situation which could be either annexed by the British or to have the very fabric of life destroyed in the country and put a halt to modernization projects commenced by Reza Shah, the modernizer of Iran." Dr. Shojaeddin Shafa, Paris Early April 2000.

At the age of sixty-one, Khomeini decided to enter politics in all its practicality! Following the death of Iran's highest source of "religious imitation" (Taqlid), Grand Ayatollah Seyed Husayn Borujerdi in 1961, the leading although quiescent, Shiite religious leader and Ayatollah Abol Ghassem Kashani in 1962, an activist agitator clergyman called

Ruhollah Khomeini saw the grounds clear for him to enter the arena and be recognized.

The Shah's "White Revolution;" modernization policy presented the farm workers with the part of the lands that they tilled for a modest return from landlords. This policy infuriated Khomeini who had to release part of the inherited land from his grandfather who had come to Iran via Iraq from India in 1834.

Khomeini continued his denunciation and attacks on the Shah whom he perceived as a tyrant and a wretched person, clinging to the so-called freedom attributed to persons like him of being senior religious figures who could neither be arrested, imprisoned, or executed. He called on the Iranian nation to rebel against Constitutional Monarchy and to replace it with the rule of the clergy, without describing the limitations, torments, and miseries it would place on the Iranian nation.

Khomeini was arrested for inciting the population to rise against the Shah on June 5, 1963. However, he was released in early August of the same year. The fiery clergyman denounced the Shah and the United States on June 5, 1964. This time he was tried for treason, sedition, and conspiracy to overthrow the Monarchy with a foreign power, usually blamed on Colonialism, England. He was sentenced to death on charges of high treason, to be hanged. However, the Shah intervened and reduced it to a simple punishment: exile.

On November 4, 1964, the garrulous clergyman was exiled to Turkey, and in less than a year, October 1965, he was allowed to move to Najaf, Iraq, where a Shiite saint is buried.

While in exile in Iraq, Khomeini's contact with the US is part of a trove of newly declassified US government documents – diplomatic cables, policy memos, meeting records. In late 1978, Saddam Hussein expelled him from Iraq; he entered France on October 6, 1978 amid fanfare and celebrations by the mass media in the United States. While in France, Khomeini conveyed a message of friendship with the administration of Jimmy Carter and the British. "There should be no fear of the flow of oil to them. It is not true that we will not sell them oil, once power is with us," Khomeini assured the British, American and the French journalists and reporters. He also assured his followers in France of their safety once they entered Iran. The documents suggest that the Carter administration helped Khomeini return to Iran by preventing the Iranian Army from launching a military coup once the Shah had left the country. Source: Ministry of Foreign Affairs and the Prime Ministry, Tehran.

Zbigniew Brzezinski (March 28, 1928 – May 26, 2017) who was National Security Adviser to Jimmy Carter from 1977-1981 speaking of the relations between Khomeini and the administration of Jimmy Carter said; "I do not have any special information particularly on the Ayatollah and his role or our role in his ascension to power. Probably in some fashion there was some involvement but nothing specific that I can recall."

According to the BBC, "these documents show that in his long quest for power, he (Khomeini) was tactically flexible; he played the moderate even pro-American card to take control but once comfortable in the seat of power, he put in place an anti-America legacy that would last for decades".

On February 1, 1979, Khomeini returned to Iran from Paris and it is from this time that poverty, bloodshed, death, and destruction has rained on Iran and the Iranian nation!

> "An Islamic government, government of the Jurist is what Khomeini had always dreamed to set up in a land not belonging in any sense to his forefathers or ancestors. He had discreetly laid the foundations for a rule of the ethnic minorities of Arab origin imposed upon an Indo-European nation. In less than five years all these people belonging to an ethnic minority who once lived in acute poverty, aggressively begged in the streets, washed and prepared dead bodies for burial, cleaned sewage and septic holes and were deeply involved in robbery, house-breaking and even murder-for-hire now came to be the rulers and murderers of the Iranian nation." Dr. Shojaeddin Shafa. Paris, May 2002

"Due to Khomeini's autocratic rule, more than a million Iranians went to their graves and nearly half a million were confined to the wheelchair for the rest of their lives. Thousands of Iranian citizens are executed every year, making the clergy administered regime the second most after China, to execute people, mostly on flimsy or trumped-up charges." Paris, May 2002

During the Iran-Iraq war (September 1980 – August 1988), hundreds of villages and dozens of cities were bombed by the Iraqis and millions were forced to flee their homes and their cities by a war commenced by Saddam Hussein Tikriti but instigated by Khomeini who called the Iraqi nation to rise up and revolt against the Ba'athist regime and to set up an Islamic Republic on similar principles as he has created in Iran. By the year beginning 2020, nine million Iranian citizens were living in exile.

Khomeini was brought to Tehran from Paris by a chartered plane paid by a certain Haj Karim Dastmalchi, a millionaire businessman from the massive Tehran Bazaar. Dastmalchi together with some twenty others, including a leftist merchant (Ahmad Javameriyan) who had helped finance the Islamic Marxist guerilla organization, "The People's Mujaheddin" and who had actively supported Khomeini's rise to power were executed on July 14, 1981 by the direct orders of Khomeini. Karim Dastmalchi was found guilty of siding with the later ousted Seyed Abol Hassan Bani Sadr, the first president of the regime. Bani Sadr was elected on February 4, 1981, and later dismissed by Khomeini on June 22, 1981.

Finally, the end came for Khomeini. His health rapidly declined since early 1986 from a myriad of illnesses. Diabetes, heart, renal and prostate problems. He died on June 3, 1989 after suffering five heart attacks in just ten days and after undergoing pain and torment for nearly two years. He told one of his doctors that he wished to die as early as possible and hopefully "painlessly." He lived the last nine years of his life as if a prisoner in Jamaran village, north of Tehran, inside a twelve square meter room, isolated because of his failing health and safety. His last years were not less than being a prisoner himself, a prisoner to his own conscience and doings.

His dead body was placed in an open coffin to be taken for his last journey but not peacefully. Crowds of thousands surrounded the coffin bearers causing his body to be thrown on the ground and the funeral procession had to be stopped. The corpse had to be flown by helicopter, five hours later, some thirty-two kilometers to "Behesht e Zahra Cemetery," for burial to the spot earlier reserved for him. The clergy-run media reported that nearly five million had come to bid farewell to the "exalted leader" while the true figure was somewhere near half a million.

Of importance is this fact that Khomeini, less than a year after his arrival in Tehran lived as an isolated person in the confides of a modest home (since January 23, 1980), adjacent to the Jamaran Mosque where he used to deliver his speeches. Seyed Mahdi Jamarani who was the caretaker of the complex offered Khomeini to reside there till his last days on June 3, 1989.

The clergyman who advocated a modest lifestyle was later to have a massive mausoleum, a complex with a golden dome and four minarets adorning his grave. It has cost the poverty-stricken Iranian nation in the equivalent of between two and half to three billion dollars and more spent each year in further embellishing his tomb. Several attacks had been launched to destroy the structure with little success.

The superstitious belief is that this controversial clergyman has been considered inviolable and even compared to Shiite Saints!

Clergyman Ruhollah Khomeini could be held responsible for the death of more than one and half million Iranians (even after his death, his religious edicts condemning people to death for their slightest infringement, considered a crime and blasphemy against "god" continue to be used against the victims of the regime). The irascible clergyman was succeeded by yet another clergyman, who also belongs to the minority sect.

Clergyman Seyed Ali Hosseini, *Ayatollah Khamenei* (April 19, 1939)

Not much is known about the background of this once obscure cleric.

"What are known is that he was linked to other Shiite revolutionaries (all clerics) in the fire of Cinema Rex in Abadan on August 19, 1978, burning to death some 499 inside the Cinema after locking the doors from the outside. Later it was learned that this horrendous murder was committed at the orders of Khomeini (while in exile) through his son Ahmed Khomeini. The clergymen culprits however managed to put the blame on the Shah's secret police arousing the hatred of the easily convinced people against the Monarchy. The people gave unquestionable credence to the clerics' false information, although years later the Shah was fully absolved of any wrongdoing, and so was the Secret Police. The Monarch later said that he felt disgusted at the cowardly act of these people in the garb of clergymen. His Majesty asked why such evil and heartless people walk on the surface of this earth and why do they claim to be the guardians of religion and if they do believe in any religion, it is definitely not the true religion of Islam but a cult, a cult that they have managed to build around this self-styled clergyman in exile." Mohammad Homayounfar, Deputy Minister of Information, The Imperial Government of Iran., Geneva, 1992

Regularly he calls on his faithful to threaten the very existence of Israel, a country recognized by most members of the United Nations and of late in the second week of September 2020 where Bahrein and the UAE signed a treaty, among others, recognizing the existence of Israel as a viable country; not a peace treaty since they were not at war with the State of Israel.

Riots and Pandemonium

As early as November 15, 2019, the clergy regime in Tehran augmented the price of gasoline three folds. Millions of Iranians took to the streets in every major city of the country, condemning the clergy run regime, calling for the elimination of the regime in all its totality, burning the effigies of clergyman Khamenei, the supreme leader, and hanging effigies of leading clergymen on tree branches, calling for their death with slogans of "death to the dictator" and vowing to exact terrible revenge on the ethnic minority who are ruling the country. Most prominent in the slogans were, "O Shah of Iran…return to Iran," "O Shah! Forgive us the way we treated you," and "Return O Pahlavi!" Reza Pahlavi succeeded his father upon his demise in Egypt and is considered the King in exile. He has been further popularized when millions of placards bearing his portrait has been distributed and even posted on banks, government buildings, hospitals, University entrances and even on armored vehicles in the streets, parked to intimidate and to threaten as a symbol of retribution against the common citizens by the clergy regime.

In this midst of turmoil, more than 1500 demonstrators against the regime were reportedly murdered, most of them by snipers, most of the snipers have been identified; as usual, the ethnic minority and a few dozen as Arab terrorists, who the public claim to be professional terrorists of Palestinian origin. More than thirteen thousand Iranians have been arrested and thrown into medieval dungeons with no recourse to an attorney or any form of legal representation. Hundreds have been murdered while in captivity! The clergyman leader Ali Khamenei appointed a notorious General Qasem Soleimani of the Islamic Republic Guard Corps to crush the uprising that could topple the theocratic regime. "Do anything to stop them – employ all means possible, just stop them" were the words spoken by clergyman Ali Khamenei."

Soleimani, labelled as a terrorist by the US administration under Donald J. Trump, had promised to slaughter every man, woman, and child, including infants in the arms of the demonstrators, to safeguard the theocracy in Tehran. Soleimani was condemned as the "child killer!" by the Iranian masses, including more than nine million Iranians in exile, mostly in European countries. More than one hundred dead bodies of children were seen besides the dead bodies of their fathers and mothers who were in processions protesting the clerical regime. He threatened to kill even twelve million Iranians, "if that will serve the wishes of our exalted Supreme Leader."

On an average, every month, a clergyman is either beaten to death or just shot. Meanwhile several senior members of the Islamic Revolutionary Guard Corps including clergymen have been shot, stabbed, strangled, or beaten to death by the tormented public. Attendance in mosques have dropped to less than a tenth! "The scaffoldings of this theocratic and autocratic regime are falling under its own weight. It is sinking and sinking fast," said a former professor at Tehran University who requested anonymity.

In the first week of December 2019, Qasem Soleimani (March 11, 1957-January 3, 2020), the much hated and feared Islamic Republic Guard Corps commander of the Quds Forces (Jerusalem Forces), the favorite general of clergyman Ayatollah Seyed Ali Khamenei, challenged the demonstrators with profanity and vowed to kill every one of them, even if the figure is twelve million and even more to protect the clergy regime and above all the exalted supreme leader.

Soleimani, dubbed the "child killer" in the third week of December 2019 said to a gathering of Revolutionary Guard Corps commanders (all of them members of the ethnic minority with a few hired Palestinian terrorists present); "I will be away on a confidential mission as ordered by our supreme leader and on my return we shall with the full blessing of our leader bring a 'final solution' to these worthless demonstrators who want their country back from you and me and other revolutionaries. It is they (the Iranians) who are thinking of wiping us out. But then, it is our duty to wipe them, their children and even their infants. Our leader has consented. We shall be successful!"

Soleimani did not return, his body was incinerated from a burst of missiles fired from a US drone near the Baghdad airport as soon as he had landed by a flight from Tehran and was being driven away from the airport, together with a certain "Abu Mahdi Al-Mohandis," who was an Iraqi citizen and an aide to Soleimani. Al-Mohandis was the leader of "revolutionary Shiites" in Iraq and like Soleimani was categorized as a terrorist. The entire Islamic Republic Revolutionary Guard Corps has been labelled and officially declared a terrorist organization.

Hossein Salami is the present commander of the Islamic Revolutionary Guard Corps a notorious individual known for allegedly stabbing to death a former maidservant of the Imperial palace. Known for his fiery and often abusive statements and threats against Israel, the United States, and Iranians in general who dare to oppose the theocratic regime in Tehran, days after the death of Soleimani on January 3, 2020, threatened to create a bloodbath to all those demonstrating against the regime.

The Revolutionary Guard Corps was created by an unspecified number of notorious and reviled individuals; two of whom were Mohsen Sazegara, a notorious figure who advocated mass murder in the early days of the sacerdotal revolution to maintain the clergy regime on the public, now lives in the United States and is involved in "research," the subject of which is unknown and Abbas Duzduzani, deceased on July 29, 2018.

Soleimani, the 'child killer" was unable to return and witness his grizzly plans of murdering innocent Iranian men, women, and children whose only fault was to take back their country after forty years of the most unpopular regime in Iranian history for the past four thousand years!

The USA has claimed that Soleimani had murderous intentions to attack several US missions and installations and diplomatic facilities in Iraq. The regime in Tehran has denied such allegations and insisted that Soleimani was on a "peace mission" to discuss ending hostilities between the Saudis and the clergy regime in Tehran.

Judging from the past and present activities of Soleimani in the region and his intentions, the truth is difficult to ascertain.

Time and often, Soleimani, a former handyman and brick layer born in Kerman (southeast of Iran) from an obscure and poverty-stricken family with virtually no formal education has repeatedly said; "the Americans and the Israeli occupiers are our enemies!"

Hatred for clergyman Khamenei is responded in kind by shouts of "Down with the Dictator" and "Death to Khamenei." Most important of all these slogans is "Oust the criminal Islamic Republic," while chanting "Death to all the murderous 'tazis' followed by Oust the 'tazis' from our Aryan homeland." (The term "tazi" is a derogative word used for these members

71

of the ethnic minority who form the rulers of the country. The origin of this word is arcane and even unknown but has a faint relation to the term "tazia" which is derived from a procession celebrated by Shia Muslims in connection with the martyrdom of Husain, grandson of Mohammed, the Prophet of Islam.) Another favorite slogan of the public is death to Arabs and the Palestinians.

Jews, Baha'is, Christians, Muslims of all denominations, Jehovah's Witnesses, Sufis, Dervishes, Atheists and Agnostics, just any individual the regime suspects and dislikes are imprisoned, tortured to death, and even executed.

For the nationalist Iranian, all clergymen are to be hunted and deprived of their peaceful existence. It is now the majority of the people who insist that the clergy in Iran have always been a hurdle for prosperity and development and it is time that they have a constructive and productive profession in life.

The vast majority now vow to oust this oppressive theocracy and somberly and ashamedly remember the golden days when prosperity, peace and calm prevailed under the Shah's reign.

The current slogan throughout the country is "Return O Pahlavi," which translates into the restoration of Constitutional Monarchy under Reza Shah the Second, (Crown Prince) and grandson of Rea Shah the Great, the architect of modern Iran. Other slogans such as "Iran that has no Shah is bereft of any law and order," "Forgive us Father," (the late Shah) "Reza Shah (the founder of modern Iran) may your soul rest in peace and be blessed."

In sacerdotal regimes, notably in the clerical regime in Tehran, the term "democracy" is openly dismissed as evil and against Islamic canonical laws!

Fanaticism, extremism in every conceivable form, terrorism and religious intolerance form the "political skeleton" of theocratic regimes! The questionable chief clergyman ruling the entire nation, reserves all rights, prerogatives, and powers for himself while allowing himself the freedom to appoint his own lackeys or to even dismiss the ruling government or to hold elections to form a government, thus reflecting some sort of an impetus to his democratic claims to the world at large! He usually "allows" an informal and an overtly fraudulent election with the formation of a government, however with extremely limited powers or no powers at all!

Radovan Karadzic (June 19, 1945) Karadzic was the co-founder of the Serb Democratic Party in Bosnia Herzegovina and served as the first President of "Republika Srpska" from 1992 to 1996. The International Criminal Tribunal for the former Yugoslavia indicted him for war crimes and genocide against the Bosnian and Croat civilians during the Bosnian war of 1992-1995.

Karadzic was a fugitive between 1996 and 2008 but was finally arrested on July 21, 2008 and brought before Belgrade's War Crimes Court. He was charged with eleven counts of war crimes and sentenced to forty years behind bars. On March 24, 2016 he was also found grossly guilty of the genocides in Srebrenica, war crimes and crimes against humanity. His sentence was increased to life in prison.

Dubbed as the "Butcher of Bosnia," he showed no remorse but arrogance and pride at what he had done. Under his "leadership" more than one million human lives were destroyed.

Ratko Mladic, (March 12, 1943), is a former Bosnian Serb General was an accomplice of Radovan Karadzic and participated in virtually every crime against the people in Srebrenica, known as the Srebrenica massacre, where an untold number of Muslim men, women and children were murdered in cold blood at his orders. Infamous for his cruelty, he ordered his men to kill, just kill, all the people of Srebrenica.

After years in hiding in several places, he was arrested on May 26, 2011. Finally, in early 2017, Mladic was sentenced to life in prison for his crimes against humanity and mass murders. He too, like other dictators lived the last decade of his freedom in hiding before being sentenced to spend his remaining life in prison.

And yet another accomplice of Karadzic and Mladic was **Slobodan Milosevic** (August 21, 1941 – March 11, 2006) a mass murderer who died in his prison cell in the Hague, awaiting trial.

Mobutu Sese Seko Kuku Ngbendu Wa Za Banga (October 14, 1930 – September 7, 1997) He was the President of Zaire between 1965 to 1997. He was an authoritarian ruler, and had his enemies thrown into dungeons for the slightest infractions against his regime. Documents indicate that the widely feared Mobutu who killed Patrice Lumumba a progressive politician, including his enabler and one-time comrade Joseph kasa-vubu, received money and weapons directly from the CIA.

King Fahd bin Abdulaziz Al Saud (March 16, 1921 – August 1, 2005) Ruled Saudi Arabia from June 13, 1982 to his death. During his rule, he confirmed the execution of five thousand Saudi and foreign nationals for various crimes.

King Abdullah bin Abdulaziz Al Saud (August 1, 1924 – January 23, 2015). He ruled Saudi Arabia from August 1, 2005 till his death. Like his predecessor (King Fahd), he too confirmed the execution of five thousand citizens for various crimes.

Benito Amilcare Andrea Mussolini (July 29, 1883 – April 28, 1945) Founder and leader of the National Fascist Party in Italy. He was responsible for 382,800 deaths in the Ethiopian invasion…half a million Italian soldiers killed during WWII and nearly fifty thousand during the initial period of the war as a result of allied bombing.

Francisco Franco (December 4, 1892 – November 20, 1975) Under his rule more than two million were killed in the Spanish civil war 1936-1939.

Idi Amin Dada Oumee (May 17, 1925 – August 16, 2003) He ruled Uganda between 1971-1979. A brutal dictator, he presided over the execution of more than half a million people and is considered one of the most brutal despots in the world.

Harry S. Truman (May 8, 1884 -December 26, 1972) Thirty third President of the United States of America, between April 12, 1945 – January 20, 1953. He ordered the dropping of the first Atom Bombs, first on Hiroshima (August 6, 1945) immediately killing 80,000…Hundreds of thousands would die in the forthcoming years due to radiation exposure. Three days later Truman ordered another atom bomb dropped on Nagasaki instantly killing 40,000 and later being the cause of the death of twice this figure due to radiation exposure. In the first fifty years after the Bomb was dropped on these two cities, historians and experts placed the figure in the excess of three hundred thousand! Later, Truman was to justify his orders to bomb Japanese cities as a mean to put an end to the war and further "save" Japanese lives.

Aung San Suu Kyi (June 19, 1945), de facto leader of Myanmar. She watched passively and most indifferently as Muslims were persecuted and murdered. She has been singled out as the main cause of the death of more than ten thousand Rohingya Muslims and the displacement of at least seven hundred thousand (800,000 originally lived in Myanmar, previously known as Burma) She has fallen from grace in the global community due to her handling of the situation of the Rohingya Muslims. She is no longer in the news in Myanmar as well as in most countries of the world.

Adolf Schickelgruber-Hiedler-Hitler, *Adolf Hitler* (April 20, 1889 – April 30, 1945…?) an Austrian, Sephardic Jew and a mentally unstable mass murderer. He was the leader of Germany's Nazi Party and was responsible for the murder of seventeen to twenty million human beings in Germany and West Europe, not counting the thirty million Russians who were killed on the Eastern front. His conspicuous act of evil was the masterminding of the Holocaust. He considered this act of intentional murder as his duty.

Study suggests Adolf Hitler had Jewish and African ancestors but vainly attempted to present himself as an Indo - European/Aryan. Article by Jennie Cohen. Updated August 29, 2018, original article published on August 26, 2010 and combined notes by several other sources.

In the decades since Adolf Hitler's death, the Nazi leader's ancestry has been a subject of rampant speculation and intense controversy. Some have suggested that his father, Alois born to an unwed woman named Maria Schickelgruber, was the illegitimate child of Leopold Frankenberger, a young Jewish man whose family employed her as a maid. (She subsequently married Johann Georg Hiedler – later spelled "Hitler" – whose surname her son adopted.)

Several historians, namely Dr. Louis L. Snyder, Professor of History, the City University of New York in his writings and speeches stated that Alois' biological father was also the grandfather of Hitler's mother, Klara Polzl, thus making Adolf's birth a result of an incestuous marriage.

In Antwerp, Belgium, in a lecture to a large audience in early August 2010, Jean - Paul Mulders, the well-respected investigative journalist and Marc Vermeeren, a historian who has researched Hitler's family ancestry collected saliva samples from thirty nine of the infamous dictator's living relatives, including a great nephew, Alexander Stuart–Houston, a resident of New York, and an Austrian cousin identified as "Norbert H." Tests were then conducted to reveal the samples' principal haplogroups, set of chromosomes that genetics use to define specific populations.

"Knack" the Flemish language magazine in Belgium, states that the relatives of Hitler's dominant haplogroup, (E1b1b), is rare in Western Europeans but common among North Africans, and particularly the Berber tribes of Morocco, Algeria, Libya, and Tunisia. The Historian Marc Vermeeren said that the results of tests (on Hitler's family and ancestral background) have shown that this is one of the major founding lineages of the Jewish population, present in 18 to 20 percent of Ashkenazi Jews and 8.6 to 30 percent in Sephardic Jews. The tests concluded that Hitler's family tree may have included Jewish and African ancestors.

During the Nuremberg trials, Hans Frank (May 23, 1900 – October 16, 1946) considered to be one of the evil politicians in the Third Reich, vainly tried to please the judges by claiming that in early 1941, he and Heinrich Himmler (October 7, 1900 – May 23, 1945), perhaps the cruelest murderer, had discreetly investigated the "Fuehrer" and discovered that he was of Jewish origin. The judges rejected his statements and refused any leniency towards him. Hans Frank was later hanged.

Several academics and DNA experts from the USA, Europe and elsewhere in their reports and lectures pointed to the fact that such tests do not necessarily conclude that the person who planned and authored the Holocaust was Jewish, African, or even a combination of an African - Jew, although agreeing to identifying him as a Sephardic Jew.

CHAPTER THREE

HOLOCAUST AND
HOLOCAUST DENIERS

Holocaust

Once the Dictator condemns a certain Nation or a country as "the enemy," the deceived nation will rarely ask the reasons but will blindly follow his orders as divinely inspired and as a postulated fact.

This Dictator (Hitler) was the root cause for the death of nearly forty million people during the Second World War! He knowingly created "Holocaust deniers" after his suicide, but at the same time there were hundreds of "Righteous among Nations" who most courageously succored the victims and save hundreds of thousands of innocent Jewish lives, old men, women, and children and even infants!

While fiercely courageous Jewish mothers with infants in their arms and leading a child to their certain death, proudly marched to the gas chambers, gallantly refusing to observe the cowardly and cruel guards in soldiers' uniform who pretended to assist them on their way to their demise, one needs to simply imagine this evil scene! Mankind thrown against mankind by a Dictator calling himself a "leader!"

Arising from the presence of the evil doers in history are conscientious heroes, men and women practicing each and very faith who rushed to the rescue of those human beings, labelled as damned.

The results of any form of dictatorial regimes are nothing short of discrimination, murder, and devastation. These are the simple reasons why the Holocaust is mentioned in this writing. It is but a result of dictatorial regimes, cruel regimes that are created by none other than human beings who later are an integral part of the sufferings.

Nazi Crimes

Bearing in mind the undeniable truth that Dictatorship was and is solely responsible for crimes against humanity, one needs to know the results of such a rule and regimes.

What was created in Germany in the early 30's was, when hysterically charged masses welcomed an Austrian born person (later identified as a Sephardic Jew through DNA results of his nephews in the USA and his family lineage and reflected in major mass media in the USA and Israel. Interestingly, he was baptized a Catholic!) who agitated vociferously and promised to return the German Nation its lost dignity and grandeur! He had earlier shown his profound animosity against the Ashkenazi Jews (not all, but most Ashkenazi Jews are Turkic-Mongol Khazars, who had converted to Judaism between the ninth and tenth century AD).

At this stage, an analogy exists between Adolf Hitler and the present occupant of the Oval Office who repeatedly damned the Muslims of the world prior to and after being "selected" by his "promoters!"

The deeds of this mentally deranged Austrian individual resulted in the planned and systematic murder of nearly six million, or even more precious Jewish lives, commonly referred to as the Holocaust!

Upon the explicit orders and consent of the dictator, death, destruction, and bloodshed spread throughout his domains. The opportunistic enablers created the dictator, and he, once the dictator, simply issued verbal orders; rarely written.

List of Death/Concentration/Extermination Camps under the Dictator

In virtually all these camps, the larger majority murdered were Jews.

The Camps and those murdered have been researched through various sources with statistics.

Herzogenbusch Concentration/Death Camp.

This camp was located in Vught, Netherlands. The "SS" (Protection Squadron) ran this camp and exterminated a total of 749 people, most of them Jews from occupied Netherlands.

Natzweiler-Struthof Concentration/Death camp.

This German run concentration camp was located in the Vosges mountains close to the Alsatian village of Natzwiller/Natzweiler in France. Out of the 52,000 inmates incarcerated. At least 22,000 were killed. Nearly all of them were Jewish men, women, and children. All were mostly from occupied France, but there were also a few thousand from other nearby countries occupied by the Nazis.

Dachau Concentration/Death camp.

This camp was the first of the several Nazi concentration camps, opened in 1933 and was located in Dachau, northwest of Munich in the state of Bavaria, in southern Germany. Nearly 190,000 political prisoners, Jews, Jehovah's Witnesses, Catholic priests, Communists and Gypsies were incarcerated of whom 41,500 were killed according to the official website of Dachau.

Although the majority killed were Jews, their exact figure is unknown.

Mauthausen Concentration/Death camp.

The Mauthausen-Gusen Concentration/Death camp complex consisted of the Mauthausen Concentration/Death camp on a hill above the market town of Mauthausen plus a group of nearly 100 further subcamps located throughout Austria and southern Germany.

This Death camp "operated" from the time of merging Austria with Germany on August 8,1938 to May 5, 1945 at the end of the Second World War.

The death toll in this massive complex remains unclear, although researchers put the figure between 122,766 and 320,000 for the entire complex. What is sure that even if the minimum figure of 122,766 is considered, the larger percentage of those murdered were Jews.

Buchenwald Concentration/Death camp. 56,000

Buchenwald was located on Ettersberg Hill near Weimar, Germany. This infamous Nazi Concentration/Death camp housed "prisoners" from all over Nazi occupied Europe and the Soviet Union which included Jews, Gypsies, Slavs, the mentally and physically challenged, Freemasons and criminals. A sizeable number of the prisoners worked primarily as forced labor in local armament factories. Hunger and poor living conditions, including executions led to 56,000 deaths at Buchenwald out of the nearly 250,000 prisoners who passed through this camp.

Gross-Rosen Concentration/Death camp.40,000

The main camp was located in the German village of Gross-Rosen, now the modern-day Rogoznica in Lower Silesian Voivodeship, Poland.

Auschwitz-Birkenau 1.1 to 1.4 million (1.1 million Jews) Some undocumented statistics estimates between 2 and 2.5 million (1.8 million Jews)

Stutthof 65000 (including 28,000 Jews)
Mittelbao-Dora 20,000
Belzec between 430,000 and 500,000 Jews
Sobibor between 200,000 and 250,000 Jews
Treblinka Nearly 1,000,000
Chelmno 152,000 and 340,000
Maidanek 78,000

Ravensbruck

Of the nearly 130,000 female prisoners who passed through Ravensbruck camp, some 50000 perished while 22000 were killed in gas chambers. The number of Jewish women who lost their lives exceeded 26000 while nearly 19000 Russian, 8000 French and 1000 Dutch women were among the victims.

Theresienstadt Transit camp

Of the nearly 150,000 Jews sent to this camp, some 35,000, nearly a fourth died there while another 90,000 were deported to Auschwitz and other death camps.

Flossenburg

More than 30,000 died of malnutrition and execution. Less than fifty percent were Jews.

Apart from these conspicuously notorious camps where human beings were murdered by fellow human beings, there were dozens, or perhaps hundreds of lesser-known camps and grounds where Jews, Gypsies, Slavs, Communists, Political prisoners, Jehovah's Witnesses, the mentally and physically challenged and those considered a threat to the Reich were summarily executed and buried in mass graves.

A respectable number of Historians have agreed that in Soviet occupied territories, German officials hunted Jews and marched them into pits earlier dug where they were executed, and their bodies piled over and covered with earth while another group was readied for execution. In occupied Russian territories nearly a million Jews were massacred while in occupied Poland, over three million Jews were murdered. This does not include Jews murdered in Germany itself. Nearly a hundred thousand were rounded up and shot.

List of Known Holocaust Deniers

Such individuals who beggar fame, attention and glory do in fact lead a life in infamy, cruelty, and shame. They existed and exist, such inglorious individuals in the tens of thousands in several countries and communities, perhaps throughout the world. As the ruthless and heartless dictators who are their heroes and whom they idolize and blindly "worship," they too take deep pleasure in mocking the innocent men, women and children murdered solely for their religious beliefs.

Most befitting response to those self-styled philosophers, historians, and thinkers who have since the past seven decades or even more, distorted the truth about the pangs of torments, death and destruction rained down on Jewish people and those of other faiths as a hoax and even a non-existent phenomenon would be the mind-shattering letter of Fanya Barbakow from the Druja ghetto, Poland (today Belarus).

Fanya Barbakov was born in 1923 in Druja, Poland. Her parents Ze'ev Velvel and Zisale had two boys and five girls: Chaim, Manos, Sonia, Bluma, Chaya, Fanya and Sima.

Members of the Barbakov family was incarcerated in the Druja ghetto together with all the Jews from that town.

The moving letter written by Fanya addressed to her family members and loved ones was in face a farewell greeting to all before death. Part of the letter reads:

"My dear ones! I am writing this letter before my death, but I don't know the exact day that I and all my relatives will be killed because we are Jews. All of our Jewish brothers and sisters were murdered and died a shameful death at the hands of murderers…I don't know who will remain alive from our family, and who will have the honor of reading my letter and my proud greetings before death to all my beloved and dear ones tortured at the hands of the murderers."

Tuesday 4 am
June 16, 1942,
Farewell to all
Yours Fanya.

In the closing lines, she added:

"God is just, and His judgement is just. We have sinned. Our meager possessions are concealed at home. But we have lost our lives. It is all finished. Brothers from all countries, avenge us. We are being led like sheep to the slaughter." Fanya

It is generally summated that Holocaust deniers usually frown upon those who accuse them of distorting the truth about the mass murder of Jews. They do not accept the "label" as being "deniers" as an appropriate inculpatory term to describe their opinions, using the term "Holocaust revisionists" instead, regardless of all the official and undeniable documents and evidence.

Several countries in Europe consider it unlawful to deny the Holocaust. Austria, Belgium, The Czech Republic, France, Germany, The Netherlands, Poland, Romania, Slovakia, Spain, and Switzerland have passed laws to jail any denier. It is also illegal in the State of Israel.

Holocaust deniers have never refrained from further wounding the soul of the millions of Nazi victims by their cowardly denial. I feel obliged to reflect the name of some of the most notorious Holocaust deniers at the cost of blemishing their odious names in my work. However, it is obligatory to send the message to both the sane world and the awakened conscience of those who may still believe this tragic genocide was a hoax.

The latest character identified is an Irish citizen, a certain Dermot Mulqueen (as reported by Harriet Sherwood Feb 10, 2020), who is reportedly half-literate and who has been given ample time on major radio and television stations in Europe, was interviewed by popular comedian David Baddiel of the USA. Dermot Mulqueen in the interview claimed that Auschwitz the most notorious death camp had no gas chambers, but instead had a swimming pool benefitting those temporarily incarcerated for further investigations. Baddiel described his encounter with Dermot Mulqueen as one of the weirdest moments of his life, said he and his film's director had wrestled with whether to interview the Holocaust denier.

One of America's most influential Holocaust deniers, Fred A. Leuchter in 1988 produced "The Leuchter Report," which purported to offer "scientific" proof that there were no gas chambers in Auschwitz. In fact, Leuchter has no qualifications whatsoever. Thoroughly discredited, the report nonetheless had a significant impact on the Holocaust denial community. Leuchter was deported from the UK in November 1991 after David Irving brought him into the country illegally to address an international Holocaust denial rally in London.

David Duke

David Duke is a self-styled white nationalist, though critics often label him a white supremacist. He says he does not think of himself as a racist, stating that he is a "racial realist" and that he believes "all people have a basic human right to preserve their own heritage." He speaks against racial integration and in favor of white separatism.

David Duke made several unsuccessful bids for political office, including runs for the U.S. Senate, U.S. House, governor of Louisiana and twice for president of the United States. However, Duke secured enough votes to serve in the Louisiana House of Representatives between 1989 - 1992.

In 2002, he pled guilty for tax evasion and fraud charges, resulting in a fifteen-month prison sentence. He is a longtime New Orleans resident and a father of two.

Mark Weber

Mark Weber has been the director of the Institute for Historical Review since 1995. This Institute, which is devoid of any academic character, is perhaps, the leading disseminator of Holocaust denial material in the western world. Weber is a former member of the Nazi National Alliance.

Robert Faurisson Aitken (January 25, 1929 – October 21, 2018)

A British-born French academic who became best known for Holocaust denial. He generated much controversy with several articles published in the "Journal of Historical Review" and elsewhere and by letters to French newspaper, especially "Le Monde," which contradicted the history of the Holocaust by denying the existence of gas chambers in Nazi death camps and the systematic killing of European Jews using gas during the Second World War.

After the passing of the Gayssot Act, making it illegal to deny the Holocaust in 1990, Faurisson was prosecuted and fined, and in 1991 he was dismissed from his academic post.

Bishop Richard Nelson Williamson (March 1940)

Williamson is an English traditionalist Catholic Bishop who opposes the changes in the Catholic Church brought about by the Second Vatican Council. He was originally a member of the Society of Saint Pius X and was excommunicated for his fiery lectures, denying the Holocaust. He was also expelled from the Society.

His excommunication was lifted on January 21, 2009, but the suspension of the bishops from the exercise of ministry within the Catholic Church, remained in force, except for certain exceptions. Popes Benedict XVI and Francis granted the exceptions to foster dialogue and goodwill, and all the priests limited ministry despite their canonically irregular situation.

Immediately afterward, Swedish television broadcast an interview recorded earlier at the Society of Saint Pius X seminary in Zaitzkofen, Bavaria. During the interview, Williamson expressed his belief that Nazi Germany did not use gas chambers during the Holocaust and that no more than 200,000 and 300,000 Jews were killed during the Holocaust.

Based upon these denials, the Bishop was immediately charged with and convicted of Holocaust denial by a German court.

Michael Hoffman II (January 2, 1957)

Michael is an unrelenting Holocaust denier. He often repeats that his maternal grandfather reminded him that elections in the United States of America were and are rigged by organized crime. He has worked on the projects of several other Holocaust deniers and neo-Nazis.

Hoffman has served as Assistant Director of the Institute of Historical Review, a Holocaust denial organization.

While residing in Idaho, Hoffman had desired to establish a museum that would detail the "Communist Holocaust against Christians," and the "Holocaust against the Germans," (the bombing of Dresden and other major German cities) where he would prove it was all deliberately planned to massacre the civilian populations of Germany. His hopes at the planned museum also included to present the "Holocaust against Japan" (the incineration of Tokyo and the Atomic bombings of Hiroshima and Nagasaki).

Hoffman has continuously denied Klan membership nor the existence of the gas chambers, but has advanced anti-Semitic conspiracy theories, and contended that "the real Holocaust of World War II was caused by the Allies."

William David McCalden (September 20, 1951 – October 15, 1990)

William David McCalden was a figure in the British political far right. He was the co-founder of the Institute for Historical Review in mid-1979. A foul-mouthed person, McCalden scoffed at those ridiculing his beliefs of the non-existence of the Holocaust.

In early 1978 McCalden emigrated to the United States and resided around El Segundo, California. Here he met noted Holocaust denier Willis Carto and together founded the "Institute for Historical Review" that lacked any academic value.

Willis Allison Carto (July 17, 1926 – October 26, 2015)

Willis Carto was an American political activist on the American far right. He had always insisted that he was Jeffersonian and Populist but was better known for his promotion of Jewish conspiracy theories and Holocaust denial.

Carto had helped create the Populist Party whose primary aim was to serve as an electoral vehicle for white supremacy and Ku Klux Klan members. It has been suggested but unproved that Carto was a close friend of Frederic Christ Trump, father of Trump, the former occupier of the Oval Office. It has been proved that Frederic Christ Trump was an active member of the Ku Klux Klan.

David Leslie Hoggan (March 23, 1923 – August 7, 1988)

David Leslie Hoggan was an American professor of History. He was anti-Jewish and maintained close relations with various neo-Nazi and Holocaust denial groups, both within the United States and abroad.

Hoggan never repented denying the death of millions of Jewish men, women and children and people of other faiths and beliefs in gas chambers and called it a "myth." On many occasions he called Adolf Hitler a man of peace!

In his lectures he often blamed the Polish government as the main instigator of the Holocaust against the Jewish people and the commencement of the Second World War in conspiracy with the British and described the Nazi regime as simply defending its historically original geographical boundaries.

The German historian and philosopher Ernst Nolte (January 11, 1923 – August 18, 2016) often defended Hoggan as one of the greatest historians of World War II. In truth, leading historians in the United States and elsewhere counter that Hoggan was an individual bereft of any eligibility to lecture History.

A few lines on Earnest Nolte throws light on the person who repeatedly acclaimed David Leslie Hoggan as a historical genius.

Ernest Nolte was a German theoretician and argued that Fascism functioned at three levels, namely in the world of politics as a form of opposition to Marxism, at the sociological level in opposition to bourgeois values, and in the "metapolitical" world as "resistance to transcendence" (in German "transcendence" translates as the "spirit of modernity").

Nolte defined the relationship between Fascism and Marxism as such:

> "Fascism is anti-Marxism which seeks to destroy the enemy by the evolvement of a radically opposed and yet related ideology and by the use of almost identical and yet typically modified methods,

always, however within the unyielding framework of national self-assertion and autonomy."

With regards to the Holocaust, Nolte contended that because Adolf Hitler identified Jews with modernity, the basic thrust of Nazi policies towards Jews had always aimed at genocide.

"Auschwitz was contained in the principles of Nazi racist theory like the seed in the fruit," Nolte wrote.

David John Cawdell Irving (March 24, 1938)

David Irving is a British Holocaust denier. In his various harangues, he has denied such a development ever took place. Elsewhere, he argues that had Adolf Hitler known of the extermination of Jews or the existence of gas chambers to murder Jews, gypsies and others deemed as undesirable by the Nazis, he would have ordered them closed immediately!

Irving's reputation as a historian was discredited, he even marginalized himself in 1988 when, based on his reading of the pseudoscientific "Leuchter report," (Fred A. Leuchter, a sympathizer of David Irving and a Holocaust denier), he began to espouse Holocaust denial, specifically denying that Jews were murdered by gassing at the Auschwitz concentration camp.

In January 1990, Irving gave a speech in Moers (Germany) where he insisted to a gathering of some fifty people that only thirty thousand people died in Auschwitz between the years 1940-45, all due to natural causes, which was equal as he claimed to the typical death toll from one Bomber Command raid on German cities.

Most shockingly and to the chagrin of the global community, Irving called the Auschwitz death camp a "tourist attraction" whose origins he claimed went back to an "ingenious plan" devised by the British Psychological Warfare Executive in 1942 to spread anti-German propaganda that it was the policy of the German state to be using gas chambers to kill millions of

Jews and other undesirables. He also claimed that the existing structures of Auschwitz camp is a mock-up constructed by the Poles.

In one of the several legal cases against him, arising from his praise for the Nazi dictator, an English court found that Irving was an active Holocaust denier, anti-Jewish and a racist who for his own ideological reasons persistently and deliberately misrepresented and manipulated historical evidence. In one legal case against him in Germany for denying the Holocaust and distorting history, Irving denounced his judge as senile and an alcoholic "cretin." Following his conviction for Holocaust denial, Irving was banned from visiting Germany. In addition, the court found that that Irving's books and all other of his writings had distorted the history of Hitler's role in the Holocaust to depict Hitler in a favorable light.

(Lady) Michele Suzanne Renouf (nee Mainwaring, born 1946)

Michele Renouf is an Australian born British political activist. Since the 1990's, she has attended and spoken at Holocaust "revisionist" conferences and written papers on this subject.

She is notorious for defending Holocaust deniers such as David Irving, Bishop Richard Nelson Williamson, Robert Faurisson Ernest Zundel, and others. She has been frequently characterized in mainstream sources as a Holocaust denier. Renouf has also described Judaism as a "repugnant and a hateful religion."

Ernst Christof Friedrich Zundel (April 24, 1939 – August 5, 2017)

Ernst Zundel was a German Publisher and pamphleteer notorious for promoting Holocaust denial. Throughout his life, Zundel claimed the non-existence of death and concentration camps.

In 1977, he founded an obscure publishing house which issued pamphlets as his co-authored book: "The Hitler we loved and Why" and Richard Verrall's (Richard Verrall is a British Holocaust denier) "Did Six Million

Really Die? The Truth at Last" which were significant documents to the Holocaust denial movement.

Bernard Schaub (born 1954)

Swiss Holocaust denier and a far-right activist. He participated in the Holocaust Conference in Tehran in 2006.

Sylvia Stolz (born August 16, 1963)

Sylvia Stolz is a German former attorney and a convicted Holocaust denier. She was a member of the defense team of Ernst Zundel, who was tried in 2006 for distributing antisemitic literature including Holocaust denial material, via a website.

Stolz disrupted Zundel's initial trial and was barred from the courtroom because of her behavior. She had said the judges deserved the death penalty for offering succor to the enemy and signed a document "Heil Hitler." In her view, Germany has been under a foreign occupation which has portrayed Adolf Hitler as a devil for more than sixty years, but that is not true. After ignoring the bar, Stolz had to be physically removed from the court. During the March 2006 trial she called the Holocaust "the biggest lie in world history."

She had also vociferously defended Horst Mahler, another Holocaust denier.

The self-imposed mental malady of denying the Holocaust.

There is no doubt whatsoever, that it was the dictator who created the Holocaust. And earthly beings "created" this monster.

It is a cumbersome task to reveal the true nature of the inner reasons and causes of Holocaust deniers throughout the world.

After tens of thousands of official documents, in the form of structures, mass graves, films of systematic shootings, gas chambers, ovens, "Death and Concentration Camps," eye witnesses in the hundreds of thousands, survivors of camps awaiting execution but freed with the advancing Allied troops, especially the Russians in the eastern front and thousands of undeniable facts, namely the undernourished frail and dying prisoners with tattoos numbered on their hands, people still exist who deny the Holocaust. They were not only among the common public who claim to be so-called historians and researchers, but also politicians who occupy posts and positions in their country's governments.

Mahmood Ahmadinejad, the former President of the Islamic Republic regime in Iran arranged a "Conference to review the Global Vision of the Holocaust," that opened a two-day meeting on December 11, 2006 in Tehran. Sceptics, deniers, anti-Jewish, and anti-Israel "delegates" from many countries of the world including the United States attended this conference that was globally condemned as further adding insult to the souls of those departed due to the Holocaust.

Clergyman Seyed Ali Hosseini Khamenei, the leader of the Islamic Revolution has time and again called for "further research" into the truth of the Holocaust. While not openly denying this terrible assault on humanity, Khamenei is known to have been aware of this calamity heaped on the Jews in Europe, he, nonetheless, insists a research on this tragedy needs to be studied and that too, profoundly researched by independent scholars.

Apart from these conspicuous holocaust deniers, there are hundreds, perhaps thousands of individuals craving for an identity or seeking name and fame; or to live in infamy and be known, even posthumously, for their cowardly deeds in attacking the defenseless deceased!

Some of these persons listed are the morally and mentally bankrupt people who in many cases, even know the terrible truth of the holocaust, but still pretend, still claim that it was a hoax.

Horst Mahler, Germar Rudolf, a convicted Holocaust denier, Gerd Honsik, Ursula Hedwick, Meta Haverbeck, Wolfgang Frohlic, Dr. Herbert Schaller, Fredrick Toben, Richard Kriege, Leonardo Clerici, Siegfried Verbeke, Paul From, Christian Lindtner, Serge Thion, Rigolf Hennig, Konstantinos Plevri, Alfonso Pergas, Carlo Mattogn, Norman Lowell, Dariusz Ratajcz, Flavio Goncalves, Oleg Anatolyevich Platonov, Nadin Ravski, Pedro Varela, Ahmed Rami, Ditlieb Felderer, and Vincent Reynouard, to name a very few, perhaps one or even less than one percent of these people who have sworn to safeguard crime, chaos, murder and assault against humanity from whatever and whichever source it comes from.

Author's note:

I will not detail the lives of all those individuals who have lived a greater part of their lives in shame and dishonor by denying the holocaust; denying the cruelty inflicted before and after the death of Jewish children, men, and women, whether young or aged. But only a few onerous names to remind the general reader that such individuals existed and exist...even today! I will not further blemish this modest literary work by naming them all.

There is no such thing as a major or a minor denier. Whether an ordinary person or a person holding office, a person with so-called spiritual convictions; a clergyman, a preacher, a priest or simply speaking, a self-appointed researcher and expert who is involved in such vile claims, a denier is a denier and beggars to be damned by the sage mind.

Cosmology, human conscience, and historical facts have and will continue to condemn such individuals both in present times and posterity. A denier of whichever gender, can never be categorized as having a soft heart if he or she has made just a few "negligent passing remarks." If that "passing remark" is not made from innocence or ignorance, then on what grounds, truth, and reasons such a remark against the existence of the holocaust has been made? A denier is created within one's person, within one's being … by the very individual who desires to become conspicuous in society and in the world, by living a life in notoriety and infamy.

Inborne cruelty of such beings forms the basics of such philosophies which the world has witnessed in astonishment during the passage of times. It is not limited to genders. There are men and women, the educated and unlearned, the rich and the poor, all have joined this doleful chorus of denying the holocaust, as if it is a form of an invitation to their existence in life. There are more than a hundred thousand of such individuals in more than a hundred countries in the world. Ironically, a sizable number of them have University level education, which is a point of disgrace, a disrespect to education where falsity and chaos has overtaken their knowledge and their inner thoughts.

Judging from the increase in geometrical proportions of the number of anti-Jewish elements in the United States of America, ostensibly from the installing of Trump into the Oval Office by arcane hands, one must consider these masses filled with anti-Jewish sentiments and feelings and also augmented that Jews must be "replaced" by "Americans" and thus their slogan "Jews will never replace us," a slogan created by the "American Nazi Party," full heartedly supporting Trump, the former President of the United States of America, one is forced to think of reason, syllogism, inductive and deductive logic and the final results of such deeds.

Those criminal elements who have been vociferously screaming obscenities against Jews are so poorly schooled that they have a crazed love for the swastika (ancient Iranian symbol of goodness from the four winds, first discovered on ceramics in Iran dating 4000 BC. Re: Encyclopedia of the Third Reich, by Dr. Louis Snyder, Professor of History, The City University of New York. Page 135), the raised hand salute (ancient Iranian salute even before the time of Cyrus the Great) and their ignorance filled adoration for the mass murderer Adolf Hitler.

CHAPTER FOUR

LIST OF RIGHTEOUS
AMONG NATIONS

I f there were and still exist hundreds, if not thousands of those human beings who continue to deny the existence of mankind's planned and deliberate assault on humanity between mid-1930's and 1945, then there were also thousands, if not tens of thousands of noble hearted human beings who selflessly dedicated their very existence into saving precious Jewish lives, especially women and children by whatever means they could.

There is no measuring rod to identify any of the righteous persons as either "most righteous" or "lesser righteous" since all those who saved lives, attempted to save lives, or even one single life in danger of being exterminated is simply speaking, the "most righteous!"

It took gallantry, inner grandeur, and the power to make the supreme sacrifice if need be, to do what it takes to save a life or lives. And they had it all. These brave people knew their own lives would be in mortal danger at the hands of Nazi occupiers, yet they dauntlessly ventured forth to play their modest role in life. Their role and part in life was to save life and prevent wanton bloodshed of innocent men, women, and children who simply happened to follow the Jewish religion.

To solemnly remember such heroes and heroines is a simple lesson for mankind to remind oneself of what happened in the past. The able minded and bodied people who rushed to rescue their fellow human beings, while others passively stood by as onlookers to a terrible tragedy that was preplanned, premeditated, and knowingly executed which created the Holocaust!

It would not be an exaggeration to hold in esteem the dignified and valorous farmer Jozef and Wiktoria Ulma of Markowa (Poland) who were murdered in cold blood for harboring eight young Jews in their home. He will always be a conspicuous example of human grandeur in saving eight lives while losing his own family including his pregnant wife and six children.

There were and will always be hundreds, if not thousands of the likes of the Ulma family throughout the world.

Names of a few of these heroes who courageously played their modest role are reflected, although thousands of others also played their role are not mentioned. Their names and identities in no way lessen those men and women of courage who are unnamed in their valiant quest to save precious lives. Saving even one individual in imminent danger of losing her or his life was and will ever be considered as a heroic act: an act of morality, courage, and human grandeur.

Here, the most important statement is these men of inner nobility sprang into action due to the evils of a single "being," a dictator!

How could one person; the Austrian born Chancellor and later Fuehrer lead a country of millions, whose culture and tradition he was an alien to, continued to torment the entire population, leading them to a war where more than forty million people lost their lives, including more than six million Jews, whose genocide was planned and executed at his orders?

He was turned into a dictator by those as depraved and as bereft of mental bearings and certitudes in life as he and his gang of criminals were.

The Dictator was most certainly created by "back-scratchers" and "yes men." It was the dictator then, and will be the dictator now, perhaps in "waiting" or "aspiring," but sooner or later if not stopped and ousted, who will be that individual to bring about an apocalyptic Armageddon on this earth!

The reasons for reflecting the names of so many individuals who daringly and selflessly made sacrifices, even endangering their own precious lives to save those facing imminent death because of a dictatorial regime was to further prove the further pains and torments inflicted upon the souls of the departed by cowardly Holocaust deniers. Self-styled savants who deny this assault on humanity exist in virtually every country in the world.

There are undeniably countless individuals who deny the existence of the dreadful genocide of the Jewish people. Some outrightly deny the Holocaust, while others, albeit knowing the truth, claim a further unbiased research is necessary! Ironically, a few of them even claim to be scholars and "men of letters!"

What has been done by a dictator in the early 1930's continues to have its tormenting effects till today. This is the "after-effects" of a dictatorial regime, created by none other than the people themselves.

Cautioning the world against the designs and hidden agenda of an "aspiring dictator" is one of the cardinal duties of every individual throughout the world. Ousting the individual with the faintest signs of even aspiring to be a dictator with far-reaching powers while under the excuse or claiming, "presidential powers" and "executive powers and privileges" must be diligently confronted, and that individual immediately ousted.

Ousting the dictators will usher in global peace and harmony!

Today we have many, perhaps millions, of those that are termed "Righteous Among the Nations", in many a garb and identity, some of those who courageously and vociferously advocate for the voiceless, the helpless and the damned.

If today and in the yesteryears, there existed and exist many who knowingly and intentionally denied and deny the Holocaust, just to further belittle the Jewish people, it must be emphatically said that there were millions then and now who acknowledge and unambiguously condemn this most deliberately authored crime against humanity!

These are only a fraction of the heroes who played their role. Many existed who bravely ventured forth to save human lives.

Henryk Goldszmit, pen name Janusz Korczak (July 22, 1878 – August 7, 1942) Treblinka extermination Camp.

An educator, Children's author, humanitarian, pediatrician and a pedagogue, and defender of Children's rights and perhaps the bravest person in Poland, Goldszmit managed an orphanage with some 192 children, some of whom were perhaps of Jewish faith. When promised of being spared although he was Jewish, if he would detach himself from the helpless children who were destined to die in the Treblinka death camp, Goldszmit rejected the offer and marched to his certain death with the children. Goldszmit's name will forever be etched among the bravest.

Georges Loinger (August 29, 1910 – December 28, 2018)

Not only Christians and Muslims played their part of saving Jewish lives by the tens of thousands, but also Jewish individuals wherever they could, contributed their share of heroism. One such person was Georges Loinger.

Using whatever means he could, he saved the lives of 350 Jewish children and helped them cross the border from France into Switzerland.

Johan Willem van Hulst (January 28,1911- March 22, 2018)

Hulst was a Dutch school director, university professor, author, chess player and politician. Dutch historians and the mass media have hailed him as a person with special convictions in life.

Using whatever means he could, Van Hulst in cooperation and coordination with other friends rescued nearly 1000 Jewish children.

Van Hulst received the Yad Vashem distinction in 1973. During a visit to the Netherlands in 2012, the Israeli Prime Minister Benjamin Netanyahu said of Van Hulst: "We say. Those who save one life saves a universe. I want to thank you in the name of the Jewish people, but also in the name of humanity." Van Hulst replied, talking about the children he could not save: "I only can hope the angels may conduct you into paradise."

Van Hulst passed away peacefully in his sleep on March 22, 2018 at the age of 107. Angels too guided him into paradise.

Irena Stanislawa Sendler (February 15, 1910 – May 12, 2008)

This Polish social worker saved more than two thousand Jewish lives. She knowingly endangered her own life to rescue more than 2500 Jewish children, men, and women from execution by the Nazi occupiers of Poland.

Arrested by the Gestapo, she was sentenced to death but managed to escape execution after Nazi guards were bribed by her supporters.

Sendler was decorated by the Governments of Israel, Poland, and the mass media in Poland as well as nearly all European countries who praised her courage.

On March 14, 2007 Sendler was honored by the Senate of Poland and a year later in July 20, the United States Congress honored her.

In 1965, Sendler was recognized by the State of Israel as Righteous Among the Nations. Earlier in 1946 she was also decorated with Gold Cross of Merit for saving thousands of Jewish lives and the Order of the White Eagle, Poland's highest honor.

Earlier, Pope John Paul II in 2003 sent her a personal letter praising her wartime efforts. She was also posthumously granted the Humanitarian of the Year award from The Sister Rose Thering Endowment in April 2009 and a month later in May 2009 was decorated with the Audrey Hepburn Humanitarian Award.

In 2013. The walkway in front of the POLIN Museum of the History of Polish Jews in Warsaw was named after Sendler.

Maria Roszak also addressed as Sister Cecylia/ Cecilia (March 25, 1908 – November 16, 2018)

A name to be remembered and whose life worthy of honor. Maria Roszak addressed as Sister Cecylia was a Polish Nun who joined the convent of the Dominican Cloisters in Krakow, taking the name of Cecylia after taking her first religious vows in 1931 and final vows in 1934.

Through her guidance and supervision, and working under the leadership of Anna Borkowska, the mother superior of the convent, hundreds of Jewish lives, especially members of the Jewish Resistance fighters as well as would-be-members of resistance fighters were saved.

The archdiocese of Krakow in Poland while praising her bravery in hiding young Jews who were being "hunted" by Nazi elements, said that Sister Cecylia (Cecilia) Maria Roszak was the oldest sister in the world when she passed away. The Government of Israel honored her.

Sir Nicholas George Winton (May 19, 1909 – July 1, 2015)

Sir Winton was a British humanitarian who established an organization to rescue children at risk from Nazi Germany. Born of German-Jewish parents who had emigrated to Britain, Winton supervised the rescue of 669 children, most of them Jewish, from Czechoslovakia on the eve of World War II. He found homes for them and arranged for their safe passage to Britain.

He personally supervised an operation which was later known as "Czech Kindertransport," (German for children's transport).

His heroism went unnoticed by the world for the next fifty years, until 1988 when he was invited the BBC television program "That's Life!" when he was reunited with several of the children whose lives he had helped save.

The British press celebrated him and dubbed him the "British Schindler." In 2003, Winton was "knighted" by Queen Elizabeth II for "services to humanity, in saving Jewish children from Nazi Germany occupied Czechoslovakia."

Sir Winton successfully rescued 669 Jewish children who faced certain death. Many of the parents of the children who stayed behind perished in the various death camps, notably Auschwitz. He also wrote letters to then President Roosevelt and other US politicians to take in more Jewish children and later said that more than 2000 would have been saved if they had helped. The last group of 250 scheduled to leave Prague on September 1, 1939, were unable to depart. With the Nazi invasion of Poland on the same day, the Second World War had begun. Of the children due to leave on that train, only two survived the war.

Sir Winton acknowledged the vital roles in Prague of Doreen Warriner, Trevor Chadwick, Nicholas Stopford, Beatrice Wellington, Josephine Pike and Bill Barazetti among others involved in this humanitarian effort. He lauded the significant role played by Trevor Chadwick in the several rescue operations.

Later Sir Winton wrote, "Chadwick did the more difficult and dangerous work after the Nazis invaded…he deserves all praise." He was decorated in 1998 by Czech President Havel among other awards.

Abdol Hossein Sardari (1914 -1981) issued Iranian passport
to nearly two thousand five hundred Jews in France.

Abdol Hossein Sardari was an Iranian diplomat stationed in Paris during
the Second World War. A lawyer by training, he used tactics to exempt
Iranian Jews from anti-Jewish measures practiced by the Nazis.

He issued more than 2500 Iranian passports to Jews who resided in and
around Paris, helping many of them to escape to neutral Iran or to other
countries outside Europe.

In a letter addressed to Yad Vashem, the Israeli National Holocaust
Remembrance Center, Sardari wrote: "I had the privilege of being the
Iranian Consul in Paris during the German occupation of France, and
hence it was my cardinal duty to save all Iranians, including Iranian Jews."

Iranian historians believe documents with the Foreign Ministry of Iran,
lists 3000 Jews, both Iranian as well as French and other Jews from other
countries who had earlier fled to France were rescued by the tireless efforts
of Abdol Hossein Sardari.

Sardari has been dubbed as the Muslim Schindler (Oskar Schindler), after
the German industrialist who saved more than 1000 Jewish lives.

Marcel Marceau (March 22, 1923 – September 22, 2007)

Marceau was a world renown French actor and mime artist in the 1940s.
During the period German troops occupied France, Marceau used mime
for the first time to keep Jewish children quiet while he helped them escape
to neutral Switzerland. He saved the lives of more than a hundred Jewish
children from certain death.

Oskar Schindler (April 28, 1908 – October 9, 1974)

A conspicuous name among "The Righteous among Nations," Schindler was a German Industrialist and a member of the Nazi Party who has been credited with saving the lives of 1200 Jews by employing them in his ammunition factories in occupied Poland.

By July 1944, Germany was losing the war, the SS ("Schutzstaffel." The "Protection Squadron.") began closing the easternmost concentration camps and deporting the remaining prisoners westward. Many were murdered in Auschwitz and the other infamous Gross-Rosen concentration camp.

Determined to save precious human lives, Schindler convinced the commandant of the nearby Krakow-Plaszow concentration camp, to allow him to move his factory to Brnenec in the Protectorate of Bohemia and Moravia, thus sparing his workers from certain death in the gas chambers.

In all, Schindler was able to save 1200 lives who after the war were termed as "Schindlerjuden" ("Schindler Jews") Most of them in later years aided Schindler and his wife who were in financial difficulties. Schindler spent his entire fortune bribing senior Nazi Officials and even guards from harming or executing the one thousand two hundred Jews whom he had saved under one pretext or the other.

Raoul Gustav Wallenberg (August 4, 1912 –
disappeared, executed, January 17, 1945)

One of the most honored among the Righteous of Nations was the Swedish architect, diplomat and humanitarian, Raoul Gustav Wallenberg. He is remembered for saving thousands of Jewish lives.

Tens of thousands of Jewish people were rescued by Wallenberg and the several rescue teams he created in Nazi occupied Hungary, while he was the special envoy of Sweden in Budapest between July and December 1944. Most outstanding feat of his was to issue "protective passports" to identify a quarter million Hungarian Jews as Swedish citizens, awaiting repatriation and thus prevented their deportation to death camps.

Through all means at his disposal, Wallenberg's determination to save the lives of hundreds of thousands of Jewish lives met with marked success. He raised money through several organizations and rented more than thirty buildings in Budapest and designated them as "extraterritorial," protected by diplomatic immunity where nearly ten thousand Jews were safely housed. Another two hundred were housed within the compounds of the Swedish Embassy in Budapest.

One of the greatest feats of bravery by Wallenberg was narrated by Sandor Ardai, his Jewish driver, when he intercepted a trainload of Jews destined for the gas chambers of Auschwitz.

> "He climbed up on the roof of the train and began handing in protective passes through the doors which were not yet sealed. He ignored orders from the Germans for him to get down, members of the Far-Right militia and political group 'Arrow Cross' began shooting and shouting at him to get away. He ignored them and calmly continued handing out passports to the hands that were reaching out for them. I believe the Arrow Cross men deliberately aimed over his head, as not one shot hit him. I think this is what they did because they were so impressed by his courage. After Wallenberg had handed over the last of the passports, he ordered all those who had one to leave the train and walk to the caravan of cars parked nearby, all marked in Swedish colors. I don't remember exactly how many, but he saved dozens off that train, and the Germans and the Arrow Cross were so dumbfounded they let him get away with it."

One of the outstanding achievements of Wallenberg was two days before the Soviet Army occupied Budapest, when he negotiated with Adolf Eichmann and with Major General Gerhard Schmidhuber, the supreme commander of German forces in Hungary. Wallenberg bribed Arrow Cross member, Pal Szalai (who was recognized as Righteous Among the Nations) to deliver a note in which Wallenberg persuaded the Germans planning to retreat, to prevent a Fascist plan to blow up the Budapest ghetto and kill an estimated 70,000 Jews. The note also persuaded the Germans to cancel a final effort to organize a "death march" of the remaining Jews in Budapest, by threatening to have them prosecuted for war crimes once the war was over.

Wallenberg was recognized as one of the Righteous Among the Nations. He was honored throughout the world for his daring and courage to save human lives.

Other heroes in Hungary at that period were **Carl Lutz**, Swiss diplomat who issued hundreds of protective passports from the Swiss Embassy; and Italian businessman **Giorgio Perlasca** posed as a Spanish diplomat and issued forged visas to the endangered Jews. Perlasca saved the lives of 5218 Jews.

Tibor Baranski (June 11, 1922 – January 20, 2019) credited with saving more than 3000 Hungarian Jewish women, men, and children. Baranski was recognized as one of the many Righteous among the Nations by Yad Vashem.

Andrée Geulen-Hersovici (Born September 6, 1921)

Geulen-Hersovici is a Belgian woman, who with others rescued one thousand Jewish children during the Holocaust. In 1942, the then Ms. Geulen was working as a schoolteacher in Brussels when the Gestapo arrived to arrest the Jewish children. She decided to join Jewish rescue organization, Comité de Défense des Juifs (Committee for the Protection of Jews). For more than two years, she moved Jewish children to live with Christian families and monasteries. She would continue to visit them and care for their needs. By keeping a secret record of the children's true identities, after the war she attempted to reunite them with their families if any survived. In 1989 Andrée Geulen was recognized as a Righteous Among the Nations and on April 18, 2007, she was granted honorary

Israeli citizenship in a ceremony at Yad Vashem, as part of the Children Hidden in Belgium During the Shoah International Conference. Upon accepting the honor, Geulen-Hersovici said, "What I did was merely my duty. Disobeying the laws of the time was just the normal thing to do."

Rudolf Stefan Jan Weigl (September 2, 1883 – August 11, 1957)

This Polish inventor of the Typhus Vaccine harbored nearly a hundred Jews in his own home, his laboratory and in the homes of trusted friends. Moreover, he had thousands of doses of vaccines smuggled into the Lwow and Warsaw Ghetto, thus saving innumerable lives afflicted by typhus.

Altogether, this heroic Polish doctor saved more than 2000 lives.

Sister Bertranda also addressed as Mother Bertranda (1900-1988)

Sister Bertranda was a Polish cloistered Dominican Nun who served as the prioress of her monastery in Kolonia Wilenska (now near Vilnius, Lithuania)

During the war years, under her leadership, the nuns of the monastery sheltered 17 young Jewish activists and helped the Jewish Partisan Organization by smuggling weapons.

Arrested by Nazi occupation authorities, she was sent to a labor camp near Kaunas, Lithuania. Her monastery was shut down and some of the nuns were arrested while others were dispersed.

After the war, Mother Bertranda asked for dispensation from her vows and left the monastery, where she adopted the name Anna Borkowska.

Frederik Jacques "Frits" Philips (April 16, 1905 - December 5, 2005)

A globally respected person for his daring, Philips was the fourth chairman of the board of directors of the famed Dutch electronics company. He helped save 382 Jews employed by telling the Nazi occupiers that their presence was indispensable for the production process at Philips.

Through his friends, he saved nearly a thousand Jewish Children belonging to the 382 persons who were employed at Philips.

Historians attribute him as saving at least 2000 Jewish lives.

Frits was recognized by Yad Vashem among the Righteous Among the Nations.

Jan Zwartendijk (July 29, 1896 - September 14, 1976)

Dutch Consular representative in Kaunas and director of Philips plants in Lithuania. He issued exit visas to 2345 Jewish refugees for Curacao (Lesser Antilles Island in the southern Caribbean, and the Dutch Caribbean region, just forty nautical miles north of the Venezuelan coast and is a considered a part of the Netherlands).

Apart from saving the 2345 Jewish lives from certain death, Zwartendijk also assisted hundreds of Jews who had already fled Nazi occupied Poland. In addition, hundreds of Polish dissidents also received his assistance.

In 1957, Yad Vashem recognized him as Righteous Among the Nations.

Jozef Ulma (1900 – March 24, 1944) **Wiktoria Ulma** nee Niemczak (December 10, 1912 – March 24,1944) resided in Markowa Poland and were farmers for several generations.

Dubbed "Servants of God." this brave and Righteous family of farmers were murdered together with their six children for helping save eight members of a Jewish family whom they hid in their attic.

Nazi occupiers of Poland murdered the entire family including their six children for hiding Polish Jewish families in their own home. Wiktoria Ulma was in an advanced stage of pregnancy and was expected to give birth to her seventh child, just days before her execution.

The Ulma family will always be remembered in the annals of written history for their bravery and convictions.

On September 13, 1995, Jozef and Wiktoria Ulma were posthumously bestowed the titles of Righteous Among the Nations by Yad Vashem. On March 24, 2004, a stone memorial to honor memory of the Ulma family was erected in Markowa.

The inscription on the monument reads:

"Saving the lives of others, they laid down their own lives. Hiding eight elder brothers in faith, they were killed with them. May their sacrifice be a call for respect and love to every human being! They were the sons and daughters of this land; they will remain in our hearts."

One must in all truth ever remember and recognize the courage, selflessness, and sacrifice of the Ulma family.

Writer and activist **Zofia Kossak-Szczucka** (August 10,1889 – April 9, 1968)

Zofia Kossak-Szczucka co-founded two wartime Polish Organizations Front Odrodzenia Polski and Zegota, which was meant to help Polish Jews escape the Holocaust.

Noting the Holocaust at close range she wrote: "England is silent, so is America, even the influential international Jewry, so sensitive in its reaction to any transgression against its people, is silent. Poland is silent… Dying Jews are surrounded only by a host of Pilates washing their hands in innocence." Our feelings towards Jews have not changed," she added." We do not stop thinking of them as political, economic and ideological enemies of Poland." But she wrote, this does not relieve Polish Catholics of their duty to oppose the crimes being committed in their country.

Her historical statements awakened millions throughout the world as to the evils of the Holocaust.

Part of it is: "We are required by God to protest," she wrote. "God who forbids us to kill. We are required by our Christian consciousness. Every human being has the right to be loved by his fellow men. The blood of the defenseless cries to heaven for revenge. Those who oppose our protest, are not Catholics. We do not believe that Poland can benefit from German cruelties. On the contrary, we know how poisoned the fruit of crime is… Those who do not understand this and believe that a proud and free future for Poland can be combined with acceptance of the grief of their fellow men, are neither Catholics, nor Poles."

In 1985, she was posthumously named one of the Righteous Among the Nations.

Karolina Juszcykowska (1899 – 1945)

A kitchen worker for "Organization Todt" (Civil and military Organization in Nazi Germany named after Dr. Fritz Todt, a construction engineer) hid dozens of Jews in her home for which she was executed. She was accused of hiding Jewish people (Janek and Paul) who were executed.

In 2011 Yad Vashem recognized her as one of the Righteous Among the Nations.

Sara Salkahazi (May 11, 1899 – December 27, 1944)

Born Schalkhaz Sarolta Klotild, she was a Hungarian Catholic religious sister who saved the lives of approximately one hundred Jews during the Holocaust. Denounced and summarily executed by the pro-Nazi Arrow Cross Party, Salkahazi was beatified in 2006.

In 1969, her deeds on behalf of Hungarian Jews were recognized by Yad Vashem after she was nominated by the daughter of one of the Jewish women she was hiding, who was killed alongside her.

Caecilia Loots. School teacher and antifascist resistance member.

Marion Van Binsbergen saved one hundred and fifty Dutch Jews.

Tina Strobos rescued more than a hundred Jews by hiding them in her house.

Johan Hendrik Weidner, head of the Dutch-Paris Organization, which saved nearly a thousand Jewish lives.

Klymentiy Sheptytsky (1869-1951) the Archimandrite of the Studite monks of Greek-Catholic Monastery who saved hundreds of Jewish lives.

Queen Elizabeth of the Belgians and **Jeanne Daman**, who helped rescue more than two thousand Jewish lives, mostly children.

The **Stoyanov Family** in Moldova who tirelessly helped in saving countless Jewish lives.

Alexsandr Stoyanov and his wife **Ludmila** and their children helped hide and rescue dozens of Jews despite warnings of severe punishment; death, by the Nazi occupiers and their agents of any individual rescuing or hiding Jews.

On November 21, 1993, Yad Vashem recognized the entire Stoyanov family as Righteous Among the Nations.

Janis Lipke (also Zanis Lipke, February 1, 1900 – May 14, 1987)

Janis Lipke was a dock worker in the port city of Riga in Latvia, who together with his wife helped smuggle out dozens of Jews from the Riga ghetto and towards freedom.

Lipke watched in horror the torments and destruction heaped on the Jewish population of Latvia, especially in the Riga ghetto and vowed to help rescue any number he could to save them from certain death.

He is honored as one of the Righteous Among the Nations.

Queen Helen of Romania (Helen of Greece and Denmark, May 2, 1896 – November 28, 1982)

Queen mother of Romania, she had her own organization to provide food, clothing and medicine for Jews who had either escaped or had been deported by the Nazi occupiers. She told her son Michael (King of Romania) that what was happening to the Jewish people in the country was unbearable, more so that her name and the King's will be connected to murder of the Jewish people and so she can expect to remain in history as the mother of "Michael the terrible." She even threatened to leave the country unless the deportations stopped immediately.

The Queen mother saved the lives of nearly two thousand Jews and saved twice that figure from disease and hunger.

On March 11, 1993, Yad Vashem recognized Helen as Righteous Among the Nations.

Traian Popovici (October 17, 1892 – June 4, 1946)

Famed attorney for saving twenty thousand Jews of Bukovina from deportation to be murdered in death camps.

He is honored by Yad Vashem memorial as Righteous Among the Nations. Through his wisdom and timely interventions, Popovici saved a large number of human lives who faced deportation to death camps.

Prince Constantin Karadja (November 24, 1889 – December 28, 1950)

The Prince was an avowed supporter of International Law and respected Human Rights.

As the Romanian Consul General in Berlin (1932-1941) and the director of Consular department of the Romanian Foreign Ministry (June 15, 1941 – October 17, 1944), in both functions, during nearly fifteen years, the Prince was determined to save Jewish lives in the "kingdom of death."

Tens of thousands owe their lives to his exceptional persistency, bravery, determination, and amplitude marking his long-term engagement in favor of the Romanian Jews stranded under the Nazi regime.

For his courageous role in saving lives, he was dismissed from the Foreign Ministry on October 17, 1944, but was re-appointed by the new Foreign Minister. On October 1, 1947 he was permanently dismissed from the Foreign Ministry. This was one of the last measures taken by minister Gheorghe Tatarescu, who one month later was forced to leave his post to Ana Pauker.

His pension was refused and in an atmosphere of incertitude and menace, he died on December 28, 1950.

On September 15, 2005 Constantin Karadja received from the Yad Vashem Institute in Jerusalem the title "Righteous Among the Nations" during a ceremony in the Israeli Embassy in Berlin.

He was credited by Yad Vashem with saving more than fifty-one thousand Jews.

Dimitar Peshev (June 25, 1894 – February 20, 1973)

Dimitar Peshev was the Deputy Speaker of the National Assembly of Bulgaria and Minister of Justice, before the outbreak of the Second World War. He rebelled against the pro-Nazi cabinet and prevented the deportation of Bulgaria's 48,000 Jews and was bestowed the title of Righteous Among the Nations.

Metropolitan Stefan of Sofia actively contributed to the rescue of hundreds of Bulgarian Jews during the war years. He was recognized as among the Righteous Among the Nations.

Metropolitan Cyril/Kyril of Plovdiv (born Constantin Markov Konstantinov January 3, 1901 – March 7, 1971)

One of the bravest of the Bulgarian Orthodox Church who in many ways helped save hundreds of lives, both Jews and Gypsies.

His historical role of bravery in the Bulgarian popular resistance to the Holocaust is recounted in the oratorio "A Melancholy Beauty" composed by Georgi Andreev with libretto by Scott Cairns and Aryeh Finklestein, first performed in June 2011 in Washington D.C.

The text describes "Metropolitan Kyril" in 1944 confronting the captors of Bulgarian Jews slated to be deported. Kyril first pledges to go with the deportees in solidarity and then tells the guards he will block the train with his own body. The guards reply that they have just received new orders to release the Jews.

Peer Anger, Ivan Danielsson, Lars Berg, Valdemar, Elow Kihlgren, Erik Perwe, Elisabeth Hesselblad, Valdemar and Nina Langlet and **Erik Myrgen** and several other Swedish citizens who jointly rescued over two thousand Jews from certain death.

Selahattin Ulkumen, Behic Erkin, Necdet Kent and **Namik Kemal Yolga** who provided sanctuary to Jews fleeing Poland. These Turkish heroes are remembered for their daring deeds in saving the lives of more than two hundred Jews.

Aristides de Souza Mendes (July 19, 1885 – April 3, 1954)

Portuguese diplomat who provided more than thirty thousand visas to Jews and non-Jews escaping Nazism in France.

As the Portuguese consul-general in the French city of Bordeaux, he defied the orders of Antonio de Oliveira Salazar's regime, by issuing visas and passports to an undetermined number of refugees fleeing Nazi Germany, including Jews.

For his humanitarian deeds and for saving countless Jewish lives, he was recognized as one of the Righteous Among the Nations.

Carlos Sampaio Garrido (April 5,1883 – April 1960)

Carlos Sampaio Garrido, a Portuguese diplomat, while serving as ambassador to Budapest, Hungary, sheltered about one thousand Jews in safe houses in Budapest between July and December 1944.

In 2010 he became the second Portuguese recognized as a Righteous Among the Nations.

Pan Jun Shun and **Feng-Shan Ho**, Chinese diplomats provided more than three thousand visas to Jews in need during their tenure as Ambassador and senior diplomat of Republic of China to Vienna in 1938. Both diplomats were recognized as Righteous Among the Nations.

Mary Elizabeth Jean Elmes (May 5, 1908 – March 9, 2002)

In mid-1942, the puppet Vichy government in France made it legal for Jewish children to be sent to concentration camps. That was the time Mary Elmes (an Irish woman) decided to do whatever possible to save the lives of as many Jewish children as possible. Together with the help of collaborators she hid at least two hundred Jewish children, some even under the age of twelve.

In 2015, she became the only Irish woman honored as Righteous Among the Nations by the State of Israel, in recognition of her work in the Spanish Civil War and World War II.

Jose Castellanos Contreras, provided Salvadorian citizenship papers to thirteen thousand Central European Jews

Mohammed Helmy (July 25, 1901 - January 10, 1982)

Mohammed Helmy, a doctor by profession was the only Egyptian to be recognized by Yad Vashem as the Righteous Among the Nations. He saved several Jews from persecution in Berlin during the period of the Holocaust.

Chiune Sugihara (January 1, 1900 – July 31, 1986)

Chiune Sugihara was a Japanese government official who served as vice consul for the Japanese Empire in Kaunas, Lithuania. He helped some six thousand Jews flee Europe by providing them transit visas, enabling them to travel through Japanese territory. At the cost of risking his job and his family's lives.

A year before he passed away, Sugihara was honored by the State of Israel as one of the Righteous Among the Nations. He was the only Japanese national to have received this honor.

Victor Bodson (March 24, 1902 – June 29, 1984)

Victor Bodson was a Luxembourg socialist politician and lawyer. He was also a former Justice Minister and Chairman of the Luxembourg House of Representatives.

He resided close to the German border just a few kilometers away from the Sauer river, which acts as a border between Luxembourg and Germany. He, with his trusted friends, helped create and operate an escape route for Jews escaping the horrors of Nazi Germany. His heroism saved approximately one hundred Jewish lives.

He was recognized as the Righteous Among the Nations.

Bosnian and Herzegovina citizens, **Zekira Besirevic**, **Mustafa and Zejneba Hardaga**, **Izet and Bahrija/Bachriya Hardaga**, and **Ahmad Sadik** combinedly saved more than a thousand Jewish lives. They were all recognized as the Righteous Among the Nations by the State of Israel.

In February 1994 members of the Hardaga family were helped by the Israeli government to leave for Israel while experiencing dangers in Sarajevo which was under attack by Serbian forces. Those same Jewish families who were saved nearly five decades earlier by the Hardagas now went to their rescue and helped them.

At this juncture, and so far, Christians, Muslims, Buddhists and people of other faiths and beliefs rushed to the help of Jews in distress. This reflects the Cosmic nature of mankind and altruism at its peak.

CHAPTER FIVE

TRUMP ANALYSIS

Trump the Mentally Disturbed, the Pernicious Charlatan,
the Master of Deceit, Falsehood, and the Prolific Liar-in-
Chief Imposed on the Nation by the Political Mafia

Covid-19 Pandemic

Considering this undeniable truth that Trump's deceitful tactics, recklessness and irresponsibility prevented the government from concentrating on ways and means to check the spread of COVID-!9, that cost the nation over half a million fatality, it is justified to momentarily divert from the original flow related to the subject. it appears inevitable to invoke the topic of the uncontrollable spread of the Coronavirus COVID-19, that had crept into every country and society on Earth and had claimed hundreds of thousands of lives and affected two million within four months since early January 2020 or even a bit earlier. By the second week of May 2021, it was claimed that more than 586,000 succumbed to this dreaded virus in the USA alone. The total cases of those affected by the virus exceeded thirty-two million people in the country. Global cases meanwhile passed over one hundred fifty million.

While all the major countries in the world, among them, the United States of America, Russia, Israel, England, China, France, Germany, Iran, Italy, and others who diligently worked on a treatment and a vaccine were reportedly working towards a vaccine to treat the several mutated forms of the virus. All, except for Pfizer manufacturers of their brand of vaccine, agreed to cooperate with all other countries in this scientific and medical research.

The evils of the Mafia Bosses do not need any elaboration after centuries of global skullduggeries. It is an established fact that they do not care an iota of what happens to humankind once they arrive at their objectives, either by creating an ignorant willing tool as their puppet dictator residing comfortably in the White House or elsewhere in the world. A vivid example was Trump, well known for his incompetency in dealing with global situations. Even though he was unfit to hold the office of the Chief Administrator of the United States of America, he was their candidate of choice.

The magnitude of Trump's follies, absurdities and incompetence coupled with his opportunist enablers in his administration was evident when he deliberately cancelled funds in 2018 meant for scientific research for virology and pandemics in the United States of America solely because President Barack Obama had paid special importance to this research institute. The institute contained the threat from both the Ebola and Zika viruses. This policy change left the United States of America unprepared to deal with the Covid-19 virus that spread like wildfire in the country and throughout the world in 2020.

Trump nullified several other programs beneficial to the health and living conditions of the nation. Those that had a positive effect on the country, and he cancelled are:

1. The National Environmental Policy Act
2. The Endangered Species Act
3. The Clean Water Act
4. The National Historic Preservation Act
5. The Migratory Bird Treaty Act
6. The Migratory Bird Conservation Act
7. The Clean Air Act

8. The Archeological Resources Protection Act
9. The Paleontological Resources Protection Act
10. The Federal Cave Resources Protection Act
11. The Safe Drinking Water Act
12. The Noise Control Act
13. The Solid Waste Disposal Act
14. The Comprehensive Environmental Response, Compensation, and Liability Act
15. The Archeological and Historic Preservation Act
16. The Antiquities Act
17. The Historic Sites, Buildings and Antiquities Act
18. The Farmland Protection Policy Act
19. The Coastal Zone Management Act
20. The Federal Land Policy and Management Act
21. The National Fish and Wildlife Act
22. The Fish and Wildlife Coordination Act

The disappearance of laws beneficial to the public has resulted in chemicals, sludge, raw sewage, and other dangerous chemicals to flow directly into the rivers, lakes and canals throughout the country creating health hazards and environmental damage.

Pastor and evangelist, Landon Spradlin, a vociferous friend and supporter of Trump and a self-acclaimed healer claimed that the Coronavirus Covid -19 was just a "mass hysteria" created and expanded into a pandemic by the opponents of Trump and was a media plot meant to weaken him from being reelected in November 2020. "This is a hoax," Spradlin repeatedly told his audience. The pastor who had claimed he regularly communicated with his heavenly father who had blessed him with supernatural healing powers of any illness, died of Covid-19 on March 26, 2020.

Statistics often Convey the Truth.

Trump initially dismissed the deadly virus as something petty and a temporary phenomenon that would disappear once summer arrives! On March 13, 2020, weeks after stating what his speech writer encouraged him to say, describing the virus as negligible, Trump declared it as dangerous to the nation's population. Lowering his regular tone of rhetoric laced with wangle and insults against his perceived enemies, in a very somber tone he declared a national emergency! Earlier in January 2020, Trump had initially dismissed Coronavirus as a hoax meant to weaken his stand since he had cut funds for virus and infectious disease research nearly two years earlier and later in his several statements called it a type of a common cold. Then on March 17, 2020 he claimed that he knew much earlier that it was a pandemic before it was declared a pandemic. His various statements, all conflicting and contradicting his prior messages to the nation, while attempting to manage a critical crisis facing the nation are evidence for the reader to judge his competency and preparedness to lead.

Beginning January 22, 2020 Trump made his opening remarks on the Coronavirus, a real calamity facing the United States of America, and in general, the entire world.

The exact wordings of Trump are reflected below:

January 22, 2020: "We have it totally under control. It's one person coming from China."

February 2, 2020: "We pretty much shut it down coming from China. It's going to be fine."

February 24, 2020: "The Coronavirus is pretty much under control in the USA...Stock Market starting to look very good to me."

February 25, 2020: "CDC (Center for Disease Control) and my administration are doing a great job of handling Coronavirus."

February 25, 2020: "I think that's a problem that's going to go away. They have studied it. They know very much. In fact, we're close to a vaccine."

February 26, 2020: "The fifteen cases within a couple of days is going to be down to close to zero."

February 26, 2020: "We're going substantially down, not up."

February 27, 2020: "One day it's like a miracle, it will disappear."

February 28, 2020: "We're ordering a lot of supplies. We're ordering a lot of, uh, elements that frankly we wouldn't be ordering unless it was something like this. But we're ordering a lot of different elements of medical."

March 2, 2020: "You take a solid flu vaccine, you don't think that could have an impact, or much of an impact on corona?"

March 2, 2020: "A lot of things are happening, a lot of very exciting things are happening and they're happening very rapidly."

March 4, 2020: "If we have thousands of people that get better just by, you know, sitting around and even going to work – some of them go to work, but they get better."

March 5, 2020: "I never said people that are feeling sick should go to work."

March 6, 2020: "I think we're doing a really good job in this country at keeping it down…a tremendous job at keeping it down."

March 6, 2020: "Anybody right now, and yesterday, anybody that needs a test gets a test. And the tests are beautiful. They are perfect just like the letter was perfect. The transcription was perfect. Right? This was not perfect as that but pretty good."

March 6, 2020: "I like this stuff. I really get it. People are surprised that I understand it. Every one of these doctors said, 'How do you know so much about this?' Maybe I have a natural ability. Maybe I should have done that than running for president."

March 6, 2020: "I don't need to have the numbers, because of one error that wasn't our fault."

March 8, 2020: "We have a perfectly coordinated and fine-tuned plan at the White House for our attack on Coronavirus."

March 9, 2020: "The Fake News Media and their partner, the Democrat Party, is doing everything within its semi-considerable power to inflame the Coronavirus situation."

March 10, 2020: "It will go away, just stay calm. It will go away."

March 13, 2020: Trump declares National Emergency.

His claim on February 26, 2020, that only fifteen people in the United States had been afflicted with the Coronavirus and that the figure will go down to zero in a couple of days was deliberately misleading, false, and absurd.

Between February 26, 2020 and April 3, 2020, the number of confirmed Coronavirus cases in the U.S. was above 245,000 according to John Hopkins University data dashboard and the death toll had surpassed six thousand and rendered more than seven hundred thousand people jobless from the business closures. On Friday, April 3, 2020, "USA Today" quoting John Hopkins University reported that Worldwide the death toll topped fifty-three thousand, and the virus had infected more than 1.6 million people. This statistic presents the geometrical proportions the virus spread within a brief period, beginning late December 2019 when the case was first seriously examined.

On Thursday, April 23, 2020, Sarah Moon of the popular CNN Channel claimed that the first case of the Coronavirus-related fatality in the United States was on February 6, 2020 and the second case was on February 17, 2020.

A more detailed statistic from combined dispatches throws further light on the developments affecting mankind from this virus. Giving randomly chosen dates and the uncontrollable rapid increase in the numbers of global and US casualties appear relevant to this silent killer.

March 1, 2020

US fatalities: 6 persons were officially said to have been deceased due to the virus.

Within a week the casualty rate rose to 6,394

The gradual but ominous increase in those affected and deceased throws light on this pandemic. Sources: Wikipedia, European Center for Disease Prevention and Control, New York Times, COVID Tracking Project

All figures are not exact. A sizable number of statistics reflected were also shown on CNN and MSNBC, trusted sources of information. This data changed rapidly and might not reflect updated numbers.

April 6, 2020

US Cases: 337,600

US fatalities: 9,600

Global Cases: 1,276,300

Global Fatalities: 69,500

January 1, 2021

US Cases: 19,990,390

US Fatalities: 346,013

Global Cases: 83,598,179

Global Fatalities: 1,821,183

January 2, 2021

US Cases: 20,350,019

US Fatalities: 349,625

Global Cases: 84,439,286

Global Fatalities: 1,833,445

The continued flow of this virus creeps unchecked into every society on earth. The undeniable statistics are ostensibly reflected for the purpose of exposing the unstable mental state of Trump who by the end of his four-year term of occupying the Oval Office most brazenly lied to the United States' Nation that he has plans and that the virus would simply disappear once and for all.

Legendry journalist Bob Woodward in his book "Rage," has exposed a nefarious lie of Trump that has proven to be too costly to the health of the country's population. Washington Post reported excerpts from the book on Wednesday, September 9, 2020 proving misleading statements by Trump to the American Nation. In one of the interviews that Woodward had conducted with Trump on March 19, 2020, Trump told him that he deliberately minimized the danger of the COVID -19 Virus and knowingly lied. "I wanted to always play it down," Trump said.

On January 22, 2020, Trump had most confidently told the nation; "We have it (the virus) totally under control. It's one person coming from China." On February 2, 2020 Trump reassured the nation; "We pretty much shut it down coming from China. It's going to be fine."

Woodward serves as an associate editor of the Washington Post and is considered a respected journalist and author in the United States and abroad.

One could only honestly judge from the tactics, pranks, falsehood, and deceits employed by Trump as to whether such an individual like him is mentally stable and fit to serve as the chief administrator of the country and if he would have the ability to take charge of any challenge facing the security and safety of the United States of America, or whether he should be stopped, ousted, or tried in an impartial Court of Laws.

On September 8, 2020, it was reported that India had more than four million cases of people suffering from the virus, while the number of fatalities were not given. Judging from the fact that rarely in India an autopsy is performed on non-violent deaths, it is a challenge to confirm any proper figure of those deceased due to the virus.

On the same day, news from Mexico said that serious concerns arose about the number of existing, new cases and those of the deceased. Official statistics were not released by the Mexican government.

The Institute for Health, Metrics and Evaluation affiliated to University of Washington School of Medicine, Seattle, Washington predicted three hundred thousand deaths by December 1, 2020. The US hit that ominous number on December 17th.

Modeling a virus and predicting their death and destruction is a challenge to Scientific Institutes. Dr. Alex McLain said modeling a virus' spread is like tracking a hurricane. But the COVID–19 predictions were so off; he said, "it's like forecasters thought a storm would hit North Carolina but hit Maine instead." Dr. McLain's statements carry scientific reason. Any predictions and forecast as to the number of cases and fatalities by COVID-19 could only be a guesswork.

Judging from the absurdity of Trump's incomplete, self-satisfying, and deceitful statements, while knowing the very rapid spread and extremely dangerous results of the Coronavirus not only throughout the United States of America but globally, an ominous event awaits mankind that could probably spell Armageddon for the planet and wipe out at least a fifth of the world's population.

This global challenge could also spell widespread hunger of unimaginable proportions throughout the world. This would create an absence of minimum nutritional requirement for the majority in overpopulated countries; some being Bangladesh, India, Pakistan, China, Brazil, and several African countries, including the sub-Sahara regions. The United States of America, a major importer of food from abroad, notably from many South American, Far-East Asian, and even Central Asian countries, could possibly face a challenge. This pandemic will trigger a massive migration from countries lacking proper medical facilities and the means to treat the ever-growing numbers of those affected to other countries having better facilities.

As a result of havoc created by unemployment, poverty and social unrests created by this pandemic, tens of millions of citizens of Spanish America from Mexico further south till Argentina including Portuguese speaking Brazil and those from the several dozens of Islands in the Caribbean will make their way to the United States of America seeking means of treatment and survival. Territorial boundaries will be meaningless for these desperate people who will enter the United States of America unceasingly and in waves after waves, overwhelming security and border forces of the United States.

Simultaneous to the above factors that could plague humankind, a partial or a total economic collapse for many countries already on the brink of financial disaster could help create large scale chaos, crime and uncontrolled migration causing demographic and social hardships for the regional nations from migrants fleeing, some by force, their own country regardless of dangerous border crossings. In this process of panic, millions of people facing unbearable poverty while leaving their homeland to seek a place just to survive will lose their precious lives; either on their way to another country or while crossing several other countries to reach their desired destination.

The United States of America, Brazil, China, India, Iran, France, Italy, Pakistan, Bangladesh, and most African countries including several countries in "Spanish America" have an exceptionally significant percentage of their population already affected by the virus, with many already deceased and many in critical condition. No form of prediction, even the most approximate, could ever be made about the final toll this virus could take on the global population and if at all the much-discussed vaccines created by the USA, Israel, England, India, Russia and elsewhere would be a hundred percent successful on a global level.

Only time will tell if the Malthusian (Thomas Robert Malthus, February 14, 1766 – December 23, 1834) theory of the Control of Population, referred to the Malthusian catastrophe, will finally prove to be of any academic reality.

About Trump

Unless and until the US nation makes a determined decision to elect a responsible, stable minded, devoid of any fraudulent past and present individual to lead the US Administration, the situation could go from bad to worse with no hope in the least for the future. That person is only and only Joseph Biden! On April 3, 2020, in an article in the Huffington Post, titled "The Worst type of Leader to Have in A Crisis" by Christopher Mathias, world famed Historian Ruth Ben-Ghiat at New York University and an expert on Fascism and Propaganda, had an urgent message during the Coronavirus crisis: "Authoritarians like Trump don't care about human life. They care about power."

Ben-Ghiat warned about the grave dangers of having an authoritarian leader like Trump in charge of America's effort to beat back the pandemic and expanded on the shortcomings of the former television reality show actor and realtor turned leader of the country, to properly lead the nation in stopping the pandemic and the imminent danger it poses for the public. She argued that Trump would seek to exploit the crisis to gain more power, to downplay the severity of the virus, and to obscure all the ways his administration fumbled the federal government's response.

Adding to her statements, she said: "For the general public, it can be hard to accept that we have a very different kind of leader. We have a leader who has an authoritarian mentality, and that kind of leader, they're often narcissistic, they are amoral, totally immoral, only power and profit matters. It's very much the end justifies the means. So, this is the worst type of leader to have in a crisis because they're incapable of acting for the public good."

The Professor described Trump as: "A foe of expertise and science of any kind of facts that gets in the way he wants reality to be, and we've seen this with abundance in the way he handled the growing crisis of Coronavirus, so he would rather send misinformation to the public – which he did recently recommending drugs that I understand put some people in the hospital – than tell the truth. And so, the broader thing is that authoritarians, they fear transparency and they fear accountability, and this is another reason they are terrible leaders to have in crises."

When confronted by PBS Newshour correspondent, Yamiche Alcindor, on March 20, 2020, that he had much earlier dismissed the virus as insignificant, Trump angrily threatened and berated the reporter and as usual lied that he had not said so.

In mass media in Europe, Canada and within the United States of America, Trump was singled out as the chief culprit for this tragedy by ignoring and even cutting off funds for research of viruses and infectious diseases. By the end of March 2020, within a short span of three months, the virus had spread throughout the world and claimed more than a hundred thousand lives and infected more than a million. How many millions will contract this virus and how many millions will finally succumb to this dreaded virus is unknown. Angela Merkel, an academic with a degree in Quantum Physics, Chancellor of Germany, and leader of the Free World, on March 11, 2020 stated that sixty to seventy percent of the population of Germany (Approximately 84 million by the end of 2019) could contract the coronavirus.

Trump's continued inconsistencies further added truth to the general feeling of the population that:

Billboards posted in various parts of the country said: "This person (Trump) didn't create this virus, but he ignored it, denied it, minimized it, joked about it, weaponized it. He is culpable for the chaos and the unnecessary illness, and yes, the preventable deaths because of it – and his supporters, too. This is the human cost of the 'make America great again' cult delusion, and we're all paying for it equally."

Speaking of mutations, scientists, bacteriologist, and virologists throughout the world continue to feverishly work towards a cure and a vaccine for the more dangerous form of the virus. The history of coronavirus is not fully examined, although virologists and bacteriologists worldwide have researched and submitted many papers. Mutated varieties continue to be counted in most countries of the world.

Abstract on Coronavirus. Progress on Research

"Human coronaviruses, first characterized in the 1960's, are responsible for a substantial proportion of upper respiratory tract infections in children. Since 2003, at least five new human coronaviruses have been identified, including the severe respiratory syndrome coronavirus, which caused significant morbidity and mortality. NL63, representing a group of newly identified group I coronaviruses that includes NL and the New Haven coronavirus, has been identified worldwide. These viruses are associated with both upper and lower respiratory tract diseases and are likely common human pathogens. The global distribution of a newly identified group II coronavirus, HKU1, has not yet been established. Coronavirology has advanced significantly in the past few years. The SARS epidemic put the animal coronaviruses in the spotlight." Source: The Pediatric Infectious Disease Journal.

Some of the most outstanding among the countries and laboratories and research institutes in Europe, Asia (especially in Turkey and Israel) and elsewhere, is the Doherty Institute in Melbourne, Australia under the lead researcher Professor Katherine Kedzierska who said that the antibodies released by the human immune system to overcome coronavirus are remarkably similar to those it uses to combat influenza – despite it never being exposed to the disease. "It suggests to us that we can fight the virus and we can drive recovery from COVID -19," Professor Kedzierska said.

Israeli scientists have in the meanwhile feverishly set upon the task to find a cure and a vaccine to deal with this mortal virus and its uncontrollable spread.

Dr. Manfred Green, a globally acclaimed epidemiologist and Director of the University of Haifa's International master's course in public health, on March 17, 2020 said developing a vaccine to prevent the virus could take up to eighteen months to reach the public.

"It takes years, not days or months," said Green, the founding director of the Israeli Center for Disease Control of the process to develop the vaccine. "There are new technologies now that we hope will speed up the process. If it's a new technology, not just a new vaccine, we don't know much about it and we need to learn about it. That would require more extensive testing. If a vaccine is developed in the next few months, you can imagine if there were a one in 1000 or one in 10,000 adverse reaction. That could be very problematic if you are giving it to millions of people." Dr. Green dismissed reports that Israeli scientists were on the verge of a breakthrough and added that: "Israel needs to be modest, make sure that we are involved… the United States, China and Europe have advanced infrastructure and talented scientists working at this."

On April 12, 2020, the "Jerusalem Post" reported that preliminary data for patients treated for COVID-19 shows a hundred percent survival rate. Pluristem Therapeutics is an Israeli company based in Haifa, Israel, and is engaged in the development of human placental adherent stromal cells for commercial use in disease treatment. According to the company's website, it extracts adult stem cells exclusively from postnatal placentas. Excerpts are:

"We are pleased with this initial outcome of the compassionate use program and committed to harnessing PLX cells for the benefit of patients and healthcare systems," said Pluristem CEO and president Yaky Yanay. "Pluristem is dedicated to using its competitive advantages in large scale manufacturing to potentially deliver PLX cells to a large number of patients in significant need."

Pluristem's PLX cells are "allogenic mesenchymal-like cells that have immunomodulatory properties," meaning they induce the immune system's natural regulatory T cells and M2 macrophages, the company explained in a previous release. The result could be a reversal of dangerous overactivation of the immune system. This would reduce the fatal symptoms of pneumonia and pneumonitis (general inflammation of the lung tissue). Previous preclinical findings regarding PLX cells revealed significant therapeutic effects in animal studies of pulmonary hypertension, lung fibrosis, acute kidney injury and gastrointestinal injury.

The United States of America, always aspiring to deliver beneficial remedies for ailments challenging humankind, has announced "good news" for the world: First COVID -19 vaccine tested in the country is poised for final testing.

The Associated Press on Tuesday July 14, 2020 stated that:

The first COVID -19 vaccine tested in the U.S. revved up people's immune systems just the way scientists had hoped, researchers reported Tuesday – as the shots are poised to begin key final testing.

"No matter how you slice this, this is good news," Dr. Anthony Fauci, the U.S. government's top infectious disease expert, told The Associated Press.

The experimental vaccine, developed by Fauci's colleagues at the National Institutes of Health and Moderna Inc., will start its most crucial step around July 27, 2020; a 30,000-person study to prove if the shots really are strong enough to protect against the coronavirus.

Tuesday, July 14th, researchers reported anxiously awaited findings from the first forty-five volunteers who rolled up their sleeves back in March. Sure enough, the vaccine provided a hoped-for immune boost. Those early volunteers developed what are called neutralizing antibodies in their bloodstream – molecules key to blocking infection – at levels comparable to those found in people who survived COVID -19, the research team reported in the New England Journal of Medicine.

"This is an essential building block that is needed to move forward with the trials that could actually determine whether the vaccine does protect against infection," said Dr. Lisa Jackson of the Kaiser Permanente Washington Research Institute in Seattle, who led the study. "There's no guarantee but the government hopes to have results around the end of the year – record-setting speed for developing a vaccine."

The vaccine requires two doses, a month apart.

There were no serious side effects. But more than half the study participants reported flu-like reactions to the shots that are not uncommon with other vaccines – fatigue, headache, chills, fever, and pain at the injection site. For three participants given the highest dose, those reactions were more severe; that dose is not being pursued.

Some of those reactions are similar to coronavirus symptoms but they are temporary, lasting about a day and occur right after vaccination, researchers noted.

"Small price to pay for protection against COVID," said Dr. William Schaffner of Vanderbilt University Medical Center, a vaccine expert who was not involved with the study. He called the early results "a good first step," and is optimistic that final testing could deliver answers about whether it is safe and effective by the beginning of next year.

"It would be wonderful. But that assumes everything's working right on schedule," Schaffner cautioned.

Moderna's share price jumped 15 percent in trading after U.S. markets closed on July 14, 2020. Shares of the company, based in Cambridge, Massachusetts, nearly quadrupled in that year.

July 14th's results only included younger adults, passing the first step. Testing later expanded to include dozens of older adults, the age group most at risk from COVID-19. Fauci said final testing included older adults, as well as people with chronic health conditions that make them more vulnerable to the virus — and Black and Latino populations likewise affected.

Two dozen possible COVID-19 vaccines continue in various stages of testing around the world. Candidates from China and Britain's Oxford University also are entering final testing stages.

The 30,000-person study will mark the world's largest study of a potential COVID-19 vaccine so far. And the NIH-developed shot is not the only one set for such massive U.S. testing, crucial to spot rare side effects. The government plans similar large studies of the Oxford candidate and another by Johnson & Johnson; separately, Pfizer Inc. is planning its own huge study. Already, people can start signing up to volunteer for the different studies.

People think "this is a race for one winner. Me, I'm cheering every one of them on," said Fauci, who directs NIH's National Institute of Allergy and Infectious Diseases. "We need multiple vaccines. We need vaccines for the world, not only for our own country."

Around the world, governments are investing in stockpiles of hundreds of millions of doses of the different candidates, in hopes of speedily starting inoculations if any are proven to work.

All said, while the world awaits the vaccine, it is a real challenge facing humanity in general as to when the vaccine will be introduced on a mass scale. Virologists have pointed to several dates. In the first week of April 2020, reports claimed that the vaccine will not be ready to be administered to the tens or even hundreds of millions awaiting it before the end of 2022. That special vaccine which could be the response to several forms of the mutated virus.

Some virologists have reservations about the efficacy of the vaccine when it is finally introduced to the public, albeit the fact that all the Coronavirus family are known to constantly mutate.

On July 28, 2020, it was reported that a new study of COVID -19, based on data from a symptom tracker application, determined that there are six distinct types of the disease involving different clusters of symptoms. It was claimed that the discovery could potentially open new possibilities for how doctors can better treat individual patients and predict what level of hospital care they would need.

On Wednesday, July 29, 2020, Mathew Chance of CNN reported that "Russia claims it's on track to approve COVID -19 vaccine by mid-August 2020. But speed of process raises questions."

Russian officials claimed that their country intends to be the first in the world to approve a coronavirus vaccine within two weeks, by August 10 or even earlier. The Moscow-based Gamaleya Institute has been feverishly working to create a vaccine. Russia has more than a million confirmed cases of people affected by the virus, but they give no clear figures of fatalities.

On Tuesday October 13, 2020, the prominent American Drugmaker Johnson & Johnson said that on Monday it had paused the advanced clinical trial of its experimental coronavirus vaccine because of an unexplained illness in one of the volunteers.

On October 16, 2020, reports circulated that Pfizer COVID -19 Vaccine rolls off production line amid hopes for emergency approval. Pfizer, one of the front-runners in developing a COVID-19 vaccine for the United States, says its result will not be ready by mid-November at the earliest.

Pfizer Chairman and Chief Executive Officer Alberta Bourla said in a public statement that it is indeed possible the company could have enough data to know this month whether the vaccine it is developing protects people from COVID -19. But the company will not have data showing the vaccine is safe before the third week of November 2020, at the earliest.

"We estimate that we will reach this milestone in the third week of November," Bourla wrote.

The company has been waiting for a certain number of people in its study to come down with COVID -19. When that threshold has been reached, scientists can analyze the data and see whether those who got sick were in the group that got vaccinated or in the comparison group, which received a placebo shot. The vaccine must reduce the risk of infection by at least fifty percent to be considered for the Federal Drug Administration emergency authorization.

A survey has shown that many Americans are hesitant about taking a coronavirus vaccine and concerned that politics could drive the approval process. But vaccine companies have said they will not let that happen, and Pfizer said its announcement underscores its commitment to safety. (Statements included from National Public Radio science correspondent Richard Harris)

As of late October 2020, nine million cases of those suffering from the virus have been identified in the United States and since early 2020, more attention has been paid towards the creation of a vaccine to stop this calamity threatening humanity in the United States of America and globally. Several countries have come up with hopes of a vaccine, but few have discussed the treatment of the existing cases of the virus, which is nearing fifty million, although all cases have not been fully identified. On October 22, 2020, the drug maker "Gilead Sciences" said that the US Food and Drug Administration has approved "Remdesivir" for the treatment of COVBID -19. The drug sold under the brand name "Veklury," has been used under emergency use authorization since May 2020.

Earlier on October 16, 2020, the World Health Organization said the anti-viral drug Remdesivir has "little or no effect on mortality" for patients hospitalized with coronavirus and it does not seem to help patients recover any faster, either.

On October 29, 2020, Moderna Therapeutics claimed it is prepping for the global launch of its potential coronavirus vaccine, already taking in 1.1 billion dollars in deposits from governments, throughout the world. The Cambridge, Massachusetts-based company said it was in ongoing talks with the World Health Organization-backed COVAX initiative on a tiered pricing proposal for its potential vaccine tentatively calling it mRNA-1273. It claimed it already has supply agreements in North America, the Middle East and in other regions of the world. This was a promising and a welcome news throughout the world.

Latest research identifies COVID-19 as a vascular disease.

Salk researchers and collaborators show how the protein damages cells, confirming COVID-19 as a primarily vascular disease.

May 2, 2021 *SciTech Daily*

Scientists have known for a while that SARS-CoV-2's distinctive "spike" proteins help the virus infect its host by latching on to healthy cells. Now, a major new study shows that they also play a key role in the disease itself.

The paper, published on April 30, 2021, in *Circulation Research*, also shows conclusively that COVID-19 is a vascular disease, demonstrating exactly how the SARS-CoV-2 virus damages and attacks the vascular system on a cellular level. The findings help explain COVID-19's wide variety of seemingly unconnected complications, and could open the door for new research into more effective therapies.

"A lot of people think of it as a respiratory disease, but it's really a vascular disease," says Assistant Research Professor Uri Manor, who is co-senior author of the study. "That could explain why some people have strokes, and why some people have issues in other parts of the body. The commonality between them is that they all have vascular underpinnings."

Salk researchers collaborated with scientists at the University of California San Diego on the paper, including co-first author Jiao Zhang and co-senior author John Shyy, among others.

While the findings themselves aren't entirely a surprise, the paper provides clear confirmation and a detailed explanation of the mechanism through which the protein damages vascular cells for the first time. There's been a growing consensus that SARS-CoV-2 affects the vascular system, but exactly how it did so was not understood. Similarly, scientists studying other coronaviruses have long suspected that the spike protein contributed to damaging vascular endothelial cells, but this is the first time the process has been documented.

In the new study, the researchers created a "pseudovirus" that was surrounded by SARS-CoV-2 classic crown of spike proteins, but did not contain any actual virus. Exposure to this pseudovirus resulted in damage to the lungs and arteries of an animal model—proving that the spike protein alone was enough to cause disease. Tissue samples showed inflammation in endothelial cells lining the pulmonary artery walls.

The team then replicated this process in the lab, exposing healthy endothelial cells (which line arteries) to the spike protein. They showed that the spike protein damaged the cells by binding ACE2. This binding disrupted ACE2's molecular signaling to mitochondria (organelles that generate energy for cells), causing the mitochondria to become damaged and fragmented.

Previous studies have shown a similar effect when cells were exposed to the SARS-CoV-2 virus, but this is the first study to show that the damage occurs when cells are exposed to the spike protein on its own.

"If you remove the replicating capabilities of the virus, it still has a major damaging effect on the vascular cells, simply by virtue of its ability to bind to this ACE2 receptor, the S protein receptor, now famous thanks to COVID," Manor explains. "Further studies with mutant spike proteins will also provide new insight towards the infectivity and severity of mutant SARS CoV-2 viruses."

The researchers next hope to take a closer look at the mechanism by which the disrupted ACE2 protein damages mitochondria and causes them to change shape.

Trump had on several occasions claimed to know more than a doctor, and more than an epidemiologist, then denied it just a few hours later. He had added that statement to his chains of follies on Thursday, April 23, 2020, the day fifty thousand US citizens had died of Coronavirus infection.

Trump is that individual who once stared directly into the solar eclipse albeit the admonishments of those around him, and who had confidently offered researchers and scientists his personal ideas about an effective method to treat Coronavirus. Present in his press conference were reporters and a host of public health experts including Dr. Deborah Birx, Coronavirus Task Force Coordinator. Addressing a surprised and uneasy appearing Dr. Birx in the most serious manner and to the bewilderment of the all those present, Trump said: "So supposing we hit the body with a tremendous, whether it's ultraviolet or just very powerful light – and I don't think you said that hasn't been checked but you're going to test it – and then I said suppose you brought the light inside the body, which you can do either through the skin or in some other way. And I think you said you're going to test that too. Sounds interesting. Then I see the disinfectant where it knocks it out in a minute, one minute. Is there a way we can do something like that by injection inside? Or almost a cleaning, because you see it gets into the lungs and it does a tremendous number on the lungs. So, it'd be interesting to check that. So, you are going to have to use medical doctors, but it sounds interesting to me, so we'll see but the whole concept of the light. The way it kills it in one minute, that's pretty powerful."

On the same day (April 23, 2020), Washington Post reporter Philip Rucker pointed to the misinformation of Trump. He told Trump: "People tuning into these briefings, they want to get information and guidance and want to know what to do. They are not looking for rumors." An angry Trump replied, "I am the president and you're fake news," adding that his recommendations "are just suggestions." After being condemned and mocked by the news media and the general public, Trump on the next day claimed that his remarks were made sarcastically.

Trump's former Food and Drug Commissioner Scott Gottlieb addressed Trump's unorthodox suggestion, telling CNBC television channel on

Friday, April 24, 2020 that, "under no circumstance you should take a disinfectant or inject a disinfectant for the treatment of anything." Dr. Deborah Brix also cautiously let Trump know that, this is not a promising treatment option.

The United States of America, under Trump refused to take part in a joint global effort to find a vaccine and a cure for this pandemic, was effectively cutting itself off from the more than 170 countries in discussion to join the COVID-19 Vaccine Global Access Facility, or COVAX. The initiative is "aimed at working with vaccine manufacturers to provide countries worldwide equitable access to safe and effective vaccines" and is co-led by the WHO, the Coalition for Epidemic Preparedness Innovations, and the vaccine alliance and GAVI, The GAVI COVAX AMC is the innovative financing instrument that will support the participation of 92 low-and middle-income economies in the COVAX facility – enabling access to donor-funded doses of safe and effective COVD -19 Vaccines.(Excerpts from NPR)

It is worthy to note that billionaire philanthropist Bill Gates had warned the world as early as 2015, that the coronavirus (SARS and its variations) could invade the world and suggested a global preparedness to combat this deadly virus.

The World Health Organization (WHO) Secretary General Tedros Adhanom Ghebreyesus warned against a "vaccine nationalism" in light of the fact that the Trump administration repeated in a statement in the first week of September 2020, that the United States of America would not participate in a global push to develop a COVID-19 vaccine, in part because the effort was led by the World Health Organization, which the White House described as "corrupt" and had accused of initially aiding China in covering up the scope of the pandemic.

The topic dealing with the coronavirus does not relate much to the real subject matter of the book but is nevertheless presented to prove the mental instability of the person planted into the White House in dealing with a national crisis and emergency, let alone a global crisis that may either arise from China or Russia or from both. Bemusedly, he fiddled away as the nation under his administration suffered from his inefficiency and inability to allocate his much-needed attention to combat this terrible virus through proper channels.

It is claimed that the USA is armed to the teeth with the most advanced systems to confront an enemy; nuclear as well as conventional, while claiming all possibilities for manufacturing, replenishment and restocking of weapon systems within a short notice. At the same time, it was alarming and incredible as to how the USA was crippled when it came to its preparedness to deal with a national health crisis, by not having enough hospital beds, respirators and the required medical facilities meant to combat this deadly virus.

Donald J. Trump is a prolific liar and a harbinger of false hopes, statistics and promises. At regular intervals, he insulted and demeaned the nation whom he was obliged to protect and assist according to the US Constitution. Trump is that rumbustious master of deceit and falsity who had time and often claimed superhuman achievements but could not describe or give a simple example. When confronted to elaborate on his claims of "achievements" he either ignored the journalists, outrightly insulted them and flew into a rage for their questions, or simply chose to walk away from the interview.

"I have done more than any other person or President," but for whom and what? He never clarified what he had done or achieved or, he was doing. He never elaborated on what he claimed. The facts are simple. He did not do anything constructive or helpful for the nation. He had undone an overwhelming number of rules and regulations beneficial to the public in terms of health, living standards, natural environment, waterways, lakes, rivers, wildlife, education, and a host of other laws meant to ameliorate life in the country.

Trump, when asked about the timeframe of the COVID-19 vaccine, said: "We are working on treatments for this, you know it is bad, this virus, terrible, but the team is amazing, fantastic and the Vice President, and it is bad, but we will make it through this war, it is a war, terrible we are testing, tests, and I have ordered the FDA to remove blocks, there are blocks, lots of blocks for medicine, treatments, yes treatments soon, very soon."

"What do you think they [protesters] want?" Harris Faulkner of Fox News asked the president. "What do you think they need, right now from you?" ... As to what Trump thought protesters are demonstrating against following the Memorial Day death of George Floyd (died, May 25, 2020) while in police custody in Minneapolis, Minnesota.

Trump's answer, verbatim: "Protesters for different reasons. You're protesting also because, you know, they just didn't know. I've watch – I watched very closely. Why are you here? They really weren't able to say, but they were there for a reason, perhaps."

In an angry tone, Trump appeared displeased with the question. "But a lot of them really were there because they're following the crowd. A lot of them were there because we witnessed was a terrible thing. What we saw was a terrible thing. And we've seen it over the years. We haven't you know, this was one horrible example, but you've seen other terrible examples. You know that better than anybody who would know it, And I know it. I've seen it, too. I've seen it before I was president. I've seen it. I Think it's a shame. I think it's a disgrace. And it's got to stop."

Since early 2019, Trump regularly stated, "I have done so much for this country that no president in the history of this country has ever done. So many good things, many good things." after he became aware that the general public in the country had condemned him as a mentally challenged person. The facts resulting from his misrule and misuse of presidential powers were officially made public.

On July 14, 2020 sensing his chances of being re-elected for a second term had dwindled by leaps and bounds he said:

"I think by election day (November 3, 2020), you're going to see incredible numbers." Donald Trump, White House Press Conference.

The facts:

Unemployment rate under Trump: 11.1% (up by 6.5 points)

Budget deficit under Trump: Three Trillion Dollars. (up by 400%)

National debt under Trump: Twenty-six trillion and five hundred billion dollars. (up 33%)

Misery index" under Trump: 11.7% (up 5.5 points)

Satisfied Americans under Trump: 20% (down 16 points)

Competitive economy rank under Trump: 10 (down 9)

Recent health coverage loss under Trump: (5.4 million)

Recent food stamp use increase under Trump: 15%

Number of lies told publicly by Trump: 20,055 (from a year before the presidential elections of 2016 till July 15, 2020)

Coronavirus statistics: By February 15, 2021 Global cases were a shocking 108, 994,619, while global fatalities recorded 2,403,462. US cases reached 27,683,116 while US fatalities reached nearly 488,000.

On Monday, February 22, 2021, it was announced that the grim figure of fatalities in the USA exceeded half a million. How many more will ultimately succumb to this virus is unknown and could never be accurately predicted.

A reminder that Donald J. Trump on January 22, 2020 had addressed the nation that there should be no fear at all since; "We have it (Coronavirus). It is totally under control. It's one person from China."

More than a month later, on February 27, 2020, Trump confidently announced that; "One day it's like a miracle, it will disappear."

Psychiatrists and virologists (especially with regards to his statements on his achievements, personal embellishments, the Coronavirus) have made it clear that the above sentences spoken by Trump are absurd, ridiculous, and meaningless and such words only flow from a mentally disturbed mind!

The infamous blusterer had regularly contradicted himself and had at times brazenly distanced himself from his own past statements and aggressively passed scatological remarks at journalists who questioned his reasons of misleading the public and lying. After finding the questions "unpalatable," Trump habitually loosened a barrage of insults at the journalist and ordered his security personnel to remove his antagonists from the group of journalists.

No definition and description befit the tricks played by the actor who was termed as a tyrant and a dictator better than what was portrayed by the popular scholar and academic, Prof. Robert Bernard Reich. Excerpts from his statements on January 27, 2020

> "Throughout history, tyrants and dictators have constructed cults of personality in order to consolidate their own power. They project their own invincibility and superiority forging a loyal group identity out of heightened chaos and division. Donald Trump and his enablers are now employing many of the same tactics to keep his political base together and silence critics. At the heart of Trump's cult of personality is the idea that he can do no wrong, even when he brazenly breaks the law."

Michael Cohen

Michael Cohen was Donald Trump's "fixer" and personal lawyer. Cohen was sentenced to three years imprisonment for wrongdoings and felonies. One of the accusations was transferring one hundred thirty thousand dollars to a porn star with whom Trump had sexual encounters in the past and Trump wanted to present a normal image of himself to the public. Trump denied it, but there was enough evidence that the payment was done at his behest for the sole purpose to cover Trump's past. Cohen pleaded guilty.

The main charges against Cohen which sentenced him to prison were pleading guilty to lying to Congress in November 2018 about negotiations concerning a proposed Trump Tower in Moscow, a project that never materialized. Cohen emphasized that Trump implicitly directed him to lie about this project. Trump denied all allegations. Cohen made a brief confession on several topics:

"For more than a decade, I was Trump's right-hand man, fixer, and confidant. I was complicit in helping conceal the real Donald Trump. I was part of the illusion."

"I'm here to tell you he can't be trusted – and you shouldn't believe a word he utters." Cohen cautions the American nation that Trump will "blatantly lie."

Cohen indicated that he, of all people, should know this, and said Trump thinks the American people are a "bunch of fools."

"I was a part of it, and I fell for it," he said. "If you think he cares about working class Americans, you're dead wrong."

John Bolton

Being frustrated and enraged by the truth and facts the news media suggested about him, Trump demanded a special television station be created solely to present him and admire his achievements for the US nation, insisting that he was the best, most educated, and most handsome. He deserved laurels, not only from the nation, but also from the world in general.

John Bolton, the former National Security Advisor of the United States (April 9, 2018 – September 10, 2019) in his memoir, "The Room Where It Happened: A White House Memoir." Claims that: "Trump does not do any official work until his hair and makeup are finished, and his hair takes another hour and half to sculpt into a mop that obscures the reality that Trump is almost entirely bald." This reflected Trump's irrelevance towards priorities and exigencies related to matters of State.

Bolton went far bolder in his book, beyond expectations which made him one of the most hated individuals by Trump and Trump's paid lackeys. He threw several of Trump's skeletons out of the closet. Trump was exposed for the fraudulent and deceitful individual that he was. Short of using expletive adjectives in his book against Trump, Bolton spared no effort to tell the public what he believed and insisted to be the truth.

CNN news, one of the most dependable news media around the world presented some of the highlights of Bolton's writings.

- Trump virtually pleaded with President Xi Jinping for help in getting reelected.

In his book, Bolton detailed a conversation between the two leaders at the June 2019 G-20 meeting in Osaka, Japan where Trump told Xi that Midwestern farmers were key to his reelection in November 2020. Trump urged Xi to buoy his political fortunes by buying American agricultural products, linking a promise to waive some tariffs on China in exchange. Trump "stressed the importance of farmer and increased Chinese purchases of soybeans and wheat in the electoral outcome."

- Trump had no problem with China's concentration camps.

Bolton described several instances where Trump waffles on China-related issues with Xi, regarding the concentration camps created by China for a million Uyghur Muslims. Trump most shamefully nodded in consent and said that that it was the right thing to do.

- Pompeo, supposedly loyal to Trump, trash talked him.

In his book, Bolton described a meeting between Trump and Kim Jong Un, in which the North Korean tyrant blamed relations between his country and the United States on the actions of prior administrations. Kim informed Trump that they could dispel mistrust and work quickly toward agreement. After Trump told Kim that he would seek Senate ratification of any agreement with North Korea, Bolton stated that Secretary of State Mike Pompeo passed him a notepad. On it was scribbled the message, he (Trump) is "so full of shit."

"I agreed" Bolton wrote, going on to note that Kim promised no further nuclear tests.

- Trump offered to help Turkey's leader avoid a Justice Department probe.

Bolton wrote that in December 2018, Trump offered to help Turkish President Recep Tayyip Erdogan with a Justice Department investigation into a Turkish Bank with ties to Erdogan that was suspected of violating US Iran sanctions. When the Turkish leader presented Trump with a memo from the law firm representing Halkbank of violating US Sanctions related to Iran., Trump flipped through it and then declared he believed the bank was totally innocent. Trump told Erdogan he would take "care of things," and explained that the southern District prosecutors "were not his people but were Obama people" and the problem would be fixed when they would be replaced by his people. Bolton wrote that "this was all nonsense" because the Justice Department prosecutors were career employees who would have taken the same path with the Halkbank probe regardless of who was the president.

- Trump's ignorance magnified.

Before the summit with Putin in Helsinki, Trump asked his advisers if Finland was a part of Russia or whether it was a "kind of satellite of Russia."

On his way to Helsinki meeting, Trump stopped to see then-British Prime Minister Theresa May in the UK. During that meeting, May's national security adviser, speaking about the Skripal poisoning, referred to the attack as one on a nuclear power. "Trump asked, 'Oh, are you a nuclear power?' which I knew was not intended as a joke," Bolton wrote.

And on multiple occasions, Bolton said Trump repeatedly confused Afghan President Ashraf Ghani with former President Hamid Karzai.

- Trump told people that Venezuela is "really part of the US" and wanted to invade.

Bolton wrote that in discussions about toppling the regime of Nicolas Maduro, Trump "insisted on military options for Venezuela," telling advisors that the country "is really part of the United States." During a March 2020 meeting at the Pentagon, Trump grilled military leaders about why the US was in Afghanistan and Iraq, but not in Venezuela.

Trump's repeated insistence that military options be considered to oust Maduro often shocked aides, lawmakers and advisors, Bolton wrote. In a meeting with Florida Republicans, "Trump still wanted a military option," leaving Senator Rick Scott and Governor Ron Desantis "plainly stunned," while Senator Marco Rubio, who had heard Trump on the subject before "knew how to deflect it politely."

- Trump wanted Attorney General Bill Barr to make CNN reporters "serve time in jail."

When news leaked about a hush-hush meeting on Afghanistan at Trump's Bedminster resort, Trump complained that CNN had reported the summit was taking place, Bolton wrote. Trump told the White House Counsel Pat Cipollone to call Attorney General Bill Barr about his desire to "arrest the reporters, force them to serve time in jail, and then demand they disclose their sources."

Author's note. I would always honor and hold in high esteem the entire gallant staff of CNN in their bravery of communicating factual news to the entire world.

Why now in his book and not at the time of Trump's continued assault on the Institute of American Presidency? Bolton could have earlier while holding office, briefed the press and the mass media about the chaotic behavior, corruption and illegal means and methods applied by Trump and his enablers to destroy the very foundations of democracy, transparency, and honor of the Office of the President of the United States of America?

Was Bolton one of the past enablers of Trump fallen out of favor or did he finally see the light that Trump was not only a danger to the integrity of the United States of America but also posed a grave danger to global peace? Or did Bolton finally discover that Trump was a puppet of foreign powers identified as arch enemies of the United States of America and that they were manipulating him when needed, and that he was their willing tool to serve them as long as he was embedded safely in Office of the President of the United States of America? Only Bolton could answer this.

All said, Bolton should not be coronated as a friend of either the US nation, the truth, or of the free world or a person with the slightest degree of any form of convictions. He is in the least a warmonger and had time and again asked Trump to commence a war with Iran, with him (Bolton) creating the groundworks of a false flag as an excuse to launch an attack with the backing of the equally war-mongering Binyamin Netanyahu, the crisis beleaguered Prime Minister of Israel. Netanyahu has been accused of fraud and corruption.

Bolton was oblivious to any form of consequences of his actions. He did not pay the least importance to the loss of hundreds of thousands, perhaps millions of fatalities should the USA enter a war with Iran.

He was impervious to the fact that in case there would be a land invasion on Iranian territory by US Forces, it would not be an easy victory. Moreover, if the US Forces would trade infantry for infantry or armor for armor, it would be exceedingly difficult to predict the winner, but what could be predicted would be the massive number of casualties on both sides. The Iranians, historically known for their chauvinism, may openly challenge the clergy dominated regime set up in 1979, but would never welcome the US Armed Forces. They would confront the invaders.

Bolton was a "bribe-accepting" individual just like most other US politicians seeking a few worthless US dollars. He accepted tens of thousands of dollars from the Mujaheddin Khalq Organization (MEK) also called "People's Mujaheddin," for a speech favoring them to succeed the Theocratic Regime in Tehran. Bolton, on several occasions, praised the "People's Mujaheddin," (MEK) a corrupt Marxist-Islamic group of terrorists and murderers as the future of Iran, to replace the unpopular clergy dominated regime. The Mujaheddin are despised by the sane world and are described by the Iranian masses as fanatic clerics in a three-piece suit. Both Bolton and Rudy Giuliani, the former Mayor of New York and Attorney for Trump, had received large sums of money whenever they participated in speeches favoring the "MEK", who had in fact murdered several US Citizens in Iran, before the creation of the Islamic Republic. To repeat it was the Carter administration hiding under the garb of a sacerdotal administration of his own, obeyed his masters, (perhaps the Henry Kissinger-Bernard Lewis doctrine of vivisecting large West Asian countries, especially throwing Iran and the entire region in perpetual turmoil, by overthrowing Monarchy in Iran) behind the curtains who had planned and executed a bloody revolution in Iran by creating the most unpopular regime on earth in the Annals of Iranian history. The self-styled, peace-loving Carter had answered the call of those who had ushered him into the Oval Office!

Impeachment

Trump was impeached on December 18, 2019 on charges of abuse of power and obstruction of Congress. He was then acquitted by the Senate whose thin majority at the time belonged to the Republican Party, through the Senate majority leader, Mitch McConnell, an uncompromising supporter of Trump, dubbed as the "enabler-in-chief" who accepted tens of millions of dollars as "donation" (bribery) for his office. His second wife, Elaine Lan Chao of Chinese origin, born in Taipei, Taiwan, was employed by Trump as Secretary of Transportation, the rest being self-explanatory.

McConnell's unwavering support to Trump and his policies, however unpopular, appeared to be a response to Trump's favor to his wife.

The House of Representatives voted 232-197 on January 13, 2021 to impeach Trump for an unprecedented second time for his role in the January 6, 2021` riot and breach of the Capitol, which occurred as a joint session of Congress was ratifying the election of President Biden. Impeachment proceedings against Trump were commenced in the Senate on February 9, 2021 and he was again acquitted.

By the second week of February 2021, the cordial relations between Trump and Mitch McConnell diminished and even turned into animosity. Trump accused McConnell of unfaithfulness and lack of support for his demand to overturn the election results in his favor.

However, Trump will always remain as an impeached individual who occupied the White House. To be precise and repeat, Trump was not exonerated, he was acquitted on the first and the second impeachment trial.

Other charges against Trump that were not included were sedition, treachery, and treason by collaborating with Russia for his personal gains, whether financial, business or even political. Russia has been and will always be considered as the arch enemy of the United States of America.

An outstanding charge was for encouraging violence and even bloodshed, by refusing to stop the rioters whom he addressed in an endearing manner. Main characters targeted for assassination were Speaker Nancy Pelosi and Trump's own Vice President Mike Pence. In case the two were assassinated, Trump could use his plenipotentiary powers to declare martial law, suspend the Constitution and declare himself the "martial law administrator" until further notice.

Cases of tax evasion, child rape and molestation (documented), misuse and expropriation of funds (in collaboration with his sons) and of donations meant for children suffering from terminal ailments, exploitation of workers were similarly not included while he was impeached for the first time.

Most outstanding of Trump's illegal wrongdoings is his fraudulent approach in paying his income tax. It has always been a question among the educated strata of the country as to how and through what ploys Trump has evaded his taxes. On September 27, 2020, the widely read New York Times reported that it obtained Donald Trump's tax information (that Trump had been refusing to show the public since the last five years for obvious reasons that he was a defaulter) extending over more than two decades, revealing struggling properties, vast write-offs, an audit battle, and hundreds of millions in debt coming due.

Donald J. Trump paid only seven hundred fifty dollars ($750) in federal income taxes in 2016 and another seven hundred fifty dollars ($750) in 2017, the year he began the presidency. He paid no income taxes at all in ten of the previous fifteen years, largely because he reported losing more money than he made. Trump has a decade long audit battle with the Internal Revenue Service over the legitimacy of a 72.9-million-dollar tax refund that he claimed, and received, after declaring huge losses. An adverse ruling could cost him more than one hundred million dollars.

The tax returns that Mr. Trump had long fought to keep private tell a story fundamentally different from the one he had sold to the American public. His report to the Internal Revenue Service portrayed himself as a businessman who took in hundreds of millions of dollars a year yet racked up chronic losses that he aggressively employed to avoid paying taxes. Excerpts from New York Times, reported by Russ Buettner, Suzanne Craig, and Mike McIntire.

By contrast to tax evasion in the United States of America, Trump, including his companies paid nearly sixteen thousand dollars as taxes in Panama, more than one hundred forty-five thousand dollars in India and nearly one hundred fifty-seven thousand dollars in the Philippines. It is still unclear the tax payments to foreign countries listed related to which year.

On Trump and Others and What was Especially Spoken of Trump

"Trump has brought death, suffering, and economic collapse on truly an epic scale. And let's be clear. This isn't happening in every country around the world. This place. Our place. Our home. Our country. The United States. We are the epicenter. We are the place where you're the most likely to die from this disease. We're the ones with the most shattered economy. And we are because of the fool that sits in the Oval Office behind the Resolute Desk." (Referring to the Coronavirus) Steve Schmidt, longtime Republican strategist, and a founder of the Lincoln Project.

"He (Donald Trump) is essentially a predator" and a successful sociopath. His focus on his personal benefit at any cost is why he's a successful sociopath," Lance M. Dodes, MD, a former assistant clinical professor of psychiatry at Harvard Medical School, is yet another mental health expert to call into question the Trump's state of mind." Professor Dodes in statements made public added; "It's very hard to get this across to the general public, because every time people talk about Trump, they start out with the unspoken unconscious assumption that he's basically like the rest of us. But in order to explain and predict Trump's behavior, you have to begin with awareness that he is essentially a predator. Once you keep in mind that Trump lacks a conscience and lacks empathy, he becomes very easy to follow. Unlike normal people, who are complex, he's basically running on a very simple and very disordered program."

Trump was ousted from his seat of power in the 2020 November elections, while impartially judged by the US nation who did not deserve this form of "comeuppance." Still, Trump has enablers in the Senate and blind followers in the streets (reminiscent in the streets of Germany in mid-1920, who supported Adolf Hitler, resorting to violence, mayhem, and destruction, without even knowing his true character and beliefs). It would have been a global catastrophe, had Trump been re-elected for a second term.

Several predictions were made in late July 2020, whereby Trump would receive a mere thirty five percent of the popularity votes while more than sixty percent of the votes would be awarded to Joseph Robinette Biden (Joe

Biden), the former Vice President to President Obama. From England to France, Germany, Canada and in the United States of America, nearly all "pundits" predicted a landslide victory for Biden.

Any mentally challenged person has no place occupying the Office of the most powerful Presidency on earth. This, according to psychiatrists and psychologists, relates most befittingly to Trump, who could have created a global catastrophe through his mental illness. No other person in the ruling administration of the United States of America merited an ignominious dismissal than Trump! Trump was the paragon of insanity propelled into the Oval Office to serve his foreign masters.

Among several presentations, reports, and books on the mental case of Trump by qualified and reputed Psychologists, Psychiatrists and Physicians in the United States of America, it is deemed exigent of initially informing the reader with the mental case of Trump, by the statements of a prominent Physician and Psychiatrist.

> "Trump has no policy on any issue because his mental impairment means he cannot think strategically or in abstract terms. He cannot weigh options, assess risk, or foresee consequences. Concepts like fairness, justice, honor, and integrity quite literally do not register. You can see this in every interview or press encounter. He never states an abstract thought or idea. Instead, he falls back on simple adjectives: disgraceful, horrible, low-intelligence, perfect, innocent, nasty, stupid, fake, etc. He's driven by negative emotion, often paranoid and often insulting, vulgar vitriolic."

Dr. John Talmadge, M.D. specializing in Psychiatry and Addiction Medicine. Clinical Professor of Psychiatry at University of Texas, Southwestern medical Center.

Carl Bernstein the untiring reporter who exposed the "Watergate scandal" of Richard Nixon and his appointees, in a report on the most popular and dependable CNN news network, painted a particularly damning portrait of Trump and his administration.

"In hundreds of highly classified phone calls with foreign heads of state, President Donald Trump was so consistently unprepared for discussion of serious issues, so often outplayed in his conversations with powerful leaders like Russian President Vladimir Putin and Turkish President Recep Erdogan, and so abusive to leaders of America's principal allies, that the calls helped convince some senior US officials — including his former secretaries of state and defense, two national security advisers and his longest-serving chief of staff — that the President himself posed a danger to the national security of the United States, according to White House and intelligence officials intimately familiar with the contents of the conversations.

The calls caused former top Trump deputies — including national security advisers H.R. McMaster and John Bolton, Defense Secretary James Mattis, Secretary of State Rex Tillerson, and White House chief of staff John Kelly, as well as intelligence officials — to conclude that the President was often "delusional," as two sources put it, in his dealings with foreign leaders."

Chauncey DeVega, a prominent journalist, on July 2, 2020 wrote on "Salon;" "For four years Donald Trump has willfully and repeatedly violated the presidential oath of office and its promises to 'faithfully execute the Office of the President of the United States," and "preserve, protect and defend the Constitution of the United States."

DeVega is in concord with many psychiatrists, psychologists and experts who believe and feel assured of Trump's mental ineptitudes. He wrote: "As many of the nation's and the world's leading mental health professionals have warned, Trump appears mentally unwell in the extreme. His evident mental pathologies, likely including malignant narcissism, an addiction to violence, a God complex and near-psychotic levels of delusional thinking, have only served to exacerbate his many defects of character and values. In total, Donald Trump is unfit to be the president of the United States of America. If he is not removed from office by the 2020 election, he will continue to pose an extreme threat to the health and safety of the American people and the world."

Dodes issued another ominous warning on July 2, 2020: "From his callous response to the coronavirus pandemic to his threats of violence against journalists and leading Democrats, Donald Trump is incapable of human concern and empathy — and he will find a way to follow through on his threats of death and destruction if given the opportunity."

"If I were to run, I'd run as a Republican. They're the dumbest group of voters in the country. They believe anything on Fox News. I could lie and they'd still eat it up. I bet my numbers would be terrific." Donald Trump, People Magazine, 1998

The Quote of Wil Zeus gives the final message, even to the enablers of the dictator and the dictator as the person!

> "Always forgive, but never forget, else you will be a prisoner of your own hatred and doomed to repeat your mistakes forever."

Before going further, one needs to know the inspirations and mind of Trump, and what factors turned this individual into an undependable person! His feelings and thoughts about himself and the world at large appear self-explanatory:

"Reading Mein Kampf in college had a profound effect on me. Very, very interesting. Of course, there were many problems in Germany at the time, they were losers, they lost. But Adolf Hitler, that is to say, I don't agree with everything he was saying at the time of course but I do respect him. As a leader, Tremendous respect. And I suppose you could say. I try to incorporate some of his teachings into everything I do to this day. In business, my daily life and my politics." Donald J. Trump (interview with Time Magazine, 2002). It is very doubtful if Trump did actually read the book or had it read to him.

Having understood the mind of this individual who had hailed Hitler as a paragon and a person guiding his life, it is but natural that only an insane mind would admire another insane, cruel and a pathetic mind; a reflection of himself in modern days.

The elections in the United States of America, whether local, state, or federal, is always tainted with some form of blemish. Money is always poured into the coffers of the candidates by those who believe that the winner would favor them in augmenting their wealth. The roots of legitimizing this form of blatant corruption and bribery masquerading as donation for the party or the individual candidate is unknown.

A simple, yet a vivid example of the wrongdoings in the US method of elections comes to light when a comparison is made, at least to one country in Europe.

In Norway, elections are seventy four percent government funded. Political advertisement on television and other mass media is banned. Voter turnout is eighty one percent which is ranked fifteenth highest in the world.

In the United States of America, elections are eighty percent funded by corporations and the super-wealthy. The bulk of the amount is used for negative television and radio advertising, often using explicit terms for the opponents with plenty of slanders and untrue accusations. The naive audience pay little or no attention to the validity of the accusations and defamations. They simply believe a candidate who makes them comfortable without caring to know his or her background. Voter turnout is between forty and forty eight percent which is ranked one hundred twenty out of one hundred sixty-nine ranking countries in the world.

Whenever a mercurial and an "aspiring dictator" has his hands on the "Nuclear Button" in the Oval Office while claiming "executive privilege" any untoward action can be prevented by simply ousting him through legal means. Any lackadaisical approach to this issue will in fact be construed as support of an imminent global danger posed by this adventurous individual resulting in death, destruction, and misery throughout the world on a massive scale.

To be more specific, one could have in all truth imagined the tragedy that may have afflicted mankind in general and hastened a general war ending in the destruction of more than a billion human lives, would have been the handiwork of this mentally unstable individual; who had shown signs of an "aspiring dictator," claimed his ultimate power of the Judiciary, called himself nothing less than god, embellished himself as the most handsome person and almost as "The All Knowing, the All Wise" and who was very apparently seated into the Oval Office of the United States of America, through arcane hands and powers, one being definitely the Russian mafia through the explicit orders from President Vladimir Vladimirovich Putin.

Mr. Trump the infamous glorified realtor is a proven failed businessman, a predator, a known philanderer, a proven child-molester, a derided television showman did all he could to create in his person a dictator. Fortunately, it did not happen. The Ballots ousted him in the 2020 presidential elections.

A simple research has shown that under Trump, the United States of America was under a very unpopular Administration led by a quixotic, inexperienced, inept, mentally challenged and a volatile individual with a very questionable past and a more dubious presence. Most fortunately his term in the Oval Office ended.

He inherited the Office of America's former popular and scholarly President, Barack Obama. The former president is a noted scholar, an academic in the true sense, a man of dignity, honesty, honor and family values and a Nobel Peace Prize Laurette.

On Friday, June 28, 2019, former President Jimmy Carter questioned the legitimacy of Trump's presidency. Mr. Carter said that the president would not be in the White House if not for Russian interference in the 2016 presidential elections.

"The president should himself condemn it, admit that it happened, which I think sixteen intelligence agencies have already agreed to say," Carter said at a panel on human rights hosted by the Carter Center in Leesburg, Virginia.

"There is no doubt that the Russians did interfere in the election, and I think that the interference, although not yet quantified, if fully investigated, would show that Trump did not actually win the election in 2016. He (Trump) lost the election, and he was put into office because the Russians interfered on his behalf," Carter added.

Former president Carter also said: "Every day we send a disgraceful signal around the world, that this is what the present U.S. government stands for, and that is torture and kidnapping of little children." (statement made on children being separated from their parents at the southern borders, where people from "Spanish America" and elsewhere attempt to cross into the United States of America to seek asylum.) Several children who were separated lost their lives. The separation of children from their parents was a plan suggested by Stephen Miller a senior policy advisor to Trump. It was also said that Miller had time and often taken credit for being the chief architect of Trump's policies whether foreign or State.

Mental Health of Trump

Donald Trump is "in severe mental decline" and "won't make it" to the next election, Anthony Scaramucci, who was White House Communication director for just eleven days, before he was dismissed in 2017, said of the President's mental behavior. It is getting worse since he saw him last.

"The Independent" on September 7, 2019 quoted Scaramucci as saying; "he's in full meltdown, it's like the episodes of Chernobyl where the reactor's melting down and people are trying to figure out whether they're going to cover it up or clean it up."

Whenever and wherever Trump spoke and usually lashed out at his imagined foes while forwarding false statistics and figures of development under his administration, and albeit the fact that he babbles to his selected audience with his usual gesticulation and body movements and gimmicks, a soporific atmosphere overtakes the event. An analogy of such an atmosphere are other cases, reminiscent of known dictators; Benito Mussolini, Francisco Franco, Sukarno, Adolf Hitler, Herman Goering,

Joseph Paul Goebbels, Rudolph Hess, Joseph Stalin, Vladimir Lenin, Nikita Khrushchev, Leonid Brezhnev, Mao Zedong, Idi Amin, and Mobutu Sese Seko, are some of them, who whenever had the opportunity to "lecture" scolded, demeaned, insulted, and threatened their imagined foes to a carefully chosen supportive crowd and paid agitators.

On many occasions, Trump made the same gesticulations, body and facial movements, hysterias, anger, hatred, mockery, contempt, promise of retributions, self-glorification, satisfaction, and empty promises as most of the named dictators, especially those of Adolf Hitler and to a lesser extent of Benito Mussolini!

Trump Scandals

Apart from the "political scandals" that plagued him, Trump's "social scandals" require volumes to write.

On June 24, 2019, Samantha Cooney, presented an article whereby well-known writer E. Jean Carroll said Trump assaulted her in a dressing room in the late 1990's, making her at least the nineteenth woman to allege sexual assault and misconduct by the president of the United States.

Other victims of assault and misconduct by Trump were:

Jill Harth (Years of incidents 1992-1993), Bridget Sullivan (Year of alleged incident: 2000), Cassandra Searles (Year of alleged incident: 2013), Tasha Dixon (Year of alleged incident: 2001), Jessica Leeds (Year of alleged incident: early 1980), Rachel Crooks (Year of alleged incident: 2005), Mindy McGillivray (Year of alleged incident: 2003), Natasha Stoynoff (Year of alleged incident: 2005), Mariah Billado (Year of alleged incident: 1997), Temple Taggart McDowell (Year of alleged incident: 1997), Lisa Boyne (Year of alleged incident: Mid-1990's) Summer Zervos (Year of alleged incident: 2007), Kristin Anderson (Year of alleged incident: early 1990's), Samantha Holvey (Year of alleged incident: 2006), Cathy Heller (Year of alleged incident: 1997), Karena Virginia (Year of alleged incident: 1998), Jessica Drake (year of alleged incident: 2006), Ninni Laaksonen

(Year of alleged incident: 2006), E. Jean Carroll (Year of alleged incident: Late 1995 or early 1996).

Most of the allegations by women of various ages from eighteen and upwards accusing Trump of indecent behavior towards them, either attempted rape, and acts condemned by law had little or no impact on him. Each time he just used the limited words and phrases he had mastered. "That's a lie, never happened, don't know her, never met her!" When confronted with his pictures with the then young or even underage girls, Trump nodded in disapproval of the authenticity of the pictures.

For the record, an article by David Mikkelson published on June 23, 2016, accusing Trump; alleging he raped a thirteen-year-old girl. The case was dismissed in California in May 2016, refiled in New York in June 2016, and dropped again in November 2016.

The article had named Katie Johnson who had accused Trump and billionaire Jeffry Edward Epstein in a one hundred million dollars lawsuit, accusing them of soliciting sex acts from her at sex parties held at the Manhattan homes of Epstein and Trump back in 1994, when Katie Johnson was thirteen years old. Katie Johnson said Trump physically violated her at age thirteen.

Some of the several official allegations filed were:

- The plaintiff Katie Johnson, alleges that the Defendants, Donald J. Trump and Jeffrey E. Epstein, did willfully and with extreme malice violated her Civil Rights under 18 U.S.C.; 2241 by sexually and physically abusing plaintiff Johnson by forcing her to engage in various perverted and depraved sex acts by threatening physical harm to plaintiff Johnson and to her family.

- The Plaintiff, Katie Johnson, alleges that the Defendants, Donald J. Trump and Jeffrey E. Epstein, also did willfully and with extreme malice violate her Civil Rights under 42 U.S.C, ;1985 by conspiring to deny Plaintiff Johnson her Civil Rights by making her their sex slave.

- The Plaintiff, Katie Johnson, alleges she was subject to extreme sexual and physical abuse by the Defendants, Donald J. Trump and Jeffrey E. Epstein, including forcible rape during a four-month time span covering the months of June-September 1994, when Plaintiff Johnson was still only a minor of age thirteen.

- The Plaintiff, Katie Johnson, alleges she was enticed by promises of money and a modeling career to attend a series of underage sex parties held at the New York City residence of Defendant Jeffrey E. Epstein and attended by Defendant Donald J. Trump.

On July 17, 2019, Trump rendered a harangue which he believed was a speech to the general public of North Carolina. His diatribes contained misleading statements laced with falsehood and inculpation aimed at the four legally elected Congresswomen through popular votes. He had earlier defined himself as a patriot by asking those who according to his accusations did not like the country to leave and return from where they came and mend the broken situation in their own countries. The chosen crowd roared in unison to "send her back!"

Trump, the opportunist and coward, attacked them for being anti-Semite. "These people are against Israel and are anti Semites," he thundered to the applause of those chosen attendees who barely knew the meaning of the word "Semite!" This statement had no relations whatsoever to his accusations levelled against the four women, three of them born in the USA and the fourth from Somalia who was an American National.

Trump's Scandals and Social Life

Paragraph 15 of the document filed against Trump the pedophile and against his accomplice Jeffrey Edward Epstein states:

- Shortly after this sexual assault by the Defendant Jeffrey E. Epstein, on the plaintiff, Katie Johnson, Plaintiff Johnson was still present while the two Defendants were arguing over who would be the one to take Plaintiff Johnson's virginity. The Defendant, Donald

J. Trump was clearing heard referring to Jeffrey E. Epstein, as a "Jew bastard" as he yelled at Defendant Epstein, that clearly, he, Defendant Trump should be the lucky one to "pop the cherry" of plaintiff Johnson.

Paragraph 16 of the document filed against Jeffrey E. Epstein and Donald J. Trump states:

- That the third and final sexual assault by the Defendant, Jeffrey E. Epstein, on the Plaintiff, Katie Johnson, took place after Plaintiff Johnson had been brutally and savagely raped by Defendant Donald J. Trump. While receiving another full body massage from Plaintiff Johnson, while in the nude, Defendant Epstein became so enraged after finding out that Defendant Trump had been the one to take Plaintiff Johnson's virginity, that Defendant Epstein also violently raped Plaintiff Johnson. After forcing Plaintiff Johnson to disrobe into her bra and panties while receiving a massage from the Plaintiff, Defendant Epstein attempted to enter Plaintiff Johnson's anal cavity.

Court Documents filed during the presidency of Donald Trump bear witness to the acts of an individual, who in truth must serve and behave as a paragon to the nation but had not in any way. This document is reflected in all its originality.

Reports stated that Mr. Epstein, 66 years old, the child-molester, rapist, kidnapper, and financier hanged himself in his Manhattan jail cell while awaiting his trial. At 6.30 a.m. prison guards found him dead. His several high-profile friends including Prince Andrew, Duke of York, filmmaker Woody Allen, Physicist Lawrence Krauss, former Maine Senator George Mitchell, Former New Mexico Governor Bill Richardson, Financier Glenn Dubin, Modeling executive, Jean Luc Brunel, Hotelier Thomas Pritzker and Donald Trump, former president Bill Clinton, Attorney Alan Dershowitz, ignored his suicide, although Trump was very closely associated with Jeffrey Epstein and his criminal deeds. Not all, but most of these individuals also visited Epstein's small and secluded island to "enjoy life."

Lest it be forgotten or lost in any documents, reference is made to earlier paragraphs of the accusations levelled against Trump and his criminal accomplice Epstein, two conspicuous pedophiles in the case of the documents and allegations against the rape of an underage girl: Katie Johnson.

Paragraph 15 of the same deposition states:

For his part, Trump asserted that the charges were "not only categorically false but disgusting at the highest level and clearly framed to solicit media attention or, perhaps, are simply politically motivated," adding that "there is absolutely no merit to these allegations."

Another underage girl is identified as Jane Doe being victimized by Epstein and Trump. And yet, another anonymous woman, identified in additional testimony as Tiffany Doe, corroborates Jane's allegations.

Trump once described Epstein as a "terrific guy;" a very close friend and said that "he's a lot of fun to be with, it is even said that he likes beautiful women as much as I do, and many of them are on the younger side." now claims he hardly knew him!

The additional charges against financier and billionaire Epstein can carry a forty-five-year sentence. Epstein was born on January 20, 1953 and he was close friends with Trump since 1987. If he had been convicted and sentenced to forty-five years, he would have died in prison either of illness or old age. Prison inmates throughout the United States of America have always been hateful of child molesters and on many occasions, child molesters and sex traffickers like Jeffrey E. Epstein have been beaten to death, stabbed, or simply strangled.

The lifetime of such prison inmates like Jeffrey E. Epstein in any prison in the United States rarely exceeds five years!

It is to be noted that the unmarried Jeffrey E. Epstein owns the famed Herbert N. Straus home on East 71st Street in the Upper East Side of Manhattan at 21,000 sq. feet (2000 sq. meters). The now accused financier's other properties include a residence in Palm Beach, Florida., an apartment in Paris, a 7500-acre ranch near Stanley, New Mexico, and a private island near Saint Thomas in the Virgin Islands called Little Saint James, which includes a mansion and guest houses, and some properties in the neighboring island of Great Saint James. Epstein was building a compound on the latter including an amphitheater and an "underwater office and pool" but ran into problems when a stop-work ordered was issued in late 2018; work continued despite the order.

It was reported that in the early hours of Saturday, August 10, 2019, Jeffrey E. Epstein was found dead in his prison cell where he was awaiting trial for his crimes against young girls. Epstein had no will to live any longer. He killed himself in his Manhattan jail cell.

Only posterity coupled with forensic investigations will finally prove the reasons and causes of his questionable suicide, since he was under a suicide watch and "unfortunately" the cameras monitoring his cell were not "functioning" at the time of his death.

Whenever Trump held his so-called "pageant show" on Epstein's property, Trump committed indecencies on young participants. In an interview he gave to Howard Stern, a radio talk-show host, he spoke frankly with him.

In a 2005 interview with Howard Stern, a radio talk-show host, unearthed by CNN during the presidential campaign of 2016, Trump said that he went backstage during pageants. "I'll go backstage and everyone's getting dressed, and everything else, and you know, no men are anywhere, and I'm allowed to go in because I'm the owner of the pageant and therefore I'm inspecting it, "Trump told Stern. "You know, I'm inspecting because I want to make sure that everything is good."

IN THE UNITED STATES DISTRICT COURT
SOUTHERN DISTRICT OF NEW YORK

JANE DOE, proceeding under a pseudonym,	)
	)
Plaintiff,	)
	)
v.	) Case No.:
	)
DONALD J. TRUMP and	) JURY TRIAL DEMANDED
JEFFREY E. EPSTEIN,	)
	)
Defendants.	)

COMPLAINT FOR RAPE, SEXUAL MISCONDUCT, CRIMINAL SEXUAL ACTS, SEXUAL ABUSE, FORCIBLE TOUCHING, ASSAULT, BATTERY, INTENTIONAL AND RECKLESS INFLICTION OF EMOTIONAL DISTRESS, DURESS, FALSE IMPRISONMENT, AND DEFAMATION

Plaintiff Jane Doe, proceeding under a pseudonym, brings this action against Donald J.

Trump and Jeffrey E. Epstein, and alleges that:

MEHR A. KALAMI

11. On the third occasion involving the Defendant, Donald J. Trump, the Plaintiff, Katie Johnson, was forced to engage in an unnatural lesbian sex act with her fellow minor and sex slave, Maria Doe, age 12, for the sexual enjoyment of Defendant Trump. After this sex act, both minors were forced to orally copulate Defendant Trump by placing their mouths simultaneously on his erect penis until he achieved sexual orgasm. After zipping up his pants, Defendant Trump physically pushed both minors away while angrily berating them for the "poor" quality of their sexual performance.

12. On the fourth and final sexual encounter with the Defendant, Donald J. Trump, the Plaintiff, Katie Johnson, was tied to a bed by Defendant Trump who then proceeded to forcibly rape Plaintiff Johnson. During the course of this savage sexual attack, Plaintiff Johnson loudly pleaded with Defendant Trump to "please wear a condom". Defendant Trump responded by violently striking Plaintiff Johnson in the face with his open hand and screaming that "he would do whatever he wanted" as he refused to wear protection. After achieving sexual orgasm, the Defendant, Donald J. Trump put his suit back on and when the Plaintiff, Katie Johnson, in tears asked Defendant Trump what would happen if he had impregnated her, Defendant Trump grabbed his wallet and threw some money at her and screamed that she should use the money "to get a fucking abortion".

13. On the first occasion involving the Defendant, Jeffrey E. Epstein, the Plaintiff, Katie Johnson, was forced to disrobe into her bra and panties and to give a full body massage to Defendant Epstein while he was completely naked. During the massage, Defendant Epstein physically forced Plaintiff Johnson to touch his erect penis with her bare hands and to clean up his ejaculated semen after he achieved sexual orgasm.

14. On the second occasion involving the Defendant, Jeffrey Epstein, the Plaintiff, Katie Johnson, was again forced to disrobe into her bra and panties while giving Defendant Epstein a full body massage while he was completely naked. The Defendant, Donald J. Trump, was also present as he was getting his own massage from another minor, Jane Doe, age 13. Defendant Epstein forced Plaintiff Johnson to touch his erect penis by physically placing her bare hands upon his sex organ and again forced Plaintiff Johnson to clean up his ejaculated semen after he achieved sexual orgasm.

3

CV-126 (09/99)   PLEADING PAGE FOR A COMPLAINT

On July 14, 2019, Trump the prolific creator of tension said that four minority congresswomen should "go back" to the countries they came from rather than "loudly and viciously telling the people of the United States" how to run the government. Within yet another racist trope identifiable with him, he indirectly pointed at them as foreigners; the fact was that only one was born abroad, although a United States citizen.

Trump the antagonist-in-chief, had forgotten that his first wife and his third and present "trophy wife" are originally "foreigners" and so was his own mother!

Two days later, the absent-minded Trump denied asking for the deportation of one of the popular members of Congress, Ilhan Omar, originally from Somalia, a naturalized American citizen, and an American citizen longer than Trump's third wife, a woman from Slovenia whose parents, virtually the same age as Trump, gained United States' citizenship through chain-migration; this all said, Trump had railed against chain-migration!

On July 22, 2019, Trump met with the Pakistani Prime Minister Imran Khan, where he boasted he could slaughter ten million Afghans and thus bring an end to the war in Afghanistan!

His arrogance and ignorance knew no bounds when he insisted that he could kill ten million in just eight days and end the situation in Afghanistan. He forgot the old proverb that "Afghanistan was the graveyard of Empires and invaders." He also forgot the very ancient saying among foreign invaders, particularly that of the British who have reminded themselves; "God protect me from the revengeful sting of a scorpion, the vengeance of a tiger and the revenge seeking Afghan."

During the same meeting in which the Press was present, Trump most shamefully lied that President Obama had given Iran 150 billion dollars plus 1.8 billion in cash to appease the murderous regime in Tehran to sign the Nuclear Protocol with Tehran in 2015, which he (Trump) unilaterally abrogated against the wishes of the European principles and the Russian principles involved in this agreement.

The truth is far from what Trump the "professional liar" claimed. That money, in the amount stated, was not American money in the least, directly, or indirectly.

First, it was Iranian money frozen due to sanctions, first levied by Jimmy Carter, the individual grossly guilty and responsible for creating the sacerdotal revolution in Iran, leading to the Islamic Revolution as per the orders of his bankrollers and the various Internationals who had authored his rise to the presidency of the United States of America.

Second, and more important is that the full amount of Iranian money (156 billion dollars that was frozen in various foreign banks, not in the United States of America) was not returned, but less than 56 billion dollars, and the 1.8 billion in cash was returned since there was no banking mechanism between the USA and Iran. That was not money belonging to the United States of America in any shape or form. But the shameful lies, obfuscation, and bamboozlement of the public by the deceit and falsehood of Trump had taken root in the minds of the simple-minded people who found it a challenge to read or to comprehend simple facts but believed in rumors and hearsay!

Such a blatant lie of the United States of America giving away money to the Iranians had been regularly trumpeted wherever and whenever possible by Republican lawmakers, some of them with dual citizenship and extra territorial loyalty.

This was explicitly done to demean and lower the values of service rendered by the Obama administration to the United States of America and in general to the world to create peace and understanding through dialog.

Trump, the apostle of falsehood, had followed the notorious Adolf Hitler's theory of incessantly lying and obfuscation to the general public until it becomes imbedded in the mind of the simple-minded people as a fact!

Trump's most ridiculous act in the meeting with the Pakistani Prime Minister came when he claimed with total absurdity that Prime Minister Narendra Modi of India had asked him to mediate between India and

Pakistan and that he (Trump) had offered to get involved in a bid to resolve the long-standing dispute over the Kashmir territorial dispute.

Indian officials in New Delhi quickly and strongly dismissed such a claim as what many others have said earlier of Trump and his statements, that Trump was a pathological liar!

Documents and undeniable facts proved that Trump made twenty false claims at his North Carolina Rally on September 10, 2019. Some are:

- On Crowds. "We haven't had an empty seat in any event, I don't believe, that we've ever been to. I don't think we've ever had … we always had people … we haven't had an empty seat," Trump said. Popular Bloomberg News reporter Josh Wingrove tweeted a photo of what he described as a "smattering" of empty seats in the almost full eight thousand capacity venue.

- Facts first: There were empty seat at this rally. There have also been empty seats at various other Trump events.

- On Ilhan Omar: "Omar laughed that Americans speak of al Qaeda in a menacing tone and remarked that you don't say America with this intensity. "You say al Qaeda makes you proud. You don't speak that way about America," Trump said.

- Facts: Omar did not say that the terrorist organization al Qaeda made her proud. Trump was inaccurately describing remarks she made in 2013 about how one of her college professors acted when he discussed al Qaeda.

- Hispanics and the wall: "Unemployment among Hispanic Americans, where we are really doing well. You know why?"

In summation, Trump's struthious philosophy in life considered his "arranged crowd" as those suffering from amnesia and would swallow any lies and disinformation he spewed. Since the day he took Office till the first week of September 2020, he had lied and misled the nation more than twenty thousand times.

This was from a person claiming strictness, truth, honor, and sanctity.

The All Knowing, the All-Wise Trump, or "And Thus Lied Trump!"

Trump's self-embellishment knew no boundaries. He had continuously reflected his highest degree of knowledge and expertise on every subject under the sun. "I am that chosen one who knows everything, far better than those who are supposed to hold the highest degree of expertise on that particular subject."

To just name a few of such claims recorded:

"Nobody is a greater military leader and commander than I am."

"Nobody knows more about taxes than I do, maybe in the history of the world."

"Nobody knows more about construction than I do."

"Nobody knows more about campaign finance that I do."

"Nobody knows more about technology than me."

"Nobody in the history of this country has ever known so much about infrastructure than Donald Trump."

"I know more about drones – this type of technology certainly – than I do."

"Having a drone fly overhead – and I think nobody knows much more about technology, certainly, than I do."

"I understand politicians more than anybody."

"Who knows more about lawsuits than I do?"

"I know more about ISIS than all the generals do, believe me."

"I know more about the courts than anyone does."

"I am the king of debt. I'm great with debt. Nobody knows debt better than me."

"I understand money better than anybody."

"I am the greatest economist that ever was."

"Nobody knows more about trade than me."

"I think I know more about the economy better than the Federal Reserve."

"Nobody knows the U.S. government system better than I do."

The above claims were just a small portion of what Trump said, reflecting his bloated degree of super-human glory, albeit the fact of being semi-literate and fighting mental illness.

And Thus, Further Spoke Trump!

Of the hundreds of ridiculous, meaningless, and incoherent statements that Trump made, a few randomly chosen reflect the mental capacity of this much glorified realtor and self- acclaimed expert on every subject under the sun.

In March 1990, concerning Domestic Policy:

"I think if this country gets any kinder or gentler, it's literally going to cease to exist."

On his dealings with Saudi Arabia:

"I have no financial interests in Saudi Arabia, never had any."

Facts:

- In 1991, a Saudi Prince bought a Trump yacht for 20 million dollars to save Trump from bankruptcy.

- In 1995, the Trump Plaza Hotel was saved by a 325 million investment from the Saudi prince.

- In 2001, the 45th floor of Trump World Towers was sold to the Saudi government for twelve million dollars.

- In 2017, the Saudi Arabian government spent 270,000 dollars at Trump's Washington, D.C. hotel.

- In 2018, Saudi Arabia's crown prince stayed at Trump's New York hotel and boosted the hotel's revenue by 13%.

On September 27, 2015, on "60 Minutes" concerning Immigration:

"We're rounding them up in a very humane way, in a very nice way. And they're going to be happy because they want to be legalized. And, by the way, I know it doesn't sound nice. But not everything is nice."

On June 15, 2015, at a campaign launch rally concerning Border Control:

"I will build a great, great wall on our southern border, and I will have Mexico pay for that wall. Mark my words."

In early 2019, Trump suggested to his advisers that soldiers should shoot migrants in the legs (just to only cripple them), to slow them down, and that the border wall should be electrified with spikes on top and fortified with an alligator-infested moat. It was widely reported that his son-in-law,

Jared Kushner, and Stephen Miller were the ones who had earlier advised the dyslexic Trump, who accepts whatever is told to him by these two individuals without even comprehending the global repercussions of such statements. Trump, due to his mental afflictions and other related ailments could neither read, speak in complete sense, properly pronounce proper nouns, nor could he write well and remember what he blurted a few moments earlier. He denied everything which is the best way out of a quagmire he created for himself.

In October 2015, on Twitter concerning Global Warming:

"It's really cold outside, they are calling it a major freeze, weeks ahead of normal. Man, we could use a big fat dose of global warming!"

On June 15, 2015, at a campaign launch rally concerning the Greatness of America:

"Our country is in serious trouble. We don't have victories anymore. We used to have victories but [now] we don't have them. When was the last time anybody saw us beating, let's say China. In a trade deal? They kill us. I beat China all the time. All the time."

On June 10, 2012, on Twitter concerning Global Warming:

"The concept of global warming was created by and for the Chinese in order to make U.S. manufacturing non-competitive."

On February 8, 2016, on This Week with George Stephanopoulos concerning Fighting Terrorism:

"When you see the other side chopping off heads, waterboarding doesn't sound very severe."

In March 1990, in Playboy magazine concerning Running for President:

"Well, if I ever ran for office, I'd do better as a Democrat than as a Republican - and that's not because I'd be more liberal, because I'm conservative. But the working guy would elect me. He likes me. When I walk down the street, those cabbies start yelling out their windows."

On June 8, 2015, at the Fox news Republican debate concerning Political Correctness and regularly lying to the public with false claims:

"I think the big problem this country has is being politically correct. I've been challenged by so many people and I don't, frankly, have time for total political correctness."

On September 19, 2019, in the New York Times concerning Why People Would Vote for Him:

"To be blunt, people would vote for me. They just would. Why? Maybe because I'm so good looking."

On Not Losing Any Vote:

On January 23, 2016, in Sioux Center, Iowa, Trump boasted: "I could stand in the middle of 5th Avenue and shoot somebody, and I wouldn't lose voters!"

He later added: "I can say I have no intention of shooting anybody in this campaign." Moments later he claimed it was a joke, after being prompted by his aides that such a statement could be legally challenged and have dire consequences.

On September 5, 2013, on Twitter referring to his Intelligence:

"Sorry losers and haters, but my IQ is one of the highest – and you all know it! Please don't feel so stupid or insecure, it's not your fault."

Note: Trump has always evaded an IQ test under one pretext or the other.

On November 1, 2018, at a White House meeting concerning Africans and Immigration:

"Why are we having all these people from shithole countries coming here?"

On November 11, 2017, on Twitter concerning Kim Jong-un.

"Why would Kim Jong-un insult me by calling me 'old, ugly, and stupid,' when I would never call him 'short and fat?' Oh well, I try so hard to be his friend – and maybe someday that will happen!"

If all the ridiculous statements of Trump were to be ever fully compiled, it would go into volumes – volumes of disgust and hatred, coupled by a disturbed mind that spoke it. He created disharmony and demeaned the substantial population of the country with his divisive statements and presented to the world a nation full of hatred against the entire world.

At the United States Mission to the United Nation on 9/26/2019 Trump spoke thus:

> "They talk about me, and I don't do anything. I don't know if I am the most innocent person in the world. But you know you look at that ... most presidential, I just said I am the most presidential except for possibly Abe Lincoln when he wore the hat, that was tough to beat. Honest Abe, when he wore that hat, that was tough to beat. But I can't do that, that hat wouldn't work for me. Yeah, I have better hair than him. But Honest Abe was tough to beat. Remember we used to do that during the campaign. They used to say, when I speak, the crowd would be crazy, I'd go crazy ...we had

a lot of fun together. We had 25,000 …We've never had an empty seat. From the day I came down the escalator, with a potential … unbelievable woman who became a first lady."

Shortly after these remarks Trump suggested that people who speak with whistleblowers should be executed. (This related to his secret conversations with Volodmyr Zelenskiy on helping him find dirt on Joe Biden, his strongest opponent in the Presidential Elections of 2020, and his son Hunter Biden. Other alleged participants in this illegal act of asking a foreign power to help Trump regain the Presidential Election, were named as William Barr, the Attorney General and Mike Pompeo.) On Thursday October 1, 2019, the Washington Examiner reported that two controversial conservatives and Trump supporters had offered a fifty-thousand-dollar reward for information about the National Security whistleblower.

Trump's lies, deceits, misleading statements and overt falsity in his conversations and speeches made it difficult for any major country to trust him, which directly means any "Letter of Understanding," any covenant or pact was meaningless due to the unstable mechanism within the succeeding US administrations, since any and all agreements can unilaterally be declared null and void by the newly elected individual in the Oval Office.

Trump Ignorance

Trump's cabinet members and associates were:

Racists writing immigration policy, thieves writing economic policy, warmongers writing foreign policy, polluters writing environmental policy, ignoramuses writing science policy, a hired goon heading the Department of Justice and a mentally sick and evil individual ruling them all.

And one is reminded of two types of people never to be trusted; A politically motivated religious leader, whether a Muslim clergyman, a monk, a priest or a preacher and a politician who tells you how to pray, and finally, a draft dodger (in this case Trump, who had fabricated medical papers, claiming physical deformities in order to escape serving his obligatory military service) who tells you how to be patriotic.

Writer, novelist, and thinker Philip Roth called Trump an ignorant con man with a "vocabulary of seventy-seven words."

Other speech experts had lowered his vocabulary prowess to between sixty-eight and seventy-two.

Most of the adjectives he used were; "wonderful, terrible, disgusting, tremendous, disastrous, horrible, terrific, lovely, beautiful, losers, I am the best, I am the finest, most educated, most handsome, never heard of him, never heard of her, never had dealings with him or her, don't know these groups, etc."

To sum up the fraud and the failure that Trump was in every sphere of life, one is reminded that:

"How sad it must be – believing that scientists, scholars, historians, economists, and journalists have devoted their entire lives to deceiving you, while a charlatan and a reality TV star with decades of fraud and exhaustively documented lying is your only beacon of truth and honesty."

Unknown

Former Republican strategist Steve Schmidt on Donald J. Trump

"Fox news is now projecting Joseph R. Biden is the President-Elect of the United States."

"The American people are going to throw you out of office. You will be repudiated and disgraced. No American has ever failed this country worse than you. None. Your incompetence, ignorance, ineptitude, and old-fashioned stupidity have caused economic collapse and made the US the epicenter of Corona virus death and suffering. You have shattered American Alliances and weakened our military. You are a disgrace. Your name will be a synonym for losing, failure and weakness. Biden is crushing you. You want to know why? It's because he is a good man, and you are a bad one. He cares about the American people and you do not. He is respected on the world stage and you are laughed at like sone type of grotesque and buffoonish clown. He is capable and you are not. You attack because you are scared. Take a minute to look at the picture of Fred Trump on your desk. Do you think he would be surprised by your failures? He would not. He bailed you out over and over again. He bailed you out because you couldn't cut it as anything other than a Conman. There will be no monuments and no encomiums for you. The whole country has watched you fail. The whole country is watching your increasingly feeble state. The whole country is watching you lose. We will all watch you return to your golf clubs as the biggest loser the American Presidency has ever produced."

Trump on his agendas for his second term in Office.

In the third week of June 2020, Trump was posed with "pleasant questions" by Sean Hannity, one of his enablers from Fox Tv. What would be his plans and priorities in case he would be reelected for a second term. What are his goals to achieve for the United States of America?

Trump's response: "Well, one of the things that will be really great – you know, the word experience, we always said that, but the word experience is a very important word. It's a very important meaning. I never did this before. I never slept over in Washington. I was in Washington, I think, seventeen times, all of a sudden, I'm President of the United States. You know the story, I'm riding down Pennsylvania Avenue with our first lady and I say, this is great. But I don't know very many people in Washington. It wasn't my thing. I was from Manhattan, from New York. Now, I know everybody, and I have great people in the administration. You make some mistakes like, you know, an idiot like Bolton. All he wanted to do was drop bombs on everybody. You don't have to drop bombs on everybody. You don't have to kill people."

Author's Note. These statements by Trump appear self-evident as to whether they flow from the mouth of a sane person or otherwise.

Throughout his term in Office, this curmudgeon apoplectic stooge of global Mafia in the Oval Office and his appointees (usually imposed on him by the same masters who were the architects of his "success" in winning the elections) agreed to live and behave as if independent, unaware that the clear majority of the general public were aware of their dubious lifestyle.

Such a trend was not limited to the United States of America, but rather, in most countries claiming to be the guardians of Democracy with freedom of Press, Expression and Thoughts!

All said and argued, it was widely believed that in the United States of America, there was a form of stochastic terrorism haunting the nation itself and in a broader sense, the entire globe, under the aegis of the same "Political Mafia" that created Trump; a mentally deranged individual, and his hordes of cut-throats threatening global peace.

Trump Mental Problems

It had been alleged that Trump suffers from Frontotemporal Dementia and those suffering from this ailment have:

- Stiffness and awkwardness in gait.
- Poor judgement.
- Loss of empathy.
- Socially inappropriate behavior.
- Lack of inhibition.
- Repetitive compulsive behavior.
- Inability to concentrate or plan.
- Frequent, abrupt mood changes.
- Speech difficulties.

- Problems with balance or movement,
- Memory loss.

Apart from these alleged ailments, Trump appeared to be shaky, weak, trouble walking and speaking in a complete sense.

It was a challenge for the sane mind to "discover" who were the persons responsible for introducing some of the least eligible individuals to serve in the Cabinet of Trump. Psychiatrists and psychologists had repeatedly proven Trump as being a dangerous "being" with his nervous hands on the nuclear button.

"Trump is a sociopathic maniac, capable of provoking a 'civil war' if he doesn't win the forthcoming presidential elections." Avram Naom Chomsky, linguist, philosopher, cognitive scientist historian, social critic, and political scientist and one of the founders of cognitive science.

John Bolton (National Security Advisor in Trump's administration, ousted on September 10, 2019 in a bitter tirade against him by Trump. He took office on April 9, 2018) after Trump dismissed him, penned a book in which he wrote very unfavorably of Trump, virtually mocking and demeaning him.

Bolton's book titled "The Room Where It Happened" appears self-explanatory. Bolton in an exclusive interview with Martha Raddatz of ABC News presented the salient points of his views and opinions about Trump and his administration. Bolton in keeping with his principle of reflecting the truth, albeit bitter, chose this interview with Martha Raddatz the respected ABC journalist. (The ABC television channel reports the most accurate and verified news in the United States of America. It has been researched that ABC Network is one of the most appreciated media channels for National and International News. To be also added is that Martha Raddatz is perhaps one of the best reporters and journalists in the country.)

On Tuesday, June 23, 2020, the much-awaited book went on sale throughout the United States of America and the world. Trump had frantically attempted to prevent the book from being published but a Federal Judge rejected Trump's wishes. Bolton was throughout his life an agitator and a professional provocateur.

The excerpts of the written text of the interview are reflected in the original form it appeared on the various mass media.

Excerpts:

RADDATZ: So, you walk into the White House on April 9, 2018. You'd worked for three other presidents, both Bushes and [Ronald] Reagan. When you walked into the White House, what was immediately different about the Trump White House?

BOLTON: Well, I could see even before my first day, when I would go over to talk to Trump and others that this was not like a White House I had ever seen before. It was not functioning in the same way as any of the three previous presidents I had worked for.

And the very first thing that I encountered on – my opening day was, of course, the chemical weapons attack by the Syrian government against innocent civilians in Syria. We responded by the end of the week. But I have to say, it was a very disappointing process we went through.

I felt there was obstruction from the Defense Department. I don't think the president fully understood – all of the implications of what he was doing. And I thought – that – while the immediate response appeared satisfactory, that it was an indication of serious decision-making problems, and a serious lack of an overall strategy –

RADDATZ: What were his briefings like? Was he reading his briefings? How often did he get intelligence briefings?

BOLTON: Well, my experience was he very rarely read much. The intelligence briefings took place perhaps once or twice a week.

RADDATZ: Is that unusual?

183

BOLTON: It's very unusual. They should take place every day. The president should read extensively the material he's given. It's not clear to me that he read much of anything. I think too many people attended the briefings. There were perhaps eight, ten people in the room most times.

RADDATZ: You say he didn't – you don't think he read anything, or much? How do you function if you don't read those briefings?

BOLTON: Well, I – you know, it's possible that there was more reading going on than I saw. But it wasn't evident in the conversations. I found it very difficult, therefore, to have sustained conversations about policy development over a period of time.

But I think it emphasized the way the president normally works, which is on any given day, he's capable of making almost any given decision. And – and that is not, in my view, the way you should do national security policy. Maybe it works in other areas. But even in trade, which I describe in the context largely of the trade dispute with China and the European Union – I thought that – that it was almost impossible to sustain a consistent coherent policy over time.

RADDATZ: And you wrote the president was not just uninformed, but stunningly uninformed. Can you give us some examples?

BOLTON: Well, there are parts of history that you would expect a president to learn over time. No, no president comes to office with 360 degrees knowledge of every aspect of our affairs. But there were things that we went over again and again and again, that just didn't seem to sink in, like why was the Korean peninsula partitioned in 1945 at the end of World War II, and what did that lead to and how did we get to that point? There are just bits of history that help to inform the current context of a lot of situations. And we just never made headway on many of them.

RADDATZ: You say in the book that Trump asked Gen. John Kelly if Finland was part of Russia, or thought Venezuela is really part of the United States.

BOLTON: He said those things, absolutely. And this is when people talk about the– what the policy making process was, when you're dealing with somebody who asks questions like that. It's very hard to know how to proceed. And this sort of incident occurred time and time again, as well as the fact that the president received information from people outside the normal process.

RADDATZ: I want to talk about politics and reelection again. Bob Gates wrote that President Obama, his decision making, was based on domestic political concerns as well. But you do seem to be going much further here, writing, "It's the only thing that Trump couldn't tell the difference between his personal interests and the country's interests."

BOLTON: Well, this is a very serious aspect of the national security policy of the Trump administration. The president over and over again seemed to think that a good personal relationship with Xi Jinping, Vladimir Putin, Kim Jong Un, the ayatollahs, Erdogan of Turkey, was equivalent to a good relationship between the United States and their respective countries.

Again, there's absolutely no doubt that good personal relations between world leaders, between counterparts, foreign secretaries, defense ministers, that kind of thing, it's all a positive. But nobody should misunderstand that a personal relationship is somehow equivalent to better relations between the two nations.

And on any number of occasions, Xi Jinping and Vladimir Putin and others would say things like, "Look, you pursue the interests of the United States. We pursue the interests of our countries." I had no doubt they knew what that meant. I'm not sure that Donald Trump did.

But we keep going back to them, quite apart from the fact that as important as trade is between the United States and China, it is not the entire geopolitical strategic picture. There's the Chinese advance in nuclear weapons; their weapons designed to counteract American presence in space, their effort to push us out of the South China Sea, and make it a Chinese province, which are issues that were very hard to get the president to focus on.

RADDATZ: The president has referred to himself as a stable genius. Is that what you saw?

BOLTON: Really? Well, how can anybody call himself a stable genius? It's hard for me to imagine somebody who would say that. He did say it a couple times when I was in his presence. And I just didn't react to him.

RADDATZ: Let's move to Vladimir Putin. How would you describe Trump's relationship with Vladimir Putin?

BOLTON: I think Putin thinks he can play him like a fiddle. I think Putin is smart, tough. He plays a bad hand extremely well. And I think he sees that he's not faced with a serious adversary here. And he works on him, and he works on him, and he works on him.

RADDATZ: You wrote that on a few occasions, President Trump was eager or even desperate, as you describe it, to meet with Vladimir Putin. What are some examples of that? And you said he also took steps to reduce U.S. pressure.

BOLTON: Well, I think there was the same fascination with speaking with a leader like Putin that we saw with respect to Xi Jinping and Kim Jong Un. It was hard to explain. The president himself used to comment on how strange it was that in one trip he took to a NATO summit, a summit with Theresa May, the prime minister of Britain, and then Vladimir Putin in Helsinki that he thought the easiest, most pleasant one might be with Vladimir Putin.

The kinds of pressure that we needed to put on Russia, economic pressure through sanctions and other steps we could take always took persuading to get the president to do, even when the sanctions were seemingly required by statutes that we operated under.

He had voices in the administration that urged him not to impose sanctions time and time again. Secretary of the Treasury Mnuchin frequently took that view. But I think it also now is a reflection of that lack of strategic thinking, the lack of continuity and perseverance that you need to have policies that work over time.

That you can't just make a decision one day, and three months later, make a contrary decision, and expect that your adversary is gonna do anything—other than conclude that you're not following any policy at all. And that if they have a plan they're pursuing, they're more likely to succeed than you are.

RADDATZ: You say in in the book that Putin knew just how to play Trump, like comparing Hillary Clinton to the U.S.-backed Venezuelan opposition leader Juan Guaidó, or saying falsely that Nicolás Maduro had big rallies. You're saying that worked on the president?

BOLTON: Yeah. I think— I think many of these foreign leaders – mastered the art of ringing his bells. And some were better at it than others. Chancellor [Angela] Merkel of Germany had no success. I don't think she tried. I think she just tried to say what her position was, like a normal leader would do, and expect a response. Didn't get it. But the dictators seem to be better at it than the leaders of the democracy. And I just hope that pattern is not gonna persist if he's reelected.

RADDATZ: You say the term, "He was marked by some of those leaders."

BOLTON: I think they knew exactly what they were looking at far better than some people here in the United States. And they pursue their objectives. And this – this is, in my view, the only way you can pursue a successful policy, is persistently – with the eye on your ultimate objective, and taking Trump apart piece by piece by piece – which I'm afraid too often was the case.

RADDATZ: You say that President Putin plays Donald Trump like a fiddle. What does he do? How does he do it? What should Americans think of that?

BOLTON: President Putin prepares very comprehensively for meetings. He knows the people he's talking to. He thinks about what he wants to say. He thinks about the points he wants to accomplish. And I think he looks at somebody like Donald Trump and says to himself – as an old KGB officer, "How am I gonna get him to the place I want him to be?"

I think that's a level of preparation, of thoroughness – of – pre-planning that just would not register with Donald Trump. That's not to say Putin succeeds all the time. But he has a plan, and he pursues it. And I can just see the smirk when he knows he's got him following his line. It's almost transparent.

RADDATZ: Donald Trump, as we say, sees himself as a dealmaker. But Vladimir Putin says he's easily manipulated. What happened to the dealmaker in those situations?

BOLTON: Well, the president may well be a superb dealmaker when it comes to Manhattan real estate. Dealing with Syria, dealing with arms limitation treaties on strategic weapons dealing in many, many other international security issues are things far removed from his life experience.

Presidents don't come to the office – no president does, knowing everything. So, it's no wrap on anybody to say, "Well, they don't know about strategic arms limitations talks." But when you're dealing with somebody like Putin, who has made his life understanding Russia's strategic position in the world– against Donald Trump, who doesn't enjoy reading about these issues or learning about them – it's a very difficult position for America to be in, notwithstanding our objective superiority over the Russians in all these areas.

RADDATZ: And you talk about other adversaries and dictators who looked at Donald Trump in the same way and marked him. Who are they?

BOLTON: Well, I think Xi Jinping would be right up there with Putin in his ability to look at Donald Trump and say, "This is somebody that we can move ultimately on our side." Now, we're in a period today, and we will be in that period up until Nov. 3, Election Day, when rhetoric about Chinese behavior is tough. It's harsh.

And some steps have been taken because of the thoroughly impermissible behavior of China with respect to Hong Kong, with respect to the Uighurs, with respect to a whole range of important issues. But how long after Nov. 3 will the harsh rhetoric prevail if Donald Trump wins? How long will it be before he's calling Xi Jinping and saying, "Let's together on those trade negotiations again?"

That's part of the problem. You could argue about the wisdom of a policy that was hard on human rights, hard in defense of Hong Kong, hard in defense of American interests in the South China Sea – versus some other policy. But when the policy one day is harsh and the next day it's not, next day it's something else, that's not a policy at all.

And the attorney general, as the Supreme Court said in the famous case, the attorney general is the hand of the president in fulfilling the president's duty to take care that the laws be faithfully executed. But that means faithful execution means execution that's not politically motivated. And – this idea that you give Erdogan and his family, who use Halkbank like a slush fund – in exchange for, what? – some hope down the road of some other kind of treatment for Trump or the country – was very troubling.

RADDATZ: You describe the president as "erratic, foolish, behaved irrationally, bizarrely. You can't leave him alone for a minute. He saw conspiracies behind rocks and was stunningly uninformed. He couldn't tell the difference between his personal interests and the country's interests." When you put all that together, how can anyone come away, after reading your book, and make any conclusion other than that you don't think he is fit for office?

BOLTON: I don't think he's fit for office. I don't think he has the competence to carry out the job. I don't think he's a conservative Republican. I'm not gonna vote for him in November. Certainly not gonna vote for Joe Biden either. I'm gonna figure out a conservative Republican to write in. But this comes back to the point of why I wrote the book.

RADDATZ: What about your own relationship with the president? Throughout the book you said you were close to resigning on a handful of occasions. You said one of those occasions, a turning point, was the night there were no retaliatory strikes against Iran at the time for bombing some ships in the Persian Gulf or placing explosives on the side of them, for shooting down one of our very high-tech drones. That was a turning point for you?

BOLTON: Yes. I think at that point – if I look back on it, it only became a matter of time – when I actually resigned. And this is something people can disagree with me, that maybe I shoulda resigned right then. But I felt and I understand how others in analogous situations still in the government can feel, that there were still contributions I could make.

But I thought that was the most irrational decision I'd ever seen any president make in my own personal experience serving in the government. It wasn't a mega crisis. Although it was a crisis. And it was a failure of decision making that – that convinced me it was a serious, serious problem.

RADDATZ: He did, obviously, follow up – killing [Iranian military leader Qassem] Soleimani – with a missile strike a drone strike.

BOLTON: Well, there are subjects – and – this is obviously an issue of controversy now that involve classified information that I don't talk about. And, you know, if I had put classified information in the book, it might've been 500 pages longer. But I had plenty to talk about without dealing with classified information. I'm glad Soleimani's dead. I wish it had happened earlier.

RADDATZ: Let's talk about other Republicans. You're a conservative Republican. If the president is all of these things you've claimed he is in the book and in this interview, why are almost all of your fellow Republicans still supporting him?

BOLTON: Well, I think they're in a very difficult position. And I view the circumstance we're in now really as the beginning of the fight for the soul of the Republican party, post Trump. Whether Trump wins in November or loses in November, that battle begins immediately.

And I think a lotta people regret that they're not able to express their views more fully.

I think the issues for the country are so grave domestically and internationally, that we need a functioning Republican Party that can stand up for the same principles that we all agreed to before Trump and that we're gonna agree to after Trump.

RADDATZ: I wanna close with where the country is right now and a couple of things. And I know you talk about Gen. Kelly at one point worried about the president's style and worried about how he would be in a crisis, another 9/11 type crisis. We're in the middle of a pandemic. How do you think the president has handled that?

BOLTON: I think he's handled it very poorly. There're a lot of criticisms about what happened– who was responsible and so on. The main problem the administration has had with coronavirus is the empty chair behind the resolute desk in the Oval Office. In early January, people, whether on the staff of the National Security Council or the Centers for Disease Control and elsewhere were saying, "This is a potential problem."

Donald Trump didn't wanna hear about it. He didn't wanna hear about it because he didn't wanna hear bad things about Xi Jinping. He didn't wanna hear bad things about China covering up what had happened with the outset of the disease. He didn't wanna hear bad things about the Chinese economy that could affect the fantastic trade deal he was working on, No. 1.

And No. 2, he didn't wanna hear anything about an exogenous variable that could have a negative effect on the American economy, which he saw as his ticket to reelection. So, for months, it was contained. It wasn't a problem. There was no economic effect.

And I think we lost a lotta time because of that. That is an example of making policy out of your hip pocket, without systematic consideration of what needs to be done, despite being warned by the people charged with making the warnings that it was coming.

RADDATZ: You say President Trump is unfit for office and you're talking about the election, do you worry about his commitment to the democratic process?

BOLTON: I don't think he fully understands the democratic process. I don't think he fully understands the Constitution.

Apart from John Bolton's book revealing Trump's lifestyle and behaviors, several other books have been written about him, some inculpatory and accusative levelled on his fraudulent ways of life and living. His niece Mary L. Trump penned a book titled "Too Much and Never Enough: How My Family Created the World's Most Dangerous Man." Mary L. Trump set to expose the various wrongdoings and the uncouth character of her uncle, Donald Trump.

"In this revelatory, authoritative portrait of Donald J. Trump and his toxic family that made him, Mary L. Trump, a trained clinical psychologist and Trump's only niece shines a bright light on the dark history of their family to explain how her uncle became the man who now threatens the world's health, economic security, and social fabric."

Mary Trump spent much of her childhood in her grandparents' large, imposing house in the heart of Queens, New York, where Donald and his four siblings grew up. She describes a nightmare of traumas, destructive relationships, and a tragic combination of neglect and abuse. She explains how specific events and general family patterns created the damaged man who occupied the Oval Office, including the strange and harmful relationship between Fred Trump and his two oldest sons, Fred Jr., and Donald.

(Brief notes on her and the book as reflected on Amazon.com)

Stephen Miller, Stephen Kevin Bannon, Jared Kushner, Ivanka Trump, Sebastian Gorka and even Sean Hannity of Fox Television infamy to name a few, had all claimed to be the guiding "star" of Trump. Some of these opportunists had allegedly labelled Trump as a dangerous clown who could be manipulated as they wished.

This self-appointed billionaire was President of the USA! He succeeded President Obama! He was "sent" to the Oval Office by a questionable institution; the "Electoral College" through the aegis of the Russians. In short, the Russians promoted his assault on the White House.

In his name, violence and death was openly practiced by ignorant people following his philosophy! Muslim men, women and children and those women and girls wearing a scarf, including those who may not be a Muslim, were simply shot or stabbed in the streets, trains and busses, a good number bleeding to death. Synagogues had been torched, and so were Mosques. Jewish cemeteries were desecrated without a single word of denouncement from the individual elected as the President and his son-in-law a Jew and his daughter who converted to Judaism!

The results for the 2016 Presidential Elections were disturbing in a country where the number of voters were very few compared to the 323.1 million population.

A total of 65,853,625 voted for Mrs. Hillary Clinton, the Democrat nominee while 62,985,105 voted for Trump. Most shockingly, 108,856,312 voters failed to cast their votes!

A closer look at the number of those, mainly Democrats who failed to vote reflects a different picture as to who should have won and who should have lost. The figures are self-explanatory since the vast majority are blacks of African origin. The media told them that their vote was not necessary since Hillary would win.

Trump won Wisconsin by 23,000 votes. In Milwaukee, 93,000 blacks did not vote.

Trump won Florida by 113,000 votes. In Miami, 379,000 blacks did not vote.

Trump won Michigan by 11,000 votes. In Detroit, 277,000 blacks did not vote.

Trump won Pennsylvania by 44,000 votes. In Philadelphia, 238,000 blacks did not vote.

Trump won Georgia by 211,000 votes. In Atlanta, 530,000 blacks did not vote.

In the USA, there is no such thing called a "popular vote!" Instead, an "American method" is "applied," whereby there are the members of the "Electoral College" representing the winning political party of each state (Most states are winner take all, no matter how close the margin.) A strange US creation!

As stated earlier, apart from the Russians behind the curtain of conspiracy, the persons responsible for the creation of this mentally unstable and dangerous individual to hold the most responsible Office in the world were owners of gambling casinos and brothels, housing developers, media owners, and others involved in dubious activities! It is a common knowledge that to oppose or expose the deeds of these "king-makers" does not forebode well! They, in all simplicity and truth, "own the President and the Presidency" as if stocks, bonds, and shares through legal means of bribery and corruption. It is legalized as "contribution and donation!" Throughout his term and tenure as the President, he was just a lackey, a toady and a "yes man" to those who "bought him!"

The "puppet-aspiring-dictator" was obliged to do, behave and act according to the orders of his "donors", whose funds flowed in at regular intervals, or face the stoppage of such funds in case he desired to be independent of their orders!

To sum up, once the individual is swept to power, he must continue to play second fiddle to his bosses for fear of losing his continued financial contributions! After all, money matters!

Religion, Evangelicals, and Trump

Ousting this potentially dangerous and aspiring dictator does not call for or advocate the least form of violence or bloodshed or even strikes. Fortunately, in the United States of America the rule of Law ultimately prevails. The USA will NEVER tolerate a dictator, no matter how the paid mass media portray him, or how the Christian evangelist preachers hailed him as the "second coming of the Messiah," an appointee of God and a redeemer of sins.

Many opportunist Christian evangelist preachers warned the public that protesting or insulting Trump was an act against God!

Trump was ceaselessly embellished as a "saintly figure" chosen and appointed by God to lead the country. In truth, it was the Electoral College and the members of this "Institution" who "selected" him. He was never elected through a popular vote.

Such is one of the hundreds of devious methods used by unprincipled people to manipulate votes in favor of a losing candidate.

To sum up, the learned and educated strata in the United States of America, who form a larger percentage of the population realized to their chagrin and despair that the individual comfortably seated at the helm of power in the Oval Office was none but a disturbed person and that he could take the nation and country to the point of disaster at any moment.

Comments on Trump's Life

Ladies and gentlemen! I need to say so!

The imminent need to pen my thoughts came just ten months after the "new" person was catapulted into the Oval Office…. It is about Donald J. Trump who imagined himself as being a dictator, at least an aspiring dictator! Such an individual could create a global catastrophe.

He had time and again reminded the startled and shocked nation of the USA that he knew more than all the generals combined, that he knew more Economics than any Economist! In all truth, his "word prowess" (also stated elsewhere) was limited to adjectives laced with profanity addressed to his opponents!

What inspired me, coaxed me, or even, compelled me to pen this work was, when at the end of more than a year of observing this "inheritor of the Oval Office" who lied more than three thousand times in five hundred days while in Office! An average of six lies, deceitful statements and claims a day! Prominent writer Steve Goldstein in an article dated April 29, 2019 in the popular "Washington Post" wrote: "The President has told Ten Thousand Whoppers (till today during his term in Office). By late August 2019, this individual's lies, and misleading statements exceeded twelve thousand and by the end of December 2019, it exceeded fifteen thousand." By the end of the year 2020, his lies had exceeded twenty thousand!

Obviously, this President had decidedly taken an oath to lie, lie and lie!

To remind:

Trump is that individual who cheated on wife number one with wife number two (who got pregnant while he was still married to wife number one); cheated on number two with future wife number three, and, then cheated on number three with a porn star and a Playboy model; is on record admitting to sexual assault and has been accused of rape by more than a dozen women, enjoys the complete and unwavering support of Conservative Evangelicals including tele-evangelical preachers, virtually all propagating "family values" and prosperity gospel. A sizeable number of these preachers have either spent time in prison or have charges of fraud filed against them.

Trump is conspicuously notorious for his other lies and deceits and is now known as: the "billionaire" who hides his tax returns, the "genius" who hides his college grades, the "businessman" who bankrupted a casino, the "playboy" who indulges in prostitution, the "Christian" who does not go to church, the "philanthropist" who defrauds charity (with his children), the "patriot" who dodged the draft and evaded obligatory military service under one excuse or the other, the "innocent man" who refuses to testify and much more notoriety.

Quotes & Comments About Trump

In mid-June 2019, the Dalai Lama told the BBC that the American president is someone with a "lack of moral principle." The Tibetan Buddhist leader also said that: "one day he says something, another day he says something, but I think a lack of moral principle is his main problem."

"A man who lies to himself, and believes his own lies becomes unable to recognize truth, either in himself or in anyone else, and he ends up losing respect for himself and for others. When he has no respect for anyone, he can no longer love, and, in order to divert himself having no love in him, he yields to his impulses, indulges in the lowest form of pleasure, and behaves in the end like an animal. And it all comes from lying-lying to others and to yourself." Fyodor Mikhailovich Dostoevosky.

It is worthwhile to note that virtually all the traits in most dictators, whether in the past or present is related to the facts noted by Dostoevosky.

Michael Bloomberg, a globally respected personality, a philanthropist and a former Mayor of New York on July 27, 2016 made the following remarks about the candidate Trump: "I have known this person for decades. We have travelled in the same business circles. He is known among other millionaires a con artist and among business owners as a cheat out to stiff everyone."

In the first week of January 2020, popular philanthropist and Media owner Michael Bloomberg who had reflected his intentions in joining the Presidential race as a Democrat, exposed Trump of not being a "billionaire" as he had time and often claimed to the public, but a fraud who refuses to show his taxes and who owes several Banks both in the USA and abroad hundreds of millions of dollars. Trump, unfailing as usual demeaned Bloomberg's physical characteristics!

Elsewhere in his statements, Bloomberg said: "Truth be told, the richest thing about Trump is his hypocrisy. He wants you to believe that we can solve our biggest problems by deporting Mexicans and shutting out Muslims. He also claimed to deport eleven million undocumented people, but he sees no problem in hiring them at his various golf clubs."

Another popular philanthropist and billionaire is Tom Steyer who in his television messages condemned Trump's lifestyle. "I will expose Trump for the fraud and the loser that he is."

The former popular president, Obama, in the second week of February 2020 remarked that: "There's no successful businessman in America who actually thinks the most successful businessman in America is Donald Trump."

Trump's Fascist Tendencies

A conspicuous sign among this particularly aspiring dictator gradually became more apparent as the months passed by! His appointment and his forced dismissal of his Cabinet members, some of whom were found guilty of wrongdoings and his insistence that they were all "the finest," created alarm throughout the educated strata of the US nation.

Early signs of several Fascistic tendencies commenced with his Administration even before being elected by the Electoral College!

Some of these are classically known signals of danger lurking within a person desiring to imitate dictators in the past. Almost all dictators finally met an ignominious and a violent end!

His other steps to empower himself gradually did not go unnoticed by the educated strata of the population! He openly commenced his plans as dictated to him by his "handlers," who in fact had swept him into the Oval Office. Some of his plans consisted in following practices of dictators in the past and present.

The simple "procedures" on the creation of a dictator.

Most of Trump's accusations and false claims against enemies, whether imagined or true were reminiscent of the dealings and philosophies of dictators in the past, Adolf Hitler, Benito Mussolini, Stalin, and Mao.

- Decrying the absence of Nationalism and an open disdain not only for Human Rights, but also those who are members of groups protecting human rights, the aspiring dictator orders such societies and organizations to be closed in the name of the country's interest.

- The dictator creates imagined enemies to be dealt with violently while calling on the masses to safeguard the integrity of the country. At times, most of the aspiring dictators make an emotional appeal to the nation to unify and declare war on the opposition who may destroy the country.

- He or she orders the arrest of any and all journalists and writers who are identified as a source of danger to the dictator's regime.

- Under various pretexts, he or she claims the urgency to empower the nation's security apparatus with plenipotentiary powers to deal with those considered as the enemies of the State. He orders the establishment of special courts for those instigating and provoking the public against the autocrat and his administration and to deal with them in the harshest manner.

- Under the dictator's administration, rampant cronyism, nepotism, chaos, and corruption and finally, fraudulent elections, of which he was and is a part of.

Trump's basis of life was partly based on the old axion of "divide and rule" but more pronouncedly on the philosophy of divide and profit, divide and benefit, divide and stay protected from personal crimes committed, divide and create disharmony, divide and create hatred among people and nations of the world.

Given such undeniable facts that this unstable and unpopular individual was comfortably seated in power with both houses at his disposal to play "Yes Sir" to his demands however appalling they may be lasted for two years. Once the Democrats won the majority seats in the Congress in the November 2018 elections, the aspirations of the aspiring dictator were appreciably weakened.

On several occasions, the aspiring dictator made a reference to be the "President for Life!" In the first week of May 2019, he even claimed that his two years were wasted and hence he required his first term of four years be extended to six years!

On May 20, 2019, Trump who held his fifth "Make America Great Again" rally in the small town of Montoursville in Central Pennsylvania claimed supernatural feats for himself. "Trump rambled about his normal complaints saying the lights were too bright, and that he preferred the sun," wrote Andrea Jefferson in the "Political Flare."

In that rally attended by a few hundred people, Trump showed his desire to serve in at least five terms (a total of twenty years)!

Most of the twelve persons interviewed who attended that rally called Trump a truly demented person, who behaved and spoke as an inebriated person and who considered those gathered to hear him as having similar characteristics as Trump.

Trump's Time and Money

Glenn Kessler, a researcher, on July 27, 2018 in an article wrote: "Since the day of taking Office on January 20, 2017 till today (July 27, 2018), the President has spent 123 days golfing, or 1/5 of his term, at a cost to the taxpayers of $72,181,957 – and still has not visited troops in a war zone."

Each trip to his golf course at Mar-a-Lago cost the common taxpayer 3.4 million Dollars. By mid-July 2019, the amount had exceeded 108 million dollars! By the end of December 2019, the amount paid by taxpayers for his "enjoyments" exceeded 125 million dollars! The amount expanded to a staggering 134 million dollars by March 4, 2020. It is to be reminded that this massive amount has been paid by the poverty-stricken taxpayers in the United States of America. A good part of this amount also went to Trump's hotels where his entourage resided during his golfing visits.

As a Presidential candidate, he was heavily critical of Barack Obama and told an audience that "I am going to be working for you. I am not going to have time to go play golf."

The Government Accountability Office released an official report looking only at the President's first four trips to Mar-a-Lago (his palatial retreat in Florida) on Feb 3-6, Feb. 10-12, Feb. 17-20 cost the taxpayer 3.4 million Dollars each trip.

On December 24, 2020, in an article written by S.V. Date, in The HuffPost, Trump arrived at his Palm Beach, Florida, resort for the thirty first golf vacation there of his presidency, raising the taxpayer-funded travel and security total for his hobby to $151.5 million.

Other news report Trump had accumulated 285 daytime visits to golf clubs since he became president with evidence of him playing on at least 142 occasions (as of November 8, 2020)

Outwardly, the aspiring dictator received Four Hundred Thousand Dollars annual salary (which he had forfeited and had instead opted to receive just One Dollar instead!), an extra expense of Fifty Thousand Dollars a year, a One Hundred Thousand Dollars non-taxable travel account and Nineteen Thousand Dollars for entertainment. He has never released his tax returns, nor has he ever given a clear picture of his wealth. On some occasions he boasted of having over Ten Billion dollars and at other times kept silent.

On May 8, 2019, Russ Buettner and Suzanne Craig wrote in the popular "New York Times" revealing the President's tax information between the years 1985 to 1994, stating his businesses were in far bleaker condition than was previously known.

"By the time, his master-of-the-universe memoir 'Trump: The Art of the Deal,' (co-written by Tony Schwartz, but revealed that Schwartz had actually written the larger part of the Book, considering Trump's limited knowledge and ability to write) hit bookstores in 1987, Trump was already in deep financial distress, losing tens of millions of dollars in troubled business deals, according to previously unrevealed figures from his federal income tax returns."

It would be only too justifying noting that on May 8, 2019, ghostwriter Tony Schwartz in an interview with Anderson Cooper on CNN stated: "If I had to rename 'The Art of the Deal' I would call it 'The Sociopath.'" Schwartz said the fact is that Trump did not write a single line of the book. "He is illiterate and does not know how to think or write," Schwartz clarified.

Schwartz said Trump was "probably aware more walls are closing around him than ever before, but he does not experience the world in a way an ordinary human being would."

During the interview Schwartz also suggested that Trump had shown losses to the tune of more than a Billion Dollars to skip paying taxes. "He has rarely paid any tax," Schwartz added.

In an article dated September 23, 2019, Jake Thomas wrote in "The Intellectualist," quoting Tony Schwartz: "Trump is the most purely evil human being I've ever met, and also the most insecure." Schwartz had earlier reflected his mind in the "Esquire" magazine.

Tony Schwartz wrote about Trump on a website: "I believe deeply that most people are better than their worst behaviors. I also believe there are some who are simply irredeemable and evil. Psychiatrist and author Scott Peck called them 'People of lie.' They lack any conscience, as Trump does, and so they are almost purely evil. Trump is the most purely evil human being I've ever met, and also the most insecure."

Schwartz, just as many other intellectuals and academics, including clinical psychiatrists, added that Trump lacked even the least interest about the country and his mission as the chief Public servant that he was supposed to be, but instead in his limited mind thought of only himself and augmenting his personal coffers at all costs.

Schwartz also said that in the following years after he was placed in the Oval Office, Trump became more nativist, racist, narrow-minded and he was just a shade of Attila the Hun.

If this was the case and it strongly appeared to be so, then this was a classic case of "comeuppance" for the masses who voted for him.

His continued false claim of being the most successful businessman in the country was again exposed, this time when a list of at least thirteen of his businesses were proven to be his biggest failures.

In an article dated March 14, 2016, Tessa Stuart wrote in the "Rolling Stone Magazine" about Trump's businesses.

"Trump (Presidential Candidate) has made his vast wealth a centerpiece of his presidential campaign; he says voters can trust him because of his keen business sense. There are some problems with that strategy, however: 1) He's not quite the self- made mogul he makes himself out to be - he got a considerable head start in business thanks to his real-estate developer father. 2) His fortune may well be considerably smaller than he says it is. And 3) his business record is less sterling than he suggests."

Independent investigators claimed that on several occasions Trump boasted of having wealth exceeding ten billion dollars while his election campaign staff disclosed to the Federal Election Commission figure of just above nine billion dollars.

Two of his nationally publicized business failures are:

1. Trump Airlines

He created this Airlines in 1988 through a loan of nearly a quarter billion dollars to buy the planes and specific routes between New York, Boston, and Washington D.C. By 1990 the Airline was losing money and proclaimed bankruptcy. The planes were repossessed by his creditors.

2. Trump Casinos

Trump filed for bankruptcy on Trump Taj Mahal in 1991 which was more than three billion dollars in debt, just a year after opening its business. By early 2004 Trump Marina and Trump Plaza Casinos and a riverboat casino in Indiana had accrued nearly two billion dollars debt.

Other losses and business failures are Trump Mortgage, Trump Steaks, Trump Travel Site, Trump Tower in Tampa, Florida, Trump University, Trump Vodka, and several other medium and large businesses.

In the first and second week of May 2019, virtually all mass media spoke and wrote about Trump's business failures and his tax payments.

Printouts from Trump's official Internal Revenue tax transcripts, with figures from his Federal Tax Form, the 1040, for the years 1985 to 1994 represent the fullest and most detailed look to date at the President's taxes, information he had kept from public view.

The numbers show that in 1985, Trump reported losses of $46.1 million from his core business, Casinos, Hotels, and retail space in apartment buildings. They continued to lose money every year, totaling 1.17 billion dollars in losses for the decade. It had been researched that Trump's core business losses between 1990-1991 exceeded $250 million each year and were more than double those of the nearest taxpayers in the Internal Revenue Service information for those years.

Overall, Trump lost so much money that he was able to avoid paying income taxes for eight of the ten years.

Comparing Trump to Hitler

This is the same individual while a candidate promised the US Nation untold wealth and benefits if he was elected!

An analogy exists where Adolf Hitler, had promised the German Nation, prosperity, and a Volkswagen car, once he was the Chancellor and Fuehrer. Instead, he delivered them death, misery, and destruction.

Trump at regular intervals prattled to his selected audience about his achievements that were never substantiated but received thunderous applause at the signal from a "floor director" present during such gatherings.

Trump's first wife, Ivana Marie Trump (nee Zelnickova), a Czech and Canadian citizen and married earlier on two occasions, stated that her husband Trump always slept with a copy of "Mein Kampf" at his bedside!

Trump appeared to have been infatuated with one of the evilest individuals in the world, who was grossly responsible for the planned murder of more than six million Jewish men, women, and children!

Researchers have compiled some of the similarities between the cruel dictator in Germany and Trump:

1. Once in power, both moved quickly to isolate their nations from other democratic nations.
2. Both sought to cancel treaties and agreements that prompted harmony with democratic nations.
3. Both expressed deep respect for totalitarian leaders and their methods of governance.
4. Both quickly moved to forge alliances with totalitarian dictatorships.

5. Both attacked the free press, claiming that media criticism of their policies was treasonous.

6. Both sought support from white nationalists by targeting racial, religious, and ethnic minorities in incendiary speeches and oppressive policies.

7. Both urged police to assault defenseless detainees.

8. Both attacked labor unions as enemies of capitalism, while abusing power to enrich far-right industrialists.

9. Both postured as military strongmen while ordering arms build-ups that served no defensive needs.

10. Both purged government officials who tried to expose their attempts to consolidate their power.

11. Both claimed that they would make their country as "great again."

12. Archbishop Stepinac had acclaimed Adolf Hitler as "God gave us Adolf Hitler." Pastor Robert Jeffress, the appointed "confessor general and apologist" of Trump, hailed him as "God has given us Trump."

13. Adolf Hitler in his "table talks" repeated that: "make the lie big, make it simple, keep saying it, and eventually they will believe it." Trump the aspiring dictator taking a cue from Hitler said, "You tell people a lie three times, they will believe anything. You tell people what they want to hear, play to their fantasies, and then you close the deal." (in the book "Art of the Deal" claimed to be partially written by Trump)

Similarities of Hitler and Trump

Striking similarity in the philosophies of Adolf Hitler and Trump.

Adolf Hitler

- Used racism to rise to power.
- Proposed mass deportations.
- Promised to make Germany "great again."
- Anti-Jew Fascist

- Blamed Jews for Germany's problems
- Thought Jews should wear special ID's.

Trump

- Uses racism to rise to power.
- Proposes mass deportations.
- Promises to make America "great again."
- Anti-Muslim Fascist
- Blames immigrations for America's problems.
- Thinks Muslims should wear special ID's.

Comparing Trump to the Worst Presidents

Speaking about the qualities of Trump both as a sitting president and in private life as a controversial "showman" and a failed businessman, his dishonesty and corrupt means in business dealings, his poor level of intelligence and education, and his racist views, one tends to compare other presidents in the past and how Trump has eclipsed them all.

Andrew Johnson (December 29, 1808 – July 31, 1875) the seventeenth president of the United States was described as the most racist until the day Trump was installed in the Oval Office.

Historians have described Warren G. Harding (November 2, 1865 – August 2, 1923) the twenty ninth president of the United States as the most corrupt president until the day the Electoral College selected Trump as the president.

Ulysses S. Grant (April 27, 1822 – July 23, 1885), the eighteenth president of the United States was considered as the least intelligent and mentally aware, until the day Trump was parachuted into the Oval Office.

Presidential historians have concluded that Andrew Jackson (March 15, 1767 – June 8, 1845) the seventh president of the United States as the most dishonest president before the arrival of Trump in the Oval Office.

Strange but true, Trump always stood and posed in front of the portraits of these four unpopular presidents in American history and held them as a paragon of his lifestyle and values.

Russian Connection

On Russia's interference and tampering with the US Presidential elections favoring Trump, John Haltiwanger wrote in "The Independent" on Monday, July 23, 2018: "Once back in the US from a trip to Europe, Trump walked back on his statements regarding Russian election meddling, stating he believed the conclusion from US Intelligence agencies that the Kremlin interfered in the US presidential election, though he also said it could be "other people also."

On the next day (Wednesday) Trump claimed Russia was not planning future attacks on US elections (which logically infers that Russia did interfere in electronically piling votes in his favor, although by a small margin!), contradicting statements made a week earlier by Director of National Intelligence Dan Coats!

On September 7, 2020, it was reported that Peter Strzok, a decorated counterintelligence agent who served with the FBI in a new book, "Compromised; Counterintelligence and the Threat of Donald J. Trump," was unable to reveal any new evidence that Trump acted as a tool of Russia. But his insider account provides a detailed refutation of the notion that a group of anti-Trump denizens of the deep state cooked up the Russia "hoax" as Trump liked to call it, to take down a president they did not support.

Strzok claims that career public servants inside the FBI and the Justice Department were utterly astonished in 2016 by what they uncovered about a presidential campaign that found unlimited time to meet with Russians, practically inviting exploitation by a foreign adversary.

"I was skeptical that all the different threads mounted to anything more than bumbling incompetence, a confederacy of dunces who were too dumb to collude," Strzok writes, summing up his views of the case for a Trump campaign conspiracy with Russia before he was removed from special counsel Robert Mueller's investigation in July 2017 over what was termed as his biased text. "In my view, they were most likely a collection of grifters pursuing individual personal interests: their own money – and power-driven agendas."

But he also believed, he wrote, that even if Trump did not formally conspire with the Russian election interference operation, the president was badly compromised. He was compromised, Strzok wrote in his book, because of his questionable business dealings, the hush money paid on his behalf to silence women, shady transactions at his charity and, most importantly, "his lies about his Russia dealings," including his secret 2015 effort to build a Trump Tower in Moscow even as he told the world that he had no business dealings with Russia.

"Putin knew he (Trump) had lied. And Trump knew that Putin knew – a shared understanding that provided the framework for a potentially coercive relationship between the president of the United States and the leader of our greatest adversaries," wrote Strzok.

The FBI dismissed Strzok in August 2018. The deputy director decided that his conduct had inflicted "long term damage" on the FBI's reputation.

Haltiwanger adds that "in this context, many are concerned that Trump is doing immense damage to America's global standing by pushing away allies and taking the word of foreign adversaries over US Intelligence Agencies. Most Americans (61%) feel the US is less respected across the globe with Trump in the White House, according to NBC poll released on Wednesday July 18, 2018. Meanwhile experts warn it could take 'years' for the world to trust the US again as Trump continues to attack the International Institutions it played a fundamental role in building following World War Two, especially the NATO alliance and the United Nations."

Maya Oppenhein, journalist of "The Independent" quoted Tony Schwartz (ghost -writer of a book that Trump purportedly wrote "Art of the Deal"); that Trump wants to be a dictator and that he harbors a deep-seated desire to become a dictator!"

Schwartz also said that the prospect of war actively excites Trump, and he lacks the emotional intelligence needed to comprehend the devastating consequences of conflict. November 15, 2017

"Donald is a very sick man. He's never going to get better. He's only going to get worse. And if it suits his purposes, he will take this entire country down with him … so please vote carefully." Dr. Mary Trump, niece of Donald Trump.

Maryanne Trump-Barry, Trump's eldest sister and a former federal judge, said her brother is a liar who has "no principles," a secret recording reveal. Maryanne describes her brother as "unprincipled, phony and cruel." In another statement, Maryanne told her niece Mary Trump; "It's the phoniness of it all. It's the phoniness and the cruelty. Donald (Trump) is cruel," according to the audio scripts and recordings.

The most noticeable part of the conversation that Maryanne Trump-Barry had with her niece (Mary Trump) was on November 1, 2018, which forms the impetus for the allegation that Trump paid someone to take his "SAT" (Scholastic Aptitude Test or College Entrance test. SAT is a standardized test widely used for college admissions in the United States of America.). This was one of the most publicized allegations in Mary Trump's book. ("Too Much and Never Enough: How My Family Created the World's Most Dangerous Man.")

According to the "Washington Post," Barry said to Mary: "He went to Fordham for two years and then he got into University of Pennsylvania because he had somebody take the exams." "No way!" Mary responded. "He had somebody take his entrance exams?" Barry then replied, SAT or whatever…That's what I believe," before saying, "I even remember the name." "That person was Joe Shapiro," Barry said. The White House denied the allegations.

All those who knew Trump from close quarters describe Trump as an amoral, mentally imbalanced, semi-literate, indecent, egomaniac, and cruel liar unfit to serve as President.

Maryanne Trump-Barry's view of her brother compares closely to others who have known Trump and served under him. They are the former White House Communications Director Anthony Scaramucci, his former personal lawyer Michael Cohen, the former Department of Homeland Security chief of staff Miles Taylor and includes several retired Generals and Admirals, to name a few.

Four Star General Barry McCaffrey (retired) on March 17, 2018; "For some unknown reasons he (Trump) is under the sway of Putin."

The highly decorated General said, "Reluctantly I have concluded that Trump is a serious threat to US National Security. He is refusing to protect vital US interests from active Russian attacks. It is apparent that he is for unknown reason, under the sway of Putin."

General McCaffrey also stated that "Trump lacks the emotional and intellectual complexity to steer a superpower and, if left unchecked, he will gradually degrade our once great country until it's as twisted, hateful, and small as he is. It really makes me sick, to be honest."

Highly decorated retired four-star Army General Stanley McChrystal called Trump an immoral and a dishonest individual.

Admiral William McRaven, a respected and a highly decorated Naval Officer (retired) wrote a letter dated August 16, 2018 to Trump after he had through Presidential prerogatives revoked the security clearance of former CIA director John Brennan.

Excerpt of the letter the Admiral wrote:

> "Former CIA director John Brennan, whose security clearance you revoked on Wednesday, is one of the finest public servants I have ever known.

> Therefore, I would consider it an honor if you would revoke my security clearance as well."

The Admiral in his letter, accused Trump, who through his wrongdoings and faulty leadership had embarrassed and humiliated the United States of America on the world stage and worst of all, divided the nation.

In unequivocal terms, the Admiral challenged that Trump's McCarthy-era tactics would never be able to suppress the voices of criticism.

Military Service

Trump was able to evade the obligatory military service by presenting medical documents that he had bone spurs by a podiatrist from Queens, New York. (the late doctor's daughters made public this news in Dec-2018).

Dr. Larry Braunstein, a podiatrist who died in 2007, often claimed of providing Trump with the diagnosis of bone spurs in his heels so he could be exempt from military service. Braunstein's daughters, Dr. Elysa Braunstein and Sharon Kessel could not substantiate their claims if ever their father had examined Trump's feet.

What was recorded in Trump's files for not serving and being exempted on medical reasons could have been easily proved if Trump had provided official X rays of his feet. When asked to dispel doubts of the Nation on this subject, he refused!

His appointed National Security chief, John Bolton, temperamental war-mongering individual, also managed to evade military service by instead serving in the National Guards. He had said:" I did not want to die in the paddy fields in Vietnam." He wrote in his Yale 25th reunion book: "I confess I had no desire to die in a Southeast Asian rice paddy. I considered the war in Vietnam already lost."

Harry John Patch (June 17,1898- July 25, 2009), British soldier, who lectured on the terrible consequences of any war said: "I felt then, as I feel now, that the politicians who took us to war should have been given the guns and told to settle their differences themselves, instead of organizing nothing better than legalized mass murder."

Daniel Nexon, associate professor in the School of Foreign Service and the Department of Government at Georgetown University, said "Americans should be extremely worried about Trump's approach to Foreign Policy if they truly care about the core infrastructure of American international leadership."

Nexon told "Business Insider" that "it's too soon to determine whether Trump has done permanent damage to America's global standing, but said that electing him to the White House, the US essentially demonstrated it's not capable of choosing 'competent' leaders."

Nexon said that European and historic US allies began to think, "even if we survive his tenure in the White House, there is nothing to stop Americans from electing another person like him."

Former CIA Director John Brennan said Trump is unstable, inept, inexperienced, and unethical in scathing interview with MSNBC, June 27, 2018.

Earlier on June 4, 2018 John Brennan, the former C.I.A. director and a Four-Star General, wrote an op-ed, describing "Trump a snake-oil salesman!" Mr. Brennan had always refrained from using the title of Trump. "I refuse to address him with his title, since he only won the Electoral Votes."

Conservative Writer Charles Krauthammer (March 13, 1950 – June 21, 2018) wrote in one of his articles about Trump's puerile and dangerous behavior:

"Trump is beyond narcissism. I used to think Trump was an eleven-year-old, an undeveloped schoolyard bully. I was off by about ten years. His needs are more primitive, an infantile hunger for approval and praise, a craving that can never be satisfied. He lives in a cocoon of solipsism where the world outside himself has value – indeed exists – only insofar as it sustains and inflates him."

"I wish Trump every moment of suffering he's brought our country. Every moment of pain he's caused our people and for every Armed Forces veteran he has called stupid or a loser. May he never draw an easy breath, may their parents haunt his every worthless, empty, cowardice breath." Cherilyn Sarkisian (Cher, popular Singer, philanthropist, and humanitarian).

Cher condemned Trump and called him a thug, to be sent to prison and assaulted by inmates, lizard brain and other adjectives after Trump had called the banning of sanctuary cities where immigrants and refugees were protected from arrest, imprisonment, mistreatment, and deportation. Cher has throughout her life always helped the sick, the dying, the hungry and the homeless from her personal earnings.

"It's not an exaggeration. Donald Trump and the Republican Party are directly responsible for hundreds of thousands of dead Americans." Rob Reiner (Movie Star)

"We've become desensitized after almost four years, but watching clips of Trump's press conference, it's just unbelievable how the leader of the most powerful country in history is so illiterate, inarticulate, ignorant, dishonest, and basically so full of (explicit)."

Thomas Juneau, musician and researcher, University of Ottawa, Canada.

"Trump reportedly took home Seven Hundred Fifty Thousand Dollars' worth of art from the home of the US Ambassador to France in 2018 after canceling a World War I cemetery visit." It is also there that Trump said, "I do not want to visit a cemetery where losers and suckers, among other disparaging remarks, are buried," referring to the gallant Marines of the US Armed forces who made the supreme sacrifice defending freedom. As usual, Trump as well as any of his family members, had never donned the honored uniform of a soldier, denied it even though many witnessed his cowardly statements about fallen heroes. Reports from the Business Insider and The Atlantic.

"For the first time in American history, a president has repeatedly shown utter and vulgar contempt and disrespect for those who have served and died serving our country. Trump cannot understand selflessness because he is selfish. He cannot conceive of courage because he is a coward. He cannot feel duty because he is disloyal. I am disgusted by him. VOTE TRUMP OUT."

Captain "Sully" Sullenberger on Trump calling American soldiers as, "losers and suckers." Chesley Burnett Sullenberger III is a retired Air Force fighter pilot and an Airline Pilot. Among his several outstanding performances was when he captained Flight 1549, an Airbus A320 on January 15, 2009 taking off from LaGuardia Airport in New York City. Shortly after takeoff, the plane struck a flock of Canada geese and lost power in both engines. Quickly determining he would be unable to reach either LaGuardia or Teterboro airport, Sullenberger piloted the plane to a crash landing on the Hudson River. All one hundred and fifty-five passengers on board survived and were rescued by nearby boats.

"I am a Republican vote for Biden. Trump ignores the truth, facts, and science. He does not fully appreciate public policy matters, including public health, the economy and foreign relations, nor does he seem to learn. Trump is a bully who lacks a moral compass. Joe Biden would bring back civility." Rick Snyder, Michigan's former Republican Governor, endorsed Joe Biden for the presidential election held on November 3, 2020.

"He is going to get worse before November 2020 by going lower and lower. This is a demagogue in action. People think he's a strongman when he is truly weak. He is afraid if he loses in 2020, he will go to jail." John Dean, former attorney General during the Nixon Administration from July 1970 until April 1973.

"I know funny, and the state of the country today is no laughing matter. Untold American lives have been ruined by the presidency of Donald Trump. The rule of law is imperiled, our unity has been shattered, the service sector has been obliterated, and major cities are suffering. In November, we must vote in historic numbers, gathering all the 'snowflakes' until there's a blizzard on Capitol Hill that no corrupt politician can survive." Jim Carrey, Actor, Producer, Author, writer, and artist.

"Trump is a draft-dodging coward who: calls the wounded and fallen 'losers,' attacked a Gold Star Family, attacked a war hero John McCain when he lay dying…and even after death. Republicans used to call themselves the 'Pro-Military Party.' Now, they're just one thing: Pro-Trump." Ana Violeta Navarro-Cardenas. American political strategist and commentator. She is a member of the Republican Party.

Joanne Rogers, the widow of Mr. Rogers on Trump: "I think he's just a horrible person. If he's re-elected, I will go into mourning. I can't even imagine. I would feel so badly. Mr. Trump seldom tells the truth. I can't believe anything he says, not even the simplest thing. He is pathologically ill. Mentally ill."

"Trump is wrecking the country. There is a genuine mass of angry people who look at this man of no character, who lies all the time, and say, we've got to stick with this fellow. It's just confounding. I hope Joe Biden wins." Retired Army four-star General McCaffrey.

"How many 'last straws' can there be before the nation finally sees trump as a demented, dysfunctional threat to our success and even survival." Laurence Tribe, Professor of Constitutional Law at Harvard Law School.

"Trump has lost the right and authority to be commander in chief. His despicable comments used to describe the honorable men and women in uniform, especially those who have given the last full measure, demonstrated the lack of respect for those he is charged to lead. He must go." Anthony C. Zinni, retired Four Star Marine General.

Seventy-three Republican National Security Officials endorsed Joe Biden and deemed Trump as "dangerously unfit" for president. In a joint statement, most of the signees who were senior officials and who served under Presidents Ronald Reagan, George H.W. Bush, George W. Bush, and Donald Trump issued a joint statement reflecting their disappointment and lack of faith in Trump. Some had served in the country's top defense and intelligence roles.

The US mass media named several well-known prominent officials who issued a group statement siding with Biden. Among them were four-star General Michael Hayden of the US Air Force and former CIA chief, former FBI and CIA chief William Webster, former National Intelligence director Michael Leiter, and Air Force secretary Mike Donley. General Hayden had earlier said that he was extremely disappointed with the functioning of Trump at the Oval Office. The group accused Trump of "aligning himself with dictators and human rights abusers," including North Korea's Kim Jong-un and Russia's Vladimir Putin, attempting to undermine the rule of law, failing to lead America through the pandemic, attacking and vilifying immigrants, and "gravely" damaging the U.S. role as a world leader. The signees believed Joe Biden would restore the dignity of the presidency and reassert America's role as a global leader.

Their joint statement further stated that "While we like all Americans had hoped that Donald Trump would govern wisely, he has disappointed millions of voters who put their faith in him and has demonstrated that he is dangerously unfit to serve another term."

Notes include excerpts from the writings of Jemina McEvoy, Forbes Magazine. August 20, 2020

"Scientific American Magazine" editors endorsed Joe Biden for president, the first time the magazine backed any presidential candidate in its 175-year history. The magazine editors said that they were motivated to back

Joe Biden for the Presidential elections after witnessing how science was ignored and politicized by Donald Trump.

> "The evidence and the science show that Donald Trump has irreparably damaged the U.S. and its people – because he rejects evidence and science," the editors of "Scientific American" wrote in their endorsement. They cited the president's response to the coronavirus pandemic, which has killed more than 195,000 Americans and continues to be a public health emergency." (In mid-February 2021, the fatality figures in the USA neared half a million)

"There are millions of people who share his anger, paranoia and his hatred. That's what bothers me. It really sounds like the dumbing down of America. Some of the people I talk to have a frenzy line between the constitution and the Bible. I think we have to stop a man who wants to be 'The Dictator.' It bothers me that people can't read him…it's such a bare exposure of greed and the lust for power." Richard Wayne Van Dyke` (Dick Van Dyke, born December 13, 1924), writer, actor, and singer.

The above documented statements and reflections from outstanding persons in the United States of America, who had honorably served the country in several fields and been globally held in esteem, bear witness to their minds and thoughts, regarding the political affairs under Trump's administration and its implications.

The question was whether Trump was seriously considered the epitome of controversies and misdeeds to befall the US Nation since he took office. He would have furthered those miseries in the future, or even continued to be the architect of more calamities, if reelected or stayed indefinitely in power, since he had repeatedly claimed that he should be president until the year 2033. Born on June 14, 1946, he will then be eighty-seven years old. Judging from a myriad of health issues that he suffers from; it would be a cumbersome task to predict that wish of Trump and the stipulations of the Constitution that a United States of America's president could serve only two terms of four years each if at all elected for the second time.

Trump was questioned by the mass media on many occasions if he seriously meant that he would continue his position in the White House, while feigning a smile he angrily refused to answer.

Unemployment rose albeit the administration's assurances, while enrollment in health care (President Obama's major contribution to the US Nation) gradually dwindled by about twelve million. The COVD-19 spread through every corner of the country. And to remind, in several sessions of interviews, Trump had told the journalist and writer Bob Woodward that he had downplayed the dangers posed by the virus, albeit being fully aware of the death and destruction it could cause.

It is a known fact that lies, false promises, and deceitful tactics is the usual "work-order" of uncouth politicians. Judging from the performance of Trump, knowing fully well that Trump's unpredictable and violent behavior and actions, whether reckless or fraught with folly, also engulfed the larger part of the world and drowned mankind in utter misery.

Trump, Religion, his Soothsayers and Backscratchers

Trump never spoke of his religious beliefs until he focused on the Presidency. His longtime spiritual advisor, since 2002, a certain Paula White-Cain who headed the New Destiny Christian Center claimed that her relationship with the President was the result of a direct "assignment" from God, who directed her to "show him who I am!"

The controversial pastor at the central Florida-based New Destiny Center was notoriously known for her luxurious lifestyle and preaching the "Prosperity Gospel" which tells followers that the more they donate to her Church (to her personally) the more God will be pleased and bless them!

The writer Jessica Glenza in "The Guardian" wrote that like many people surrounding Trump, Paula White-Cain was controversial, ill-mannered, and semi-literate. She was alternatively described as a charlatan and heretic. Her Florida Ministry and Evangelism made her a millionaire but also attracted scrutiny from Congressional investigators.

The thrice married Paula White-Cain had no educational eruditions. A private investigator who requested anonymity said he was amazed at the ignorance and poor education of Paula White. She found it embarrassingly difficult to properly pronounce the name of countries or answer the location of certain countries or major cities of the world.

She claimed that it was she who advised Trump to officially move the US embassy to Jerusalem thus identifying Jerusalem as the capital of Israel. "God told me and I in turn told the President who immediately obeyed the commands of God through me!"

After a prolonged silence, the dubious Paula White surfaced again in the second week of October 2019 at a book signing ceremony, she showed outbursts of emotions about her controversial life, and simultaneously showed her profound delight at being introduced to Trump who like her had been married several times.

She claimed that she had been charged with a divine mission ordered by God to "save" the American nation through Trump. "God had personally communicated this particular instruction to me to unforgettably relay it to the nation and also the world in general."

Paula White noting that Trump's popularity had been falling while his follies, illegal activities and wrongdoings were being more exposed and scrutinized by the Press and among the general public claimed: "One thing I said, I'll never do politics, but when it came down to it, it wasn't about doing politics, it was an assignment – to say no to President Trump would be saying no to God, and I won't do that." While sitting at the desk bedecked with her books and with just a handful of buyers, she refused to answer as to in which language God had communicated with her.

In an article dated November 7, 2019, Andrea Jefferson, a popular journalist wrote: "Paula White is a Florida pastor who led a prayer at Donald Trump's inauguration, chairs his Evangelical Advisory Council, and is now a White House employee with her salary paid for by the American taxpayer."

Befitting her association with an administration occupied by a much-disliked former reality TV star who had spent his life affiliating with various fraud enthusiasts, she was often introduced as "Dr. Paula," without even an undergraduate degree or seminary degree of any kind. Paula White lived a comically luxurious lifestyle despite having driven her previous church into bankruptcy.

Well known scholar, ethicist, and theologian Russell D. Moore, (Ph.D. in Systematic Theology) said that "Paula White is a charlatan and recognized as a heretic by every orthodox Christian, of whatever tribe."

In 2010, Paula White was photographed with controversial prosperity gospel preacher Benny Hinn, a self-acclaimed "faith healer" while the latter was married. Paula White's marital status was unknown at that time.

Benny Hinn has been accused of open fraudulent practices of "healing" the sick, the cripples and those near death." The public now ask since he has "healed" countless people on stage (all of them actors paid to play the role of a terminally sick and dying person who have been miraculously healed by his dramatic gestures) with his power to heal, why does he not visit hospitals and heal all those on the verge of death!

Benny Hinn at times grew angry when confronted of the falsity and hypocrisy of his deeds and claimed all that he does flows from God! "God communicates with me at regular intervals with instructions and I follow them all."

Both Benny Hinn and Paula White, when questioned separately of their affair, claimed God had played an important role in their meeting. Both Benny Hinn and Paula White refused to comment as to how and in which language God communicated with them.

Benny Hinn, a multi-millionaire, obviously through the donations of the unwitting millions, had in the first week of September 2019, rejected the concept of "Prosperity Theology and Gospel" as being an unacceptable act! Hinn's wealth had been estimated at forty-two million dollars after preaching the "Prosperity Gospel" for decades. Nearly two hundred men and women preachers adhere to this type of gospel in the United States alone.

Paula White regularly appears into the "limelight." In early 2018, she suggested that people across the country send her all their earnings for the month of January, or face damnation from God!

Considering the population of the United States in the vicinity of three hundred and thirty million and with some two hundred million working (this excludes the one percent of the population who are millionaires and billionaires) with a monthly pay of two thousand dollars, this adds to an unbelievable and a mind-boggling amount.

Trump's spiritual adviser also claimed that she was in fact doing a service to the people of the country by asking them to send her their income for the month of January since it would transform their lives and furthermore, sending their money to her ministries to honor the religious principles of "first fruit," which she emphasized that all "firsts" belong to God, including the first harvest and, apparently, the first month of your salary. "Receive God's blessings by sending me your money. It will save you and prove beneficial. Reap rewards after rewards by sending me money. Let the money flow in!" This is a complete misrepresentation of the Judeo-Christian tradition of tithe, ten percent of the harvest goes to the poor and needy in the community.

In the first week of November 2019, Paula White again made headlines! This time, she sensed the legal problems that Trump was facing through his contacts with foreign powers in tracking or even finding some sort of illegality with the son of former Vice President Joe Biden, whom Trump considered a danger to his 2020 reelection. After the election, Paula White accused that enemies of Trump had somehow engaged the services of demonic forces and used witchcraft to defeat Trump in the 2020 presidential elections.

In an article dated February 20, 2020, journalist Michael Stone reported that Paula White claims she "saw the face of God" while visiting heaven before being sent back to the White House. In a video recorded earlier,

Paula White tells a selected small congregation, that she had a "divine encounter" where she saw the "face of God!"

Trump's spiritual adviser told her ecstatic and frenzied crowd who reached their hands to her as if seeking her blessings that: "I literally went to the throne room of God. There was a mist that was coming off the water, and I went to the throne of God, and I didn't see God's face clearly, but I saw the face of God...I knew it was the face of God! And then God placed a mantle on me, and it was a very distinct mantle, and I saw it very distinctly, the color was like goldish, a yellowish goldish... and then I saw the earth for a moment, and then God brought me back, and he put me in certain places, one being the White House, one being certain continents."

At the end of what she had claimed to be an ethereally transmitted sermon to the wonderful and specially selected audience, the small gathering went into ruptures of praise to the "lord" for having created Trump and beside him the "heavenly Paula White!"

Paula White who had been aggressively advocating the cause of "Prosperity Gospel" had been officially employed by Trump in the White House position in the Office of Public Liaison. Her job description was described as; "Adviser to the faith and opportunity initiative" with the common taxpayer footing her salary! Her yearly salary was unknown. She joined Trump's coterie of informal religious advisers whose main job was to heap praise on Trump, albeit his continuous harangues and statements, nearly all of them laced with falsehood, baseless accusations, and obfuscations. Most of them lack simple general knowledge but appear to be well versed in the art of dramatics. The fact was that they acted as soothsayers to Trump who eagerly awaited to hear words praising him.

The last week of September 2019, Lance Wallnau, an extremist, a known Trump supporter, and an evangelical activist, passed scatological remarks against the enemies of Trump, especially Democrat members of Congress. Arguing against the possibility of commencing impeachment procedures against Trump for treason and sedition said: "If an impeachment were to happen, it would be going against the wishes of 'Six hundred million

Americans' and this would create a dangerous situation within the country." According to official statistics the US population (2020) did not exceed three hundred and thirty million people.

On March 22, 2019, Pat Robertson, a businessman-preacher described as a fraudulent person with tens of millions in cash, said that "Trump has been a fantastic president for the faith community" and added that; "In fact God told me last night that Donald Trump's name has been written in the Book of Life. He's guaranteed a place in heaven. In fact, he will also be a real estate mogul in heaven and have his own Trump Towers."

Yet another Trump "backscratcher" was a former prison inmate sentenced for embezzlement and financial fraud, Televangelist Jim Bakker. While being led to prison, Bakker was shown crying for mercy. On February 11, 2020, Bakker, the former imprisoned convict said; "I was sleeping last night, and God came to me and showed me a vision of the White House and there were pictures of presidents on the walls. I saw pictures of Donald Trump Jr., Ivanka, Eric, Barron and even some Trumps not even born. I believe that God was showing me the holy Trump line will go on because they are doing His work." Bakker claimed that God informed him that should Trump be ousted from the presidency or not reelected in 2020, there would be a civil war with bloody consequences.

Jim Bakker was indicted in 1988 after a sixteen-month grand-jury probe on eight counts of mail fraud, fifteen counts of wire fraud and one count of conspiracy. In 1989, after a five-week trial which began on August 28 in Charlotte, North Carolina, a jury found him guilty on all 24 counts and sentenced Bakker to forty-five years in Federal Prison and imposed on him a half million dollars fine. After a new trial upon Bakker's request, the sentence was reduced to eight years but was paroled in July 1994. He owed six million dollars to the Internal Revenue Service. In 1996, Bakker eschewed further the "prosperity Gospel" claiming that he had enough time to read the Bible in full while in prison and that he had realized that he had taken passages out of context and used them as proof texts to support his prosperity theology.

Trump had the ignominy of being associated with questionable characters sharing his own thoughts and of the same mental caliber. His opprobrium of having relations to persons in his Cabinet were as vile, vicious, and poorly tutored as himself was self-evident.

Stephen A. Crockett Jr. in an article dated January 31, 2019 in the "Root" wrote "Trump is not a liar. A liar is someone who occasionally writes mistruth. Trump is a broken firehose of lies. He's a broken slot machine of lies. He's a lie conveyor belt."

Trump had claimed (Monday, February 4, 2019) that America was "starting to make a turn back" to a time when Bible study was big in public schools.

Holy Nonsense, Trump and Abettors Hand in Hand

What form of politics and what form of government and administration Trump followed was as murky as his upbringing, mind, decisions, lifestyle, and philosophy. It is unknown, a total mystery, as to what form of government or administration prevailed in the United States of America with a mercurial "inspiring dictator" heading it.

Was it a form of "mob-rule" masquerading as some form of Theocracy or "Kakistocracy" or perhaps "Kleptocracy" or perhaps the initials of a dictatorship to follow through the aegis of a camarilla located elsewhere from the USA? Or were those very persons who earlier swept him to the realms of power through the manipulation of the ballot box and the invisible Electoral College steering the country?

Trump was seen on television surrounded by deceitful millionaire preachers and soothsayers holding hands in a circle while immersed in a spiritual trance. Trump was everything except divinely inspired as had been proven by his actions through the years with dozens of legal cases pending against him.

Trump on Thursday, February 20, 2020, at a rally in Colorado Springs, Colorado attended by carefully selected paid supporters and professional agitators said: "I would prefer to be the president of the United States for the next twenty-six years, till I am one hundred years old!" Later, when confronted by a few brave journalists who questioned his statements, in whispers Trump said: "I was joking!" Meanwhile, the paid agitators had believed his words, showed delight that he would be the President of the United States for the next quarter century or even more.

Earlier, before Trump had taken the stage to present his "sermon," words had spread among the small unsuspecting crowd, through the organizers of the rally, that either Paula White or Pastor Robert Jeffress, the two notorious spiritual advisers of Trump, had each seen visions where God told them that Trump will be the President till he is one hundred years old and that Trump will personally reveal it, since he too had the same vision and signs from God!

Trump's belief and his claimed religious and divine inclinations were revealed through his utter ignorance and inability to quote any statement or word from the Bible, whether the Old Testament or the New Testament.

Professor Reza Aslan, world famed scholar of Religion and author (in early April 2017) spoke of the fundamentalist Christians and the role of heads of their churches in US politics.

Professor Aslan said: "Are fundamentalist Christians a dangerous religious cult? Possible. Trump has much of his evangelical fan-base believing that he's somehow been anointed by God to become President. Never mind the Russian election scandal, his affairs with porn stars and unwarranted sexual acts towards women, or his inability to remember even a single Bible verse when asked Evangelical Christians are abandoning their core moral beliefs to follow as someone who exhibits every trademark of a cult leader."

Elsewhere in his statements, Professor Aslan said: "Eighty-one percent of white evangelicals voted for Donald Trump in the previous election. That's a record. That's more white evangelicals that voted for George W. Bush-and George W. Bush was a white evangelical. This makes no sense to people, especially when you consider that Trump is not just the most irreligious person in modern history, that his entire worldview makes a mockery of core Christian values like humility and empathy and care for the poor; that this individual who couldn't even name a single verse in the Bible, and yet received a record number of votes by white evangelicals."

One of the pivotal reasons, in Trump receiving such a large number of white evangelical votes, argues Professor Aslan, that it has to do with the pernicious influence of something called the "prosperity gospel" which has gripped the imaginations of white evangelicals. "That is the version of Christianity preached by these fraudsters like Joel Osteen and T.D. Jakes, the essential gist of which is that God wants you to drive a Bentley, that Jesus really wants for you is material prosperity-and indeed that's how you know God has blessed you, is by your material prosperity."

It would be only justifying presenting these "men of God" who have been coaxing the superstitious masses for the past decade and more to part with their money, thereby enriching themselves at the cost of mostly poor people who have been virtually mesmerized to believe what flows from their mouth as godly and ethereal statements directly from God, but through them! It is not a mystery or an arcane subject as to how these "men of God" earned such money. The "art" of suggestion and theatrics and delivering sheer lies to the unsuspecting untutored people desperately searching ways and means to escape the realities of life lies the answer. They just give whatever they have to the wily preacher.

Thomas Dexter Jakes is a burly African American who claims to regularly communicate with God, speaks in "tongues" and who feels proud of having his DNA traced back to the Igbo tribe of south Nigeria.

Jakes the preacher has asked his audience to research his rich heritage and lineage. An unbiased research speaks of the Igbo people who were until the late twentieth century a large tribe scattered in the southern sector of present-day Nigeria who still preferred to live in simple dwellings and were a modern day "hunter gatherers." It has also been proved that a significant percentage of the slaves brought into the Americas were from there.

Thomas Dexter Jakes is not the only preacher besides Joel Osteen whose hands are deep in the pockets of the poor and lesser privileged who live on a paltry income in their lives but made to part even with that petty amount, based on the powers of suggestions of these charlatans. There are other preachers who live and exist through the business of "prosperity gospel" in relieving the public from whatever they have on the promise that God would multiply their offerings of cash at least seven-fold at minimum, ten at normal if not, more. If the donor does not receive their expected rewards, as is the usual case, he is curtly reminded that he or she has not donated enough.

Videos of these "holy actors" on stage when closely monitored, reveal that all of them share a "standard method" of misleading their audience with limited phrases. Among them, scolding and chiding the population for not donating enough to the cause of God through them (the preachers) comparing their religion with other religions and beliefs while mocking other major religions and beliefs in the world and often encouraging the audience for having paid an appreciable amount as "donation" last time and asking for more to appease God! Most standard statement is that the people have invited the wrath of God, for not contributing "plentiful donations" to the cause of God, whom they represent!

In simple terms, these preachers have a message for their unsuspecting audience: "God is in danger, this Church and congregation are all in danger! Help God, help this Church! Send your offerings to God at the earliest possible...but at my address!"

They could be seen on their television programs arrogantly flaunting their expensive rings and gold and platinum chains with a "extra-large cross" while "Simple Simons" in the audience cheer them at a signal from the "floor director" stationed among these unsuspecting people. Most of these "men of God" have refused to speak with journalists about their abilities (of healing and treating the sick and dying) or their true intentions in life, except for the known fact that they are being labelled as scoundrels and crooks. Time and often they were shown to have either flown into a rage or even attacked the journalists for having dared to expose them. Their source of income is from spreading "fantastic rewards for those paying" and "lesser damnation" among the ignorant and uneducated people, some of them with a valueless High School Certificate or at best, with a worthless College education.

"I was getting into theology and studying the roots of the Bible, but then I started to discover the man-made nature of it. I started seeing things that made me ask, 'is God really speaking through this instrument?' My eyes opened to the reality of the Bible being just a document to control people." Woody Tracy Harrelson, American playwright, and actor.

"There is a cult of ignorance in the United States, and there always has been. The strain of anti-intellectualism has been a constant thread winding its way through our political and cultural life, nurtured by the false notion that democracy means that any ignorance is just as good as your knowledge." Isaac Asimov, American writer, and professor of biochemistry. (January 2, 1920 – April 6, 1992)

"Cruel men believe in a cruel God and use their belief to excuse their cruelty." Bertrand Russell, British polymath, philosopher, logician, mathematician, historian writer, social critic, political activist, and Nobel laureate. Bertrand Arthur William Russell (May 18, 1872 – February 2, 1970)

"And what I'm willing to do, which the mainstream church is not, is to denounce the Christian right as Christian heretics. You don't have to, as I did, spend three years at Harvard Divinity School to realize that Jesus didn't come to make us rich. And he certainly didn't come to make Pat Robertson and Joel Osteen (two notorious multi-millionaire evangelists) rich. And what they have done is to acculturate the worst aspects of American Imperialism, capitalism, chauvinism, and violence and bigotry into the Christian religion." Chris Hedges, American Pulitzer Prize-winning journalist, Presbyterian minister, author, and television host.

All said, not all preachers are self-serving in the name of religion. Not all are scoundrels and felons. They have not taken Christianity as a hostage unto themselves to milk their audience. They form the vast percentage compared to the unscrupulous preachers who are in the minority but extremely garrulous, vociferous and have millions of dollars in their accounts.

A recent study revealed there are more than a hundred thousand Christian preachers of various denominations in the USA alone, fifteen thousand of whom are identified as "petty" charlatans who suffice with an "income" of a few thousand dollars a week, to the "major" charlatans who are not satisfied with even a few hundred thousand dollars a week. Trained in the art of "mental-manipulation," these "confident-tricksters" time and often claim that God has given them the wealth they have, and that the public could also have that, but only if they "donate" to God through them! But the vast majority, ten times that number of preachers with moral scruples and convictions eclipse the fraudulent ones.

Trump, despite being accused of being a philanderer and a professional fraud, had an appreciable number of garrulous evangelical supporters, who were in turn accused as being fraudulent and had even spent prison terms. In simple words, all these television evangelists wholeheartedly support Trump and his way of life, that mocks and challenges the very precepts of Christianity!

Jim Bakker, a former television evangelist who spent years in prison for fraud, claimed that God anointed Trump and blessed him to be the President of the country.

During the campaign, a certain Franklin Graham, son of the late evangelist Billy Graham and Trump's most enthusiastic supporter, dismissed Trump's moral failings by comparing him favorably to the flawed patriarchs and prophets of the Bible; Moses and David. Franklin Graham has said in public that God anointed and appointed Trump to be the President of the United States of America. He also claimed that Trump's extra-marital affairs had nothing to do with the public and claimed that Trump's third and present wife, a Slovenian woman whose past life was questionable and shrouded in mystery, as someone incredibly special, although her nude and suggestive pictures presented her as not leading a chaste life.

Franklin Graham has repeatedly dodged questions as to what his real profession in life is or what does he do for a living! He is known to lead a very ostentatious life, unabashedly, as he says, with the money of the public. "They donate to my cause and I do not hesitate to take that opportunity. Let the money flow in. I will accept anything that is hard currency in the name of Jesus!"

Franklin Graham has on many an occasion demeaned not only Islam but also the Prophet of Islam. Indirectly, he has scorned the nearly two billion Muslims of the world. He has also condemned Catholics, and the Pope without knowing the true essence of Catholicism. He has insulted and belittled Muslims, Catholics, Mormons, The African Americans, Buddhists, Hindus and to an extent the Jews. On Hinduism Graham said: "No elephant with hundred arms can do anything for me. None of their nine thousand gods is going to lead me to salvation." On Islam he said, "Islam is a religion of hatred. It's a religion of war!" He has made more controversial remarks about Islam and Muslims. In a March 2011 interview with "Newsmax," Graham said the 2011 earthquake and tsunami in Japan "may be" the second coming and Armageddon."

He had also threatened those who dare to contradict and challenge his statements and lectures with dire consequences which he did not elaborate, then toned it down through legal means, insisting that he was and is exercising his "freedom of speech and opinion!"

Claiming to be a globally respected person and a man of God, he insisted he was qualified to render his opinion on any subject for the betterment of true Christianity. His message to his detractors is usually laced with threats. At the same time, he does not condone the freedom of speech and thoughts of others who describe him as a money-minded opportunist, a professional agitator, a provocateur, and a scoundrel.

Graham, who is Chief Executive Officer of the Billy Graham Evangelistic Association and of Samaritan's Purse, had, on many occasions and in his several lectures at seminaries, claimed that the Constitution of the United

States of America is based on Christian beliefs and values that the founding fathers emphasized this fact.

In truth, Graham has openly lied about this. Documents reflected below testify to Franklin Grahams deceitful tactics and forged claims.

1. "Christianity is the most perverted system that ever shone on man."- Thomas Jefferson
2. "The hocus-pocus phantasm of a God like another Cerberus, with one body and three heads, had its birth and growth in the blood of thousands and thousands of martyrs." -Thomas Jefferson
3. "It is too late in the day for men of sincerity to pretend they believe in the Platonic mysticisms that three are one, and one is three; and yet the one is not three, and the three are not one." - Thomas Jefferson
4. "There is not one redeeming feature in our superstition of Christianity. It has made one half the world fools, and the other half hypocrites." - Thomas Jefferson
5. "Lighthouses are more useful than churches." - Ben Franklin
6. "The way to see by faith is to shut the eye of reason." - Ben Franklin
7. "I looked around for God's judgments but saw no signs of them." - Ben Franklin
8. "In the affairs of the world, men are saved not by faith, but by the lack of it." - Ben Franklin
9. "This would be the best of all possible worlds if there were no religion in it." - John Adams.
10. "The New Testament, they tell us, is founded upon the prophecies of the Old; if so, it must follow the fate of its foundation." - Thomas Paine
11. "Of all the tyrannies that affect mankind, tyranny in religion is the worst." - Thomas Paine
12. "I do not believe in the creed professed by the Jewish Church, by the Roman Church, by the Greek Church, by the Turkish Church, by the Protestant Church, nor by any Church that I know of. My own mind is my own Church. Each of those churches accuse the

other of unbelief; and for my own part, I disbelieve them all." - Thomas Paine

13. "All national institutions of churches, whether Jewish, Christian or Turkish, appear to me no other than human inventions, set up to terrify and enslave mankind, and monopolize power and profit." - Thomas Paine

14. "It is the fable of Jesus Christ, as told in the New Testament, and the wild and visionary doctrine raised thereon, against which I contend. The story, taking it as it is told, is blasphemously obscene." - Thomas Paine

15. "Religious controversies are always productive of more acrimony and irreconcilable hatreds than those which springs from any other cause. Of all the animosities which have existed among mankind, those which are caused by the difference of sentiments in religion appear to be the most inveterate and distressing, and ought most to be depreciated. I was in hopes that the enlightened and liberal policy, which has marked the present age, would at least have reconciled Christians of every denomination so far that we should never again see the religious disputes carried to such a pitch as to endanger the peace of society." - George Washington

16. "The Bible is not my book, nor Christianity my profession." - Abraham Lincoln

17. "It may not be easy, in every possible case, to trace the line of separation between the rights of religion and the Civil authority with such distinctness as to avoid collisions and doubts on unessential points. The tendency to usurpation on one side or the other, or to a corrupting coalition or alliance between them, will be best guarded against by an entire abstinence of the Gov't from inference in any way whatsoever, beyond the necessity of preserving public order, and protecting each sect against trespasses on its legal rights by others." - James Madison

18. "Religious bondage shackles and debilitates the mind and unfits it for every noble enterprise." - James Madison

Robert Jeffress, the pastor of the First Baptist Church in Dallas, told a talk radio audience that Trump was a better presidential candidate than someone else who "embodies" the teaching of Jesus" because Trump fits the biblical preference for a "strongman" in government. Jeffress had even gone to the point of hailing Trump as an apostle of Christ!

Frank Amedia, an Ohio pastor who briefly had ties to the Trump campaign, explicitly cast the president as a prophet receiving divine revelations: "I believe he receives downloads that now he's beginning to understand come from God," he said in July 2017.

Without being in the least aware of the "exalted and ethereal" position bestowed on him by unscrupulous opportunists, Trump really imagined in his feeble mind that there lies a "halo of superhuman glory" upon him.

On claims that he (Trump) had revived the faith of the public in Christianity, researcher and journalist Mark Chancy of the Washington Post stated that there was no such time in American history.

Mark Taylor an obscure self-proclaimed Prophet of Christianity and a close friend of Trump on July 26, 2019 made a prediction to journalist Daniel Ott and a few days earlier to a small crowd of his supporters. Mark Taylor had considered the deep unpopularity that the majority of the US nation had harbored against Trump and his family members for using the Presidential Office to enrich himself and his fraudulent means in life, which had endangered his second term as very slim, he said; "if he will be reelected, Trump will release the cures for Alzheimer's and other terminal diseases." He went to the extent in his earlier statements to his supporters to spread his heavenly prophecies among those who were sick and dying to vote for Trump, in case they need to be healed!

Evangelist Pastor Rick Wiles was a regular supporter and apologist of Trump. He is the founder of "TruNews," a website notorious for promoting racist and anti-Jewish conspiracy theories, in which he regularly lays blames of all kinds of ills and torments afflicting the world on Jews. Pastor Wiles is also a senior pastor at "Flowing Streams Church" in Vero Beach, Florida.

In late October 2019, Wiles sensing the danger of Trump being ousted from Office for endangering the safety of the United States, by Russia and or China or simultaneously from both, before the 2020 elections, told journalist Andrew Simpson; "I warn the American public that if Trump is removed from Office, his supporters will 'hunt down' the people who did this to him." Months earlier he had told his congregation that "God's wrath shall befall those and their entire families who will not vote for Trump."

Another staunch supporter of Trump was Evangelical Bishop Edir Macedo Bezerra of the "Universal Church of the Kingdom of God." He had argued on a weekly basis that daughters should not be allowed to seek out higher education because if they do, they will be smarter than their husbands. The Brazilian Pentecostal Bishop is reported to be worth in excess of 1.1 Billion dollars. In the first week of October 2019, Macedo explained that he would not allow his daughters to go to college because he believes that an educated woman cannot have a happy marriage.

Rick Joyner, another close friend of Trump and a self-acclaimed "man of God" before and after the Presidential elections in 2016 began to praise Trump to lofty heights, time and often comparing Trump to the disciples of Christ!

Joyner, who has been accused of being a money-minded opportunist, to this day; perhaps sensing the imminence of Trump either being ousted through impeachment (on charges of treason and complicity with foreign powers and even sedition) or losing the Presidency at the 2020 elections recommended his "mantra" of lauding Trump; "If you look at the disciples that Jesus chose, they were all Donald Trump, each and every disciple of Jesus were Donald Trumps."

Time and often Trump had portrayed himself as a man of "god" who enjoys "good relations" with "god!" He had indirectly indicated that he consulted God whenever he did not feel like trusting his advisors or those near him or even his appointees in the administration. "I enjoy very special relations with God since a very long time and each time, I call upon God, I receive heavenly voices telling me what to do."

Trump had repeatedly invoked the Constitution of the United States of America without ever having read it properly, since he had claimed that the Constitution is based on Jesus and Christianity. The Constitution says otherwise. In the entire Constitution containing 4,534 words, there is no such term or words pertaining to "God." "Jesus," "Christianity," or "Bible." This also challenges the false claims of Franklin Graham, the provocateur, preacher, and messenger of hatred and malice.

Trump often spoke about his religious upbringing on the campaign trail, but the church where he was a member stated that he was not an active member.

On Tuesday, February 5, 2019 Pastor David Lewicki stated: "Not only I was the pastor of New York City's Marble Collegiate Church for about five years where Trump was on the member rolls, I have never seen Trump at the church. Not a Bible study, not a service. Never. I did not see this individual on any given day there were Church services, unless and until he managed to make himself invisible. I was not in the least interested to either greet him or shake his hands, knowing too well that he would claim that he had donated a large amount to any of the pastors in the church."

One of the pastors of Marble Collegiate Church requesting anonymity, said that he had never come across a person more deceitful and a prolific liar than Trump. "His demeanor was intimidating, insincere and laced with falsehood."

The Huffington Post stated that Trump's relationship with the Christian faith as insincere adding although he won support among evangelicals, he has an odd history of bungling his Bible references, once calling the New Testament "book 2 Corinthians" usually referred to as "Second Corinthians" – as "Two Corinthians."

Speaking of those claiming to have direct link with God, such as Paula White-Cain, Trump, and hundreds, if not thousands of preachers, priests, and pastors in the USA, one is reminded of the following lines by Oscar Wilde (1854-1900):

"Religion is like a blind man looking in a black room for a black cat that isn't there and finding it!"

Speaking of Trump and the mendacious "elite" that he had appointed through God to serve the US Nation, one must not harbor any hopes from him nor his appointees of peace and prosperity, who were stealthily dragging the country toward an Authoritarian State, while stealthily yet feverishly working toward turning this aspiring dictator into a full-fledged dictator by investing in him plenipotentiary powers to do as he pleased. Most unfortunate were his foxy soothsayers, opportunists, yes-men, lackeys, and back-scratchers who nodded in consent, applauded, and never questioned the legality and logic of whatever would be the outcome of his deeds and plans.

Trump Achievements

Trump claimed many "achievements," very few of which could be verified. He had however, enacted some activities, which he claimed would be beneficial to the nation. Prior to the 2016 presidential elections, he had vociferously promised to build a wall alongside the US-Mexican border just to appeal to his xenophobic base. Official statistics showed during his administration, work on 350 miles of replacement or secondary barrier (wall) were completed, while under construction was 221 miles of new and replacement primary and secondary barrier. A total of 157 miles of pre-construction activity involving new, primary, and secondary barriers were undertaken. Before he took office, there were 654 miles of barricades to stop pedestrians and 300 miles of anti-vehicle fencing. However, Trump did not make a distinction between these new stretches of barrier and replacement structures, regarding both as new wall. What Trump had built was far from what he promised at the start of his 2016 election campaign, when he pledged to build a concrete wall along the border's entire 2000-mile length. The wall is not made of concrete but steel strips with enough spacing to view the other side. Some amount of concrete was used to anchor the posts stationed at a distance.

His tax-cuts benefitted billionaires and those who "donated" to his election campaign. The exact and official amount is unknown but said to be in the tens of billions of US Dollars.

He had undone, cancelled, and rolled back every beneficial Law, Act and Legislation that President Obama had signed into law.

Statements made by the general population against Trump's imagined achievements appear to be uniquely similar in that they condemn him as a factor in destroying their lives.

"Whatever Obama did for us; Trump has undone it."

"Whatever Obama gave us to augment and further improve our lifestyle and livelihood, Trump snatched it from us."

Most befitting are the lines from Henry Louis Mencken (1880-1956):

"The whole aim of practical politics is the keep the populace alarmed - and hence glamorous to be led to safety, be menacing it with an endless series of hobgoblins, all of them imaginary!"

Trump's Mental Condition

Trump's regular accusations, explicit insults heaped on his true or imagined enemies, conflicting and unsubstantiated claims became the subject of interest to psychiatrists and doctors throughout the country.

Calum Stuart writing in "Political State" in late April 2019 states that "Experts reveal Trump's erratic behavior could be due to an untreated Sexually Transmitted Disease as Americans recoil in horror!"

Dr. Steven Beutler, a specialist on infectious disease and Internal Medicine, believed there must be some explanation for the bizarre, flighty, volatile behavior from Trump, and he thought that behavior may be the signs of an undiagnosed and untreated sexually transmitted disease: Syphilis.

In a book titled "The Dangerous Case of Donald Trump" released in October 3, 2017, Dr. Bandy Xenobia Lee, a world-renowned forensic psychiatrist, M.D., M. Div., assistant clinical professor Yale Law and Psychiatry Division, Co-founder and director of the Violence and Health Study Group for the MacMillan Center for International and Area Studies; as well as co-leader of Academic Collaborators for the World Health Organization's Violence Prevention Alliance strongly supported a team with the working title "Duty to Warn." She and her staff felt an urgency to get the book into the hands of the public and governmental powers-that-be as soon as possible. As detailed in the following lines, Dr. John Gartner led the team.

Dr. Lee's introduction explains in detail the risks, legal as well as professional, of writing a book like "The Dangerous Case." Those fully supporting Dr. Lee's historical awareness of Trump's dangers to the country and the world in general were Gail Sheehy; Lance Dodes, M.D., Training and Supervising Analyst at the Boston Psychoanalytic Society and Institute and retired Assistant Clinical Professor of Psychiatry at Harvard Medical School; Dr. John Gartner, Ph.D.; and Noam Chomsky, to name a few.

Dr. Lee's wisdom and opinions about the mental limitations of Trump became more apparent and read by millions on the internet when she reflected her approval at the writings of Dr. Mary Trump (niece of Donald Trump), and a clinical psychologist in her book; "Too Much and Never Enough: How My Family Created the World's Most Dangerous Man." Dr. Trump in her book strongly believed that her uncle suffers from several mental issues. "I have no problem calling Donald a narcissist – he meets all nine criteria as outlined in the Diagnostic and Statistical Manual of Mental Disorders," she wrote in the Book.

In her writings, Mary Trump suggests that Mr. Trump "meets the criteria for anti-social personality disorder and some of the dependent personality disorder."

Dr. Trump in her book also wrote that his (Donald Trump) pathologies and behaviors are so bizarre that "coming up with an accurate and comprehensive diagnosis would require a full battery of psychological and neuro-physical tests that he'll never sit for."

Dr. Lee who had fiercely campaigned to warn people about the president's mental status since the 2016 election, said most recently in the last week of July 2020, that she was "delighted" that Dr. Trump had drawn the same conclusions about the president's mental health.

"Any honest and competent mental health professional has come to the same conclusion," she said. Dr. Lee had worked since the day Trump was swept into Office by arcane hands, to raise awareness of what she saw as personality deficiencies that make Mr. Trump unfit to occupy the Oval Office.

Dr. Lee stated the reasons "lawmakers have been denying claims about the president's mental health for years" is indicative of the "poor state of mental health in our society."

Speaking of the president's boasting of how he "aced" a cognitive test, Dr. Lee said that "he is likely frantically trying to convince himself that he is mentally fit." She also suggested that Trump's attacks on Joe Biden the former Vice President, who appeared to be leading in the polls throughout the country, compared to Trump in the November 3, 2020 presidential election, are all just "defensive projection."

"Projection" is a way of disowning what you cannot tolerate in yourself by attaching it to others, and since his case is severe, what he says almost has nothing to do with Mr. Biden but is a very accurate portrayal of himself," Dr. Lee said.

Returning to Dr. John Gartner, who is the founder of "Duty to Warn," an organization of mental health professionals and laypersons who consider it their duty to warn patients, clients, and the community at large, when aware of potential danger. Dr. Gartner warned the US Nation that we were in dire trouble due to our president's mental instability. More than Sixty Thousand mental health professionals had signed Dr. Gartner's petition which states:

"We the undersigned mental health professionals, believe in our professional judgement that Donald Trump manifests a serious mental illness that renders him psychologically incapable of discharging the duties of President of the United States. And we respectfully request he be removed from office, according to Article 4 of the 25th Amendment to the Constitution, which states that the president will be replaced if he is 'unable to discharge the powers and duties of his office."

Dr. John Gartner detailed the reasons of potential dangers that Trump could pose on a global scale.

Some of the statements made by Trump reveal his imbalance and mental state. Dr. Gartner specializes in borderline personality disorder, bipolar disorder, and depression and he believes that Trump is suffering from an extremely dangerous mental illness, an illness that is identical to that suffered by Hitler, Mussolini, and Stalin.

In addition to the above statements, added impetus to this truth is an article by Eddie Krassenstein, journalist and author who presented a documented statement from Dr. Gartner on the illness and dangers posed by Trump in a widely read article dated January 30, 2019 on "Hill Reporter.com."

Some of the conspicuous statements are:

"Donald Trump truly has the most dangerous form of mental illness that you can find in a leader," Gartner told "KrassenCast," (Krassenstein's news media). "He suffers from a personality disorder called malignant narcissism. Malignant narcissism was introduced by Erich Fromm, the famed psychoanalyst, who himself escaped the Nazis. Malignant narcissism was his attempt to explain the psychology of dictators like Hitler or Stalin or Mussolini."

Gartner also said that that Malignant narcissism is a combination of four traits, which includes narcissism, paranoia, antisocial personality disorder (the psychology of a criminal and someone who routinely lies) and sadism.

241

"He has actually gotten intense pleasure from [other people's] pain. He is reveling in the chaos and the destruction he is causing," Gartner explained. "The more he feels threatened by the Mueller investigation (investigating Trump for fraudulent methods used in the presidential election and other wrongdoings for which he was subsequently impeached by the Congress. He was acquitted by the majority Republicans in the Senate, but not exonerated!), the more he needs to experience the exaltation of feeling drunk with power, through his ability to harm and humiliate and degrade other people."

Gartner also went into detail about how malignant narcissistic leaders tend to commit constant purges against their own staff. Hitler did this, as did Stalin and Saddam Hussein. Trump did this at a faster rate than any other president in American history.

Gartner also compared Trump's psychology to that of a "gangster who believes all kinds of crazy conspiracy theories."

Statements by Dr. John Gartner, Dr. Bandy Xenobia Lee and other academics including a host of Military generals, Admirals, and politicians testify to this simple fact that when renowned academics speak, serious steps by the nation's masses (in any country) must receive special attention to prevent potential danger and catastrophes by their pretentious leaders chosen to serve but in reality, usurpers of power and aspiring dictators, who if not ousted immediately will bring misery of untold magnitude, both locally, regionally and even globally. Trump's own garbled, contradictory, lies, deceitful tactics, falsehood and unsubstantiated allegations flowing from his own mouth could very well establish the fact that he was unable to serve as a public servant and the chief administrator of the USA and needed to be ousted and ousted fast!

Most recently the boldest and most straightforward article appeared on May 6, 2020 by journalist Jason Miciak in the "New York Daily News," one of the most popular major media in the country about the mental bearings of Trump and the unimaginable dangers and consequences he may pose to the nation and the world, perhaps alluring to the fact if in the White House for a second term.

The topic "The President is unwell" and "Analysts Jump to Agree" is noted for being to the point and documented. "Major insiders have noted that Trump has been mentally unwell for a long time."

According to the New York Daily News; "Less than two weeks after unimaginably suggesting injecting disinfectants might help kill off the Coronavirus, the past few days have seen him spiral out of control, proving utterly incapable of staying focused on the biggest crisis a president can face."

The vast majority of the major mass media throughout the country, except for his few vociferous supporters, had put forward his statements and acts, adding to the general consensus that Trump was indeed incapable, mentally disturbed, and very dangerous, considering the unlimited powers invested in him while having the full support of the Senate occupied by questionable Republicans who were eager to play the role of a tool, pawn and even a docile "yes man" to him. The Vice President, Mike Pence, was just a lackey and an obedient subordinate, who chose to laud Trump at regular intervals. Pence invoked the golden rule of being docile and subservient to his master whenever approached to control or nullify Trump's illogical acts on stage.

Combined mass media reported Trump's abuse of powers and his unacceptable and disturbing overtures promoting lies, deceits, ignorance, arrogance and even violence wherever and whenever he spoke.

A very few of Trump's absurdities and his unsound mental faculties are summed up by popular journalist Jason Miciak:

> Spread unfounded conspiracy theories about the origins of the coronavirus, about former President Barack Obama and about an MSNBC cable-news host.

Made statements that can only be described as delusional, like comparing himself to Abraham Lincoln, inventing a non-existent letter of apology from Joe Biden, and spewing non-science about his favorite drug, hydroxychloroquine.

Attacked two female reporters for doing their jobs, lamenting that they didn't behave like "Donna Reed," an actress synonymous with the gender role-abiding, kitchen-dwelling 1950s housewife she played on television more than 60 years ago.

Attacked another female cable-news host, calling her a "third rate lapdog."

And in the middle of the night at 12:45 a.m., displayed a 234-word rant on Twitter, complaining about an ad released by a Republican anti-Trump group whose leaders include George Conway, husband of his staffer Kellyanne, in which he used words like "deranged loser of a husband," and "Moonface" to describe him.

"Advisers have argued…they could be alienating some viewers, including senior citizens worried about their health," an Associated Press report says, and "Officials at Trump's reelection campaign have also noted a slip in Trump's support in some battleground states and have expressed concerns that the briefings, which often contain inaccurate information, may be playing a role." The giant orange elephant in the room was not that Trump's impaired judgment would cost him the election; it was that it may have cost American lives.

Trump's other incoherent statements include:

"It's a phenomenon that started two years ago. It's disgraceful, I'm 'gonna' maybe, and I'm looking at it very seriously. We're doing some other things, that you probably noticed, like some of the very important things that we're doing now, but we're looking at it very seriously because you can't do it." Trump on homelessness. Interview with Tucker Carlson, Fox News. July 1, 2019

"You know what uranium is, right? It' this thing called nuclear weapons, and other things, like lots of things are done with uranium, including bad things." Trump speaking on nuclear energy.

"The kidney, very special, the kidney has a very special place in the heart, It's an incredible thing." Trump on people working hard and kidney health.

Hence Trump had demeaned, debased, and reduced the role of the United States of America from being a globally recognized leader of peace and tranquility into a war-mongering bully, even threatening its allies.

Some targets of his insults were:

Sir Nigel Kim Darroch, Ambassador of Great Britain to the USA. Darroch had through a message to London called Trump's administration as inept and insecure.

His own Attorney General, Jeff Sessions whom he forced to resign.

James Comey the popular FBI Director who was fiercely loyal to his duties and personal convictions.

Several judges, multiple Television networks, serving and former heads of the FBI (in addition to James Comey), CIA and NSA, ambassadors, the United Nations, NATO, dependable allies of the United States of America, Treaties signed by the United States government, mayors, Governors, former presidents, the entire Supreme Court of the United States of America, reporters, newspapers, the First Amendment, people who obey subpoenas, business leaders, athletes, singers, actors, Gold Star Widows, veterans with PTSD, dead war heroes, scientists, intelligence analysts, Mexicans, almost every retired general and admiral, Muslims, various Heads of States, rape victims, school shooting survivors and his former business competitors.

What the Former Military Commanders Said about Trump's Handling of the Aftermath of the Unfortunate Cold-Blooded Murder of George Floyd

On May 25, 2020, George Floyd, an African American was initially arrested in Minneapolis, Minnesota on suspicion of attempting to make a transaction with a counterfeit twenty-dollar bill in his possession. He was subjected to inhuman brutality with a knee on his neck for more than eight minutes while he was handcuffed face down in the street. Two other officers further restrained Floyd and a fourth officer prevented onlookers from intervening. Derek Chauvin the known killer of Floyd was a police officer with a cruel and a vicious reputation. He was officially reprimanded nearly twenty times in the past for his violent and trigger-happy behavior, but not dismissed. Unfortunately, Floyd passed out and died during the last three minutes of the more than eight minutes of being restrained by the police officers. While the onlookers gazed in disbelief as life ebbed out of Floyd, it took a few hours for the entire nation to absorb the shock brought about by the resurgence of racism against the people of African origin who suffered for more than three centuries of slavery in the United States of America.

His death was clearly considered deliberate and intentional violence directed at the African American community who number nearly fourteen percent of the total population of nearly 331 million people. They are free of human bondage but never accepted as equal, even today in the United States of America.

Minnesota Attorney General Keith Ellison promised to prosecute the four officers to the fullest extent of the law if found guilty of this horrendous crime. First to be arrested was Derek Chauvin followed by the three others on charges of murder.

Floyd's cold-hearted murder ignited riots throughout the major cities of the United States. When angry crowds demanding justice neared the White House, Trump sought the safety of the "bunker" instead of addressing this terrible issue. Immediately on being brought back from the bunker, he ordered the militarized police, army, and the national guards to deal with the protesters, claiming that the governors and mayors of cities torn by riots, were inefficient and that only he could bring law and order in the country through mobilizing the Army against the unarmed nation who were just demanding their rights of being heard. He further helped to antagonize the vast majority of the population of the country through his refusal to fully acknowledge what betook the unarmed and handcuffed African American.

Statement by Four Star Marine General James N. Mattis on June 3, 2020:

In Union There Is Strength.

> I have watched this week's unfolding events, angry and appalled. The words "Equal Justice Under Law" are carved in the pediment of the United States Supreme Court. This is precisely what protesters are rightly demanding. It is a wholesome and unifying demand—one that all of us should be able to get behind. We must not be distracted by a small number of lawbreakers. The protests are defined by tens of thousands of people of conscience who are insisting that we live up to our values—our values as people and our values as a nation.

> When I joined the military, some 50 years ago, I swore an oath to support and defend the Constitution. Never did I dream that troops taking that same oath would be ordered under any circumstance to violate the Constitutional rights of their fellow citizens—much less to provide a bizarre photo op for the elected commander-in-chief, with military leadership standing alongside.

> We must reject any thinking of our cities as a "battlespace" that our uniformed military is called upon to "dominate." At home, we should use our military only when requested to do so, on very rare occasions, by state governors. Militarizing our response, as we witnessed in Washington, D.C., sets up a conflict—a false conflict— between the military and civilian society. It erodes the moral ground that ensures a trusted bond between men and

women in uniform and the society they are sworn to protect, and of which they themselves are a part.

Keeping public order rests with civilian state and local leaders who best understand their communities and are answerable to them.

James Madison wrote in Federalist 14 that "America united with a handful of troops, or without a single soldier, exhibits a more forbidding posture to foreign ambition than America disunited, with a hundred thousand veterans ready for combat." We do not need to militarize our response to protests. We need to unite around a common purpose. And it starts by guaranteeing that all of us are equal before the law.

Instructions given by the military departments to our troops before the Normandy invasion reminded soldiers that "The Nazi slogan for destroying us...was 'Divide and Conquer.' Our American answer is 'In Union there is Strength.'" We must summon that unity to surmount this crisis—confident that we are better than our politics.

Donald Trump is the first president in my lifetime who does not try to unite the American people—does not even pretend to try. Instead, he tries to divide us. We are witnessing the consequences of three years of this deliberate effort. We are witnessing the consequences of three years without mature leadership. We can unite without him, drawing on the strengths inherent in our civil society. This will not be easy, as the past few days have shown, but we owe it to our fellow citizens; to past generations that bled to defend our promise; and to our children.

We can come through this trying time stronger, and with a renewed sense of purpose and respect for one another. The pandemic has shown us that it is not only our troops who are willing to offer the ultimate sacrifice for the safety of the community. Americans in hospitals, grocery stores, post offices, and elsewhere have put their lives on the line to serve their fellow citizens and their country.

We know that we are better than the abuse of executive authority that we witnessed in Lafayette Square. We must reject and hold accountable those in office who would make a mockery of our Constitution. At the same time, we must remember Lincoln's "better angels," and listen to them, as we work to unite.

Only by adopting a new path—which means, in truth, returning to the original path of our founding ideals—will we again be a country admired and respected at home and abroad.

James Mattis

Former Chairman of the Joint Chiefs Admiral Michael Mullen who served as the top military advisor to Presidents George W. Bush and Barack Obama, wrote that the event "made it impossible to remain silent."

Mullen, a four star-admiral said President Trump had "laid bare his disdain for the rights of peaceful protest in this country" and risked politicizing the U.S. military by his actions.

In his forceful op-ed in The Atlantic magazine the admiral wrote:

I Cannot Remain Silent

Our fellow citizens are not the enemy and must never become so.

JUNE 2, 2020

Mike Mullen

Seventeenth chairman of the Joint Chiefs of Staff

It sickened me yesterday to see security personnel—including members of the National Guard—forcibly and violently clear a path through Lafayette Square to accommodate the president's visit outside St. John's Church. I have to date been reticent to speak out on issues surrounding President Trump's leadership, but we are at an inflection point, and the events of the past few weeks have made it impossible to remain silent.

Whatever Trump's goal in conducting his visit, he laid bare his disdain for the rights of peaceful protest in this country, gave succor to the leaders of other countries who take comfort in our domestic strife, and risked further politicizing the men and women of our armed forces.

There was little good in the stunt.

While no one should ever condone the violence, vandalism, and looting that has exploded across our city streets, neither should anyone lose sight of the larger and deeper concerns about institutional racism that have ignited this rage.

As a white man, I cannot claim perfect understanding of the fear and anger that African Americans feel today. But as someone who has been around for a while, I know enough—and I have seen enough—to understand that those feelings are real and that they are all too painfully founded.

We must, as citizens, address head-on the issue of police brutality and sustained injustices against the African American community. We must, as citizens, support and defend the right—indeed, the solemn obligation—to peacefully assemble and to be heard. These are not mutually exclusive pursuits.

And neither of these pursuits will be made easier or safer by an overly aggressive use of our military, active duty, or National Guard. The United States has a long and, to be fair, sometimes troubled history of using the armed forces to enforce domestic laws. The issue for us today is not whether this authority exists, but whether it will be wisely administered.

I remain confident in the professionalism of our men and women in uniform. They will serve with skill and with compassion. They will obey lawful orders. But I am less confident in the soundness of the orders they will be given by this commander in chief, and I am not convinced that the conditions on our streets, as bad as they are, have risen to the level that justifies a heavy reliance on military troops. Certainly, we have not crossed the threshold that would make it appropriate to invoke the provisions of the Insurrection Act.

Furthermore, I am deeply worried that as they execute their orders, the members of our military will be co-opted for political purposes.

Even amid the carnage we are witnessing, we must endeavor to see American cities and towns as our homes and our neighborhoods. They are not "battle spaces" to be dominated and must never become so.

We must ensure that African Americans—indeed, all Americans— are given the same rights under the Constitution, the same justice under the law, and the same consideration we give to members of our own family. Our fellow citizens are not the enemy and must never become so.

Too many foreign and domestic policy choices have become militarized; too many military missions have become politicized.

This is not the time for stunts. This is the time for leadership.

MIKE MULLEN *is a retired admiral from the U.S. Navy and was the 17th chairman of the Joint Chiefs of Staff.*

Closing Thoughts

Trump, the master of obfuscation, knowingly or otherwise, had successfully created a "Potemkin Village" for his several million enablers and supporters in the country who earnestly and sincerely believed in his success in steering the country. In truth the majority of the society suffers from one mishap to another, from one torment and to another.

The world is now facing a few dangerous dictators that pose a mortal danger to the general population where they rule.

The clergy regime seated in power in Tehran, has openly claimed that it has no obligation whatsoever to cater to the needs of the general population, since its powers are through divine grace and hence not reproachable or questionable in any form whatsoever.

The tyrannical regime in North Korea does not believe in any form of law, except whatever flows from the mouth of Kim Jong-un, their "dear respected" leader who holds life and death for any person in the country with a twist of his tongue.

Trump, the pretender to the throne of a dictator in the United States of America was the most dangerous, since at the stroke of a pen and the button, he could have unleashed an apocalypse on earth, which his enabler politicians and generals would have faithfully complied.

The case to deal with dictators and the aspiring dictator in the United States of America is quite different. In the USA it is the ballot box that threatens their downfall. Laws do exist to combat open murder of the population by any head of State, whether lawfully elected or otherwise. The United States of America, while continuing to pretend and insist that it is the bastion of freedom and democracy often falters in this claim when challenged. It is the unscrupulous rich in the country, who bribe their candidates of choice prior to and after winning the elections, then personally benefit from future laws passed by the compromised politicians. Skullduggery, crime, chaos, and corruption is even encouraged in the American system of politics where bribery is a way of life and dubbed as contribution to a candidate's coffers to pay his office staff. Meanwhile the mass media in the country continue to label this and that country among the first ten or twenty most corrupt countries in the world. The so-called statistics prudently skip the United States of America where all Senators and Congressmen of both genders gleefully accept contributions, calling it lawful and permissible.

Having said, in all the dictatorial regimes, it is the dictator and his enablers who loot the treasury and systematically imprison and slaughter the population under one pretext or the other. That befits the description of a murderous and a corrupt regime. Theocratical regime in Tehran and the cruel Kim Dynasty in Pyongyang and the most dangerous administration under Trump and his goons in Washington are conspicuous examples of corrupt, dangerous, and unpopular regimes.

On the other hand, in the largest democracy in India, the majority (Hindus) now oppress the minority (Muslims) under the present Prime Minister; Narendra Modi, a Gujarati, from a *Modh-Ghanchi-Teli* (oil-presser) family, considered to be as an "Other Backward Class" by the Indian government, identified as a Hindu fanatic has "visions" of establishing a *"Hindu Rashtra"* (a Hindu State). Modi has both directly and indirectly provoked and encouraged fratricidal hatred between Hindus who form at least seventy nine percent of the population and the Muslim population which stands at fifteen percent out of a total population exceeding 1.4 billion. It is also clear that Modi has taken a cue from Trump, the person then seated in the Oval Office, of discriminating and hating Muslims worldwide. Modi had regularly praised Trump's approach to the Muslims in America and elsewhere in the world. In the United States of America and India, it is the majority who oppress and discriminate against the minorities and those practicing a religion other than the majority religion of the country.

Trump, the instigator, on his brief thirty-six hours visit to India on February 24, 2020, showed his continued antagonism against the Muslims in the city of Ahmedabad by stating; "I have taken the required steps to combat radical Islamic terrorism wherever and whenever needed." Those words reflected tacit endorsement of Modi's religious extremist policies against the Muslim population of India, a declared "Secular State" according to its Constitution, written on January 26, 1950 and ratified by 284 members of the Constituent Assembly. Buddhism, Christianity, Zoroastrianism,

Baha'ism, Judaism, Jainism, Sikhism, Islam, and people practicing any faith or belief were to be treated and respected with equal rights.

Trump's unwarranted statements describing his "steps" against radical Islam ignited a rampage of further hatred against the Muslims by Hindu mobs, especially in the northern region of Delhi. Hindus murdered more than forty Muslims, men, women, and children in broad daylight while the police and other security officials passively stood by as "onlookers!"

Trump, who had wittingly created this tragedy, was to later say; "I didn't say anything bad. Did I?"

Modi, the fanatic Hindu later said: "nothing has happened!"

In the first week of March 2020, writer, and political analyst Sarah Repucci, through "Freedom House" examines the potential dangers posed by Trump and Modi under the topic "Democracy and pluralism are under assault."

> "Democracy and pluralism are under assault. Dictators are toiling to stamp out the last vestiges of domestic dissent and spread their harmful influence on new corners of the world. At the same time, many freely elected leaders are dramatically narrowing their concerns to a blinkered interpretation of the national interest. In fact, such leaders – including the chief executives of the United States and India, the world's two largest democracies – are increasingly willing to break down institutional safeguards and disregard the rights of critics and minorities as they pursue their populist agendas."

Elsewhere the writer observed that;

> "Ethnic, religious and other minority groups have borne the brunt of government abuses in both democracies and authoritarian states. The Indian government has taken its Hindu nationalist agenda to a new level with a succession of policies that abrogate the rights of different segments of its Muslim population, threatening the

democratic future of a country long seen as a potential bulwark of freedom in Asia and the world."

This again proves that state sponsored brutality and mayhem against a selected class is not new. It happened and continues to happen throughout the world. It has however found new vigor through the evils and cruelty of the perfidious Trump who acted according to his masters behind the scenes!

As the most dangerous individual who wielded sway and total power over the nuclear button with the powers to initiate conflict against any country he wished (as he regularly claimed), Donald John Trump was chosen as the main subject of this work. If invested with further plenipotentiary powers, he could definitely have created the "last war."

Thus Trump, the con man, a fraud and failure and a mentally ill individual was selected as a larger portion of the theme in this work.

New World Leaders

Much earlier I had foreseen that, once Obama leaves Office, and should Trump be chosen to succeed him, the baton of the leader of the "Free World" would be passed from the USA over to a group of universally acclaimed and popular persons; Emmanuel Macron, Angela Merkel, Justin Trudeau, Alexander Van der Bellen, His Majesty Felipe VI of Spain, His Majesty Emperor Akihito, and the newly enthroned Emperor Naruhito, Their Majesties Willem-Alexander, Philippe of Belgium, Carl Gustav XVI of Sweden, Harald V of Norway and King Abdullah of Jordan.

Interestingly, in the last week of May 2017, Angela Merkel, the honored Chancellor of Germany, a scientist, and a popular figure in global politics was referred to as the leader of the Free World!

Furthermore, the entire benign and progressive nation of Switzerland could be, or rather must be identified as the one and only "collective leaders of the Free World!" Their Government could also be termed as the only and sole "Joint Enlightened Democracy!"

To Further Say:

What has profoundly engrossed me in this subject is not discussing who is right and who is wrong or to lay claims to any form of academic pretensions, but to reflect the seriousness and dangers of a global war by ignorant adventurers who are in fact "political puppets" living and acting at the behest of their puppeteers, behind the "political curtains!" And to search for ways and means to bring about some form of checks and balances and limitations to what they can do to satisfy their masters behind the scenes!

Most important of all, the ultimate will of a nation undergoing misery to OUST the mentally unstable dictators or the "tension and unrest-seeking" aspiring dictators, in order to USHER in global peace, harmony, and prosperity to instead prevail. Once these individuals are OUSTED, tried, and sentenced to the harshest punishment, the nation may follow a path of recovery.

An untried person with a questionable past is seated on the throne of power by the political mafia through hysterical masses and overnight turned into a leader, embellished, and glorified, and once comfortably seated in power, the now power-wielder seizes the opportunity to proclaim himself as the source of power and fountain of wisdom! If a clergyman, he invokes the will of god as he grabs power! The same ignorant masses who had earlier proclaimed him as a savior now beg him to just let them live!

The cruel and murderous dictator is either a Military Officer, a civilian or a clergyman! Just intimidate him, shout him down and strip him stark naked of his uniform, or his suit and necktie or his robes and headgear and he is immediately transformed into a pitiable trembling coward begging for his life!

Comparison of clergyman dictator and the person formerly in the Oval Office.

In Iran, while the clergyman dictator lacks any credentials of having been voted into office through any democratic means, Trump does have some credit as having stood for elections although he lost the popular vote but was placed in office by the Electoral College thus legalizing his credentials.

The dictator in Iran belongs to an ethnic minority, a relatively obscure cleric who has some rudimentary education and has a basic knowledge of geo-politics and history and who regularly reminds the nation claiming the Creator is his mentor and guide.

The aspiring dictator formerly in the Oval Office pretended to have some knowledge, but spoke in grammatically incorrect English, lacked the ability to write in a clear manner, spoke in a threatening tone to any journalist and reporter questioning or exposing his flaws that in turn relates to his mental stability. Time and often he humiliates the Press and attacks them as "fake news" journalists.

The clergyman dictator in Iran has never entertained any form of interview, nor is he willing to answer any questions or protests. He speaks in monologue and refuses to give any form of interview to any local journalists within the country or any foreign news agency. He repeatedly claims the source of his power as coming from the Omniscient One!

The individual formerly in the Oval Office also claimed inspirations from the heavens, but through questionable individuals, whom he had appointed as spiritual guides. They were fanatic Christian preachers with instructions to remind the nation that Trump was an apostle and a savior. These soothsayers at regular intervals claim communications with the Omnipotent One, praising Trump often in exaggerated terms.

Trump's plenipotentiary powers were however limited through the US Constitution, federal judges, and the opposing political party, who attempted to rise to the occasion on behalf of the nation. Some two years after the meteoric and unchallenged deeds of Trump, the Republican Party in Congress was soundly defeated, leaving him with only the Senate to back him.

The clergyman dictator's powers are unlimited, he is the entire embodiment of the country's leadership and is not amenable in the least to any judicial body. He heads every political department of the country. He elects the group which elects him. He bestows upon himself the prerogatives and plenipotentiary powers where he dismisses, imprisons, pardons, decides the country's political direction and even orders executions of whomever he pleases. This he does in the name of his brand of religion and the claims of his communications with various prophets that he regularly has. At any instant where a challenge arises from the masses, the clergyman dictator justifies his acts as God's will and his repeated claims of being infallible. Invoking heavenly powers at any point where he is in danger of being toppled has so far succeeded. The startled and frightened nation has no recourse or the power to protest.

The individual who succeeded President Obama on the other hand, had enablers from the political party he claimed to be, rowdy and violent crowds, billionaire supporters (for their own causes and benefits) and his own wealth, most of it proven to be through dubious means. Both invoke heavenly blessings!

Comments on 2016 Election

A myriad of reasons enticed me to pen this work. Dozens of reasons, hundreds of developments, beginning the day President Obama left Office. The quality of life led by the so-called successor and his lifestyle including his continuous falsification of facts and statistics making the world a dangerous place! Most important was his mental instability! As soon as the globally respected scholar and Nobel Peace Prize Laureate President Barack Obama's last week was nearing its end, I noticed a cloud of nervousness descend upon the educated masses of the USA and an ominous feeling within the shocked World Community who desperately planned how to deal with him!

Results of Presidential Elections in the USA were manipulated when the so-called questionable "Electoral College" (unheard of in any country of the world) intervened to "select" this individual although he lost the popular votes by 2,864,974 million. Hillary Rodham Clinton, the former First Lady and Senator who was the winner in the true and correct meaning of Democracy was "condemned" as the loser by oligarchs who had earlier "paid" for her political demise! Human decency, law and norms of Democracy was squashed and laid aside in the name of bribery, chaos, and corruption to seat the most dangerous person in power. The sycophant had won; but in truth, his billionaire promoters and Corporations (whom he had earlier promised financial favors when and not "if" elected) were the real winners!

And a few words of "reminder" to the good Nation of the USA...through the historical statements of Octavia E. Butler (June 22, 1947-February 24, 2006), "Parable of Talents."

> "Choose your leaders with wisdom and forethought. To be led by a coward is to be controlled by all that the coward fears. To be led by a fool is to be led by the opportunists who control the fool. To be led by a thief is to offer up your most precious treasures to be stolen. To be led by a liar is to ask to be told lies. To be led by a tyrant is to sell yourself and those you love into slavery."

A desire to reflect facts and an inner urge to present global dangers by any powerful dictator are the cardinal factors to pen this work. Reasons that strengthened the will within me to play my modest part in relaying a message to the nations of the world in preventing a would-be dictator, especially a powerful dictator in case Trump was promoted to a full-fledged dictator where possibilities of a scenario assuredly existed with mankind meeting nothing but death, mayhem, and destruction, perhaps on a global level.

After reading and listening to experts and statements and to the individual himself on mass media, I decided that I must start this work, irrespective of the price!

I ask my readers to weigh in the appropriate reasons I employ to justify this work, only after carefully viewing the compelling reasons as presented below and to judge for themselves the merits and the dangers if Trump had continued to be in Office.

Ever since being "planted" into the Oval Office by the arcane and mysterious "Electoral College" until December 2020, Trump made more than twenty thousand false or misleading claims, most of them to the astonishment and amazement, even for the common individual in the streets.

The most befitting poem relating to this most prolific liar ever to be in the Oval Office is by famed British-French writer, historian, and poet Joseph Hilaire Pierre Rene Belloc (July 27,1870 – July 16, 1953). Among many of his notable literary works is one that today relates to the disastrous repercussions of the "Trump regime" and Trump himself as an individual who has virtually mastered the art of lies, deceits, fraud, and general obfuscations! When he tells the truth and when he lies has now become a challenge to the common educated American citizen, which could endanger the world and not have in the least a favorable outcome to the American nation. The unbridled lies of Trump and self-glorification begs the need to relate this poem most logically to him, as an individual!

Reflected is the opening verse of the poem by Hilaire Belloc.

"MATILDA WHO TOLD LIES, AND WAS BURNED TO DEATH"

> "Matilda told such dreadful lies,
> It made one Gasp and Stretch one's Eyes...
>
> Her Aunt, who, from her Earliest Youth,
> Had kept a Strict Regard for Truth,
> Attempted to Believe Matilda:
> The effort very nearly killed her..."

The readers are invited to read this poem in its entirety and to judge for themselves the degree of this poem's relation to the individual (Trump) "selected" by the mysterious "Electoral College" whose blatant lies and fraud staggers a sane mind. His unceasing lies albeit he is fully aware of its authenticity is clearly comparable; an analogy of the highest order, to that of "Matilda's lies" that finally brought her own end. The Aunt's house could be strongly compared to the destiny of the country he supposedly had vowed to protect!

Trump's relation to this poem is befitting. Trump had lied and lied so much that even if once he tells the truth, he is not believed, not even by his own hand-picked aides. Trump has already gone down in the history of the United States of America as the least competent person to be elected to the presidency. He had been proven repeatedly by dozens of psychiatrist and psychologists to be mentally unstable and unable to govern or to execute his duties as demanded by the Constitution of the United States of America.

There are dozens of mendacious ruling heads of state in this world still clinging to the gall of power and systematically tormenting, torturing, and even murdering the populace; the same people who elected them to the seat of power.

History has never recorded a single instance where an individual seeking the highest position in any country in any period has in the faintest voice openly advocated "Dictatorship" to be the final prescription for the ills facing the country for which he will be the remedy. The truth is that with a meretricious elite backing him, especially in the case of Trump in the USA, the general simple-minded nation is promised prosperity, wealth, bliss, and heaven on earth by the confidence trickster, only to create havoc once comfortably seated in power.

But why focus on the dubious and tawdry regime in the USA? This is due to the simple truth Trump's administration had destroyed the fabric of peace and harmony on earth and aimed to immerse the world in further untold miseries and hardships. Furthermore, the United States of America has unlimited power and ability to create mass destruction with its superior and modern weaponry.

The theocratic regime in Tehran is currently under the iron hands of clergyman Ali Khamenei, who sees himself as an appointee of god!

Iranians fed up with this unpopular regime, where the ethnic minorities rule, decided to finally end this onerous theocracy. The opportunity arose in the first week of July 2019, when prices of consumer goods spiraled and the price of gasoline was augmented several folds, millions of Iranians took to the streets of major cities and even far-flung villages to denounce him and to call for his ouster. The millions now roar obscenities at the clergy and the regime. "Death to the Dictator...Death to Khamenei... Death to the Islamic Republic, followed by "O King Return to Iran!" Other slogans like "Forgive us Reza Shah," and "Death to Arabs," "Death to Palestinians," Death to Seyeds," "Death to mullahs," and "We are Aryans...we do not believe in Arabs and their hateful religion," have now become common slogans.

More than two thousand Iranian demonstrators including children accompanying their parents were fatally shot, many by snipers, while two hundred were later executed by "revolutionary courts," and thousands thrown into primitive dungeons and left to die. Of late, prominent champion Greco-Style wrestler Navid Afkari, 27, was hanged on September 12, 2020 at the Adelabad prison Shiraz. He was accused of killing a Basij (a paramilitary volunteer militia affiliated to the Revolutionary Guard Corps) member (Hassan Turkman) and for participating in demonstrations against the regime in August 2018 in Shiraz. Hundreds of witnesses claimed that wrestler Afkari was a very gentle person who had never indulged in any form of violence, let alone killing the Basij militiaman. He had claimed through a letter from the prison that he was innocent of the charges of killing any person.

Persian language television stations based in California claimed that part from fomenting trouble in Iraq, Yemen, and Syria (Arab countries) and elsewhere, the sacerdotal regime has threatened Saudi Arabia and openly stated that in case Israel will attack the territorial boundaries of Iran, Tel-Aviv and Haifa would be raised to the ground! The militarily toothless regime now only concentrates on severely punishing its own people, even by extra-territorial killings through hired hands, majority of them at the hands of Arab terrorists, most of them being Iraqi, Palestinian, Syrian, and Lebanese in addition to Pakistani, Afghan, or Indian Shiites.

All told, the main focus of this writing is Trump in the USA, whose unpredictable and unstable mind holds the "nuclear button" on which he had a high degree of control! This is the crux of the writing! This is the heart of the matter! The catastrophe it could have cost humanity is not too difficult to imagine.

A close and unbiased examination of statements made by experts, psychologists and psychiatrists present a very frightful and ominous picture if this aspiring tyrant and dictator had not been ousted before it was too late.

Be aware of the formula that relieves the public of their power and grants it to the aspiring dictator.

Democracies become Dictatorships.

History suggests 10 steps.

1. First destroy labor unions, so people have no way to bargain for higher wages and less capacity for political organizations.
2. Crack down on college students, so they will not oppose you (hint: burden them with so much student debt and make it so hard for them to find good jobs that they will not dare rock the boat).
3. Undermine public education, so people are less able to think critically for themselves.
4. Cut deals with rich business executives and billionaires that if they back you, you will reduce their taxes, slash government spending on the poor, and eliminate regulations that impinge on their profits.
5. Make most people economically anxious, frustrated, angry, and insecure.
6. Convince them their problems stem from "them" – foreigners, immigrants, racial or ethnic or religious minorities, intellectuals.
7. Make them cynical about democracy.
8. Convince them all they need is a strongman who will fix everything.

9. Fill the airwaves with your big lies.
10. Get elected, and then take over.

Prof. Robert Reich.

All the above steps are related to modern day dictators, tyrants, and despots throughout the world. Most of the dictators are either deceased or have been replaced by individuals as tyrannical or even more evil than the one they replaced. Unbiased examples are the former rulers of the Kremlin, from Lenin to Stalin et.al., The Kim "dynasty" of North Korea, clergyman Khamenei who replaced clergyman Khomeini, Robert Mugabe (Zimbabwe), Than Shwe (Present day Myanmar), King Abdullah (Saudi Arabia), Muammar al-Gaddafi (Libya) and scores of other malevolent persons identified as dictators." Most are deceased and the rest remain to be ousted!

In the USA, after the end of the second term of President Obama, his successor created in himself a new brand of an "aspiring dictator," an "Electoral College elected" individual who had been catapulted into the Oval Office by arcane powerbrokers. He immediately set to deal a death kneel to the very meaning of the word "Democracy" and "Democratic values" in the USA.

And again, all the present dictators who have replaced the ones ousted before them, or benign rulers they were able to oust through deceit and lies have been known to commit untold atrocities against the same nation whose lives and living standards they promised to ameliorate. Such individuals have murdered, imprisoned, and created mass graves of those who protested their rule.

One is obligated to remember the quotes of Aldous Huxley!

> "The perfect dictatorship would have the appearance of a democracy but would basically be a prison without walls in which the prisoners would not even dream of escaping. It would essentially be a system of slavery where, through consumption

and entertainment, the slaves would love their servitudes." Aldous
Huxley (1894-1963)

The dictator through his power of suggestion orders the outright murder
of his personal enemies at the hands of those trusted men and women
who are supposedly his "favorite" citizens. The favored citizens were none
but professional provocateurs and paid agitators who agitated throughout
the cities of those countries promoting the future dictator who is by now
acclaimed with superhuman feats and abilities.

This fact applies to Lenin, Stalin, Adolf Hitler, Benito Mussolini, Mao, Pol
Pot, Ho Chi Minh, Heng Samrin, the succeeding Kim dynasty, Mobutu
Sese Seko, Idi Amin, Sukarno, Suharto, clergyman Khomeini and his
"successor" clergyman Khamenei, Fidel Castro, his brother Raul, and
dozens of other criminals, some deceased, some living in hiding and some
murdered. And then, in the USA, there was a former television showman, a
semi-literate individual, a failed businessman and an ethically questionable
person with a dubious past; the forty fifth administrator of the USA,
Donald Trump.

Lest it be late, as a reminder, it is through dictators and despots only when
genocide, mass murders and incarceration in medieval dungeons happen.

An example in infamy is King Leopold the Second of Belgium (April 9,
1835 - December 17, 1909 and king between 1865-1909), whose brutality
against the African people still shocks the world. His administration of
the Congo was marred by atrocities leading to the death of ten million
Congolese. Some historians put this figure at an alarming figure of fifteen
million! If the figures are true and substantiated, this would be the largest
genocide so far.

This is because the mass murder of human beings was pre-planned,
premeditated, and intentional just as the systematic, intentional, and
deliberate murder of six or even seven million Jews., most of them
Ashkenazi Jews. The true figures of the Holocaust will never be known,
except for the available figures mentioned in the death and concentration

265

camps. As time passes by and more research is done, a figure more startling than the murder of six million Jews could be discovered.

True, that in the two World Wars several times these figures, human beings were stolen of their precious lives. That was the outcome of Wars started by madmen at the behest of Internationals, but planning and building gas chambers, death camps and concentration camps was a different form of cruelty aimed and directed to a specific nation. And so was King Leopold's evil deeds against the African people, and Stalin's and Mao's murderous rampage in the murder of a hundred million people.

Printed in the United States
by Baker & Taylor Publisher Services